Alternative Investments and the Mismanagement of Risk

Other Published Books 1997–2003

Stress Testing: Risk Management Strategies for Extreme Events, Euromoney, London, 2003

Outsourcing, Insourcing and IT for Enterprise Management, Macmillan, Palgrave, London, 2003

Liabilities, Liquidity and Cash Management. Balancing Financial Risk, Wiley, New York, 2002

The Management of Philanthropy in the 21st Century, Institutional Investor, New York, 2002

Enterprise Architecture and New Generation Information Systems, St. Lucie Press/CRC, Boca Raton, FL, 2002

Modelling the Survival of Financial and Industrial Enterprises. Advantages, Challenges, and Problems with the Internal Rating-Based (IRB) Method, Macmillan/Palgrave, London, 2002

Managing Operational Risk. Risk Reduction Strategies for Investment Banks and Commercial Banks, Euromoney, London, 2001

Managing Risk in the New Economy, New York Institute of Finance, New York, 2001

Implementing and Auditing the Internal Control System, Macmillan/Palgrave, London, 2001

Integrating ERP, Supply Chain Management, and Smart Materials, Auerbach/CRC Press, New York, 2001

Internet Supply Chain. Its Impact on Accounting and Logistics, Macmillan/Palgrave, London, 2001

Reliable Financial Reporting and Internal Control: A Global Implementation Guide, John Wiley, New York, 2000

New Regulation of the Financial Industry, Macmillan, London, 2000

Managing Credit Risk, Volume 1 *Analyzing, Rating and Pricing the Probability of Default,* Euromoney, London, 2000

Managing Credit Risk, Volume 2 *The Lessons of VAR Failures and Imprudent Exposure,* Euromoney, London, 2000

Credit Derivatives and the Management of Risk, New York Institute of Finance, New York, 2000

Setting Limits for Market Risk, Euromoney, London, 1999

Commercial Banking Handbook, Macmillan, London, 1999

Understanding Volatility and Liquidity in Financial Markets, Euromoney, London 1998

The Market Risk Amendment: Understanding Marking to Model and Value-at-Risk, McGraw-Hill/Irwin, Burr Ridge, IL, 1998

Cost-Effective IT Solutions for Financial Services, Lafferty, London and Dublin, 1998

Agent Technology Handbook, McGraw-Hill, New York, 1998

Transaction Management Managing Complex Transactions and Sharing Distributed Databases, Macmillan, London, 1998

Internet Financial Services – Secure Electronic Banking and Electronic Commerce? Lafferty, London and Dublin, 1998

Network Computers versus High Performance Computers, Cassell, London, 1997

Alternative Investments and the Mismanagement of Risk

Dimitris N. Chorafas

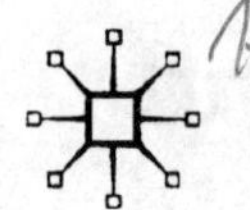

First published 2003 by
PALGRAVE MACMILLAN
Houndmills, Basingstoke, Hampshire RG21 6XS and
175 Fifth Avenue, New York, N. Y. 10010
Companies and representatives throughout the world

PALGRAVE MACMILLAN is the global academic imprint of the Palgrave Macmillan division of St. Martin's Press, LLC and of Palgrave Macmillan Ltd. Macmillan® is a registered trademark in the United States, United Kingdom and other countries. Palgrave is a registered trademark in the European Union and other countries.

ISBN 1–4039–0681–5

This book is printed on paper suitable for recycling and made from fully managed and sustained forest sources.

A catalogue record for this book is available from the British Library.

Library of Congress Cataloging-in-Publication Data
Chorafas, Dimitris N.
Alternative investments and the mismanagement of risk/
Dimitris N. Chorafas
p. cm.
Includes bibliographical references and index.
ISBN 1–4039–0681–5 (cloth)
1. Investments. 2. Risk management. 3. Hedge funds. I. Title.

HG4521 .C4548 2003
332.6–dc21 2002034884

10 9 8 7 6 5 4 3 2 1
12 11 10 09 08 07 06 05 04 03

Printed and bound in Great Britain by
Antony Rowe Ltd., Chippenham and Eastbourne

Contents

Preface

'Investors beware' is good advice in any situation, especially when dealing with the control of risk and alternative investments. An offer I received some time ago, from one of the better-known banks, was to 'buy an instrument whose performance is not correlated with the equity markets'. Not wanting to accept what seemed to be a gift horse without looking it in the mouth, I asked about the risk behind it and was told: 'There is *no* risk'. This aroused my suspicion.

- Having worked for over 40 years in risk management, I was not about to write the bank a blank cheque.
- Therefore, I set about uncovering the hidden risks.

This book is the product of my findings. It is written for investors and for those dealing in financial instruments: analysts, traders, risk controllers, auditors, and managers of institutions, including hedge funds, as well as consultants, and regulators. Also, for the *end-investors*, those people and companies to whom repackaged financial products will be sold, along with the accompanying risks. These end-investors will accumulate the exposure embedded in alternative investments along with the rewards they expect to get.

One of the lessons all investors should have learned from financial history, and from their own past practice, is that *leveraged* instruments have all the potential to impose economic pain on their holders, even if in the short term they may be offering great opportunities for paper profits. This pain is magnified by leverage, lack of transparency, and illiquidity, and it can have a devastating impact on a complacent investor who has not taken the care and time to manage current and potential risks.

The book aims to bring the risks of alternative investments under perspective and provide some solutions to the problems identified. As experience demonstrates, identifying the problem we are faced with is 50 per cent of the way to its solution. The risks that I have identified in my research, in connection with alternative investments, are laid out, including some pitfalls of which investors must be aware.

State-of-the-art management of exposure connected to alternative investment ranges from the proverbial long hard look, to risk models, stress tests, and drills. Many current solutions are partial because they primarily address one or other aspects of exposure. The so-called 'holistic' approaches, based on some secretive proprietary model, are not, I believe suitable for those alert to the polyvalence and elusiveness of financial exposure.

* * *

Chapter 1 defines alternative investments and their place among financial instruments. It explains how alternative investments differ from traditional investment strategies, identifies who are the participants in alternative investments, examines the role of hedge funds, funds of funds, special alternative investment vehicles (SAIVs) and credit institutions, as well as their relationship to and impact on the financial markets.

Chapter 2 explains the inherent risks of alternative investments and why they are not for the faint-hearted. It examines the problems arising from their low degree of liquidity and transparency, but high level of complexity. This chapter calls into question some accepted notions of the benefits of alternative investments for investors and the financial markets as a whole. It explains the intersection of credit, market, and operational risks, provides an example of prudent hedging strategies, and assesses the implications of regulatory activity.

Chapter 3 describes the process of investing in alternative investments and unravels the complex and often contradictory language of alternative investment sales pitches and documentation. It examines the reputational, legal, and technological risks (critical with such complex financial instruments), and concentrates on investment strategies followed by the aggregators and merchandisers of risk, and the high-tech models those managing alternative investments must be confident in utilising.

Chapter 4 turns the reader's attention to the activities of hedge funds and explains why, for practical purposes, they have taken over where mutual funds left off. This chapter brings under perspective, statistics identifying the exposure taken with modern financial instruments, including those used with alternative investments, and explains how to face the risks associated with them.

The subject of Chapter 5 is hedge funds and multimanagers, and the degree to which this strategy can be successful. The chapter describes six different hedge fund macrostrategies, relates these to the risks of the macromarkets and reviews transborder capital flows. The chapter also describes what has been called *tidal wave XXI* (for the twenty-frist century). This is a worst case scenario currently being studied by regulators and some credit institutions.

Chapter 6 elaborates on risk and return with derivative financial instruments. It covers the changing pattern of derivative trades, as well as the derivatives' exposure of banks and financial institutions. The text also introduces the risks associated with individual derivative products, such as credit derivatives. This chapter concludes with a view on regulatory oversight of derivatives trading.

Chapter 7 scrutinises the strategies of alternative investments that are intended to give high returns. The text looks at principal protected notes, investment tracking, disinvestment from hedge funds and the risks associated with conflicts of interest. Then, it concludes with some examples of famous hedge funds, such as Quantum and Tiger.

Chapter 8 emphasises that there are 'some' solutions to the problem of risk control with alternative investments. Stress testing is discussed as a means of assessing strategic risks, with globalisation and liquidity as basic implementation examples. Another vital subject being treated is the importance of balancing different types of risk, and how this can be achieved.

The final chapter, Chapter 9, starts with an analysis of the position of alternative investments within the economy of the early twenty-first century, including the basic law of capitalism. Then it assesses the collapse of Long-Term Capital Management (LTCM), a precedent that continues to affect investor confidence in hedge funds. Whereas in the LTCM's meltdown, the Fed of New York obliged the major banks which were LTCM's partners to contribute the billions needed for salvage, a new lender of last resort has now been found in the end-investor. The chapter considers market discipline and transparency as the ultimate strategies for managing the risks of alternative investments.

Many investment experts and financial analysts have been kind enough to offer their advice and opinions on what alternative investments are worth and the risk which they involve to both the bank and the investor. Some chose not to be quoted by name citing the case of Chung Wu, a UBS PaineWebber stock advisor who on 21 August 2001, told clients they should 'sell' their Enron shares – and he was fired that same day. Alternative investments and Enron correlate in terms of risk, among themselves and with Global Crossing as well as with other high fliers of the late 1990s, who are now defunct.

I am thus indebted to a long list of knowledgeable people and organisations, for their contribution to the research that made this book possible, and also to several experts for constructive criticism during the preparation of the manuscript. Much of this criticism is included in the text along with the answers given to the points which were raised.

The complete list of the people and organisations who participated in this research is presented in the Acknowledgements.

Let me take this opportunity to thank Stephen Rutt and Caitlin Cornish, for seeing this project all the way to publication. To Eva-Maria Binder goes the credit for compiling the research results, typing the text, and making the camera-ready artwork and index.

DIMITRIS N. CHORAFAS
Valmer and Vitznau

1
Alternative Investments Defined

1. Introduction

The term *alternative investments* is derived from the way in which capital is employed, an approach which is not the same as in traditional investment methods. Classically, a fund manager tries to obtain a maximum performance by buying a stock when it is cheap and selling it when the price has gone up. His goal is to beat the index. He is also satisfied if he has lost less value than the index, when the market has fallen.

Alternative investment strategies use different means to profit from market volatility. One of the strategies a hedge fund manager uses is to go short, when the price is high, and cover his position when the price is lower. By shorting a company, and sometimes the whole economy, he profits when the market falls. However, *shorting* has major risks because equity prices can recover unexpectedly and covering leveraged short positions becomes very expensive, if not outright ruinous.

No two financial institutions define alternative investment in the same way. In fact, few have come forward with a precise definition, other than to say that the old investment strategy of buying and holding stocks is no longer valid because the market has changed. Hence, the drive to diversify, placing something like 20 per cent of investors' capital into alternative investments (see Chapter 2).

Such an allocation of one's financial resources to highly *risky, illiquid, leveraged,* and *non-transparent* instruments is poor advice, and a bad practice which can have disastrous results. It is therefore both curious and disturbing that retail banks try to sell financial toxic waste to their clients:

- In theory, this is done to protect against the uncertainties of the market.
- In practice, it makes a mockery of 'investing' as risks may be well in excess of returns.

This is, in a nutshell, the result of my research. The 'how' and 'why' it is so is documented in the nine chapters of this book. To crack the code of how pro-alternative investments people think, besides a good deal of interviews three different persons (identified as *reviewers*) were asked to comment on this text, including research findings and conclusions. Their comments have been inserted in boxes, and they are answered in the paragraph(s) immediately following each box.

Which type of risky financial instruments make up alternative investments? The answer to this query is not linear. Not only does the definition of alternative investments tends to be imprecise, but also no two special alternative investments vehicles (SAIVs) offer the same pattern of assets and liabilities, or level of gearing: the instruments being used are too diverse. From a hedge funds viewpoint, a number of instruments may fall within the broader horizon of alternative investments:

- US long/short
- US equity short
- US emerging growth
- Macroinvestments
- Event-driven
- Market-neutral
- Europe long/short
- Europe equity short
- Emerging markets
- Fixed income long
- Fixed income hedge
- Capital-protected
- Managed currencies
- Managed futures
- Credit derivatives
- Risk arbitrage
- Private placements
- Other instruments and Cash

With a few exceptions, such as equity long, fixed income long and cash, these are not traditional-type instruments. Also a characteristic of alternative investments is the very high leverage associated with strategies being followed, and the risks involved with SAIVs, particularly due to the fact that alternative investments are now marketed to retail investors who do not necessarily appreciate the exposure they are taking.

This exposure may be vast and the investor – pension fund, mutual fund, insurance company, bank, high net worth individual or even a saver

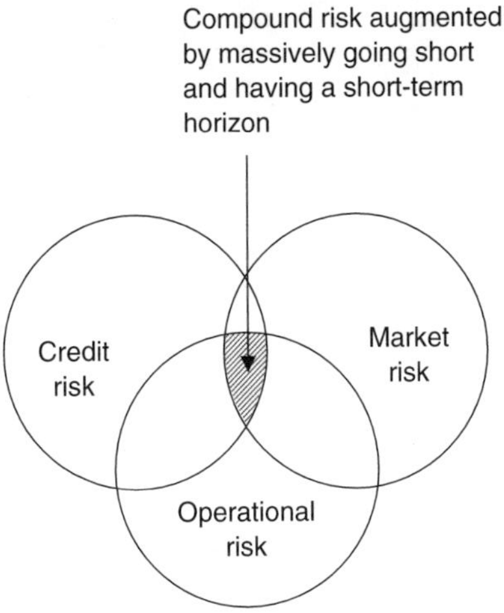

Figure 1.1 Alternative investments involve an inordinate amount of all types of risk.

who used to put his or her money in a time deposit account – can find himself at the junction of all three major types of risk targeted by the New Capital Adequacy Framework of the Basle Committee on Banking Supervision. Figure 1.1 presses this pattern of exposure which is vastly underplayed by the merchandisers of risk who always find an argument to divert the buyer's attention.

To add one more reference, when this text was written, 17 other books on alternative investments were already in the market. Why should one write an 18th? The answer is because all 17 other books *promoted* alternative investments. By contrast, this text takes a *contrarian* approach. It brings to the investors' attention the fact that alternative investments are very risky and that their returns happen to be well below the level being advertised by the merchandisers of risk.

2. Alternative investments and end-investor

People and companies who favour alternative investments do so because they believe their returns are uncorrelated with the bond and stock markets. The presumed lack of correlation is a major selling point of alternative investments but *end-investors*[1] – the people at the end of the chain who put their money into alternative investments and keep the SAIVs as assets in their portfolio – should not enter into contracts that mask or disregard the true level of risk.

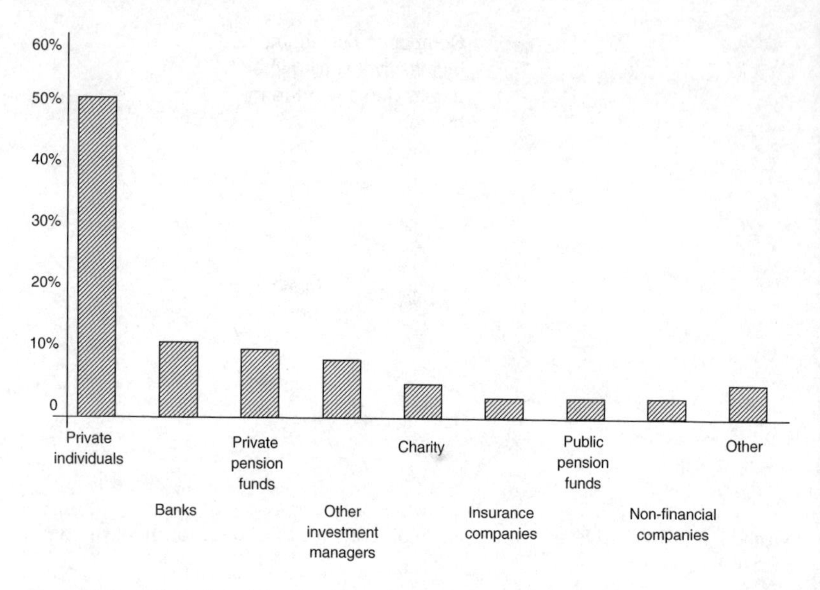

Figure 1.2 A lot of entities invest in hedge funds, with high net worth individuals taking the lead.

One of the misfortunes of the end-investor is that he or she is too far from the alternative investment instruments which suck money like a sponge. End-investors find themselves at the long end of a multilayered structure which hides the huge amount of assumed exposure, a situation made worse by the fact that hedge funds are not known for their transparency. Figure 1.2 gives an example of this new sort of pyramiding.

Alternative investments involve not only credit risk, because they are leveraged and illiquid, and market risk, given the strategies being followed, but also legal risk and technology risk (see Chapter 3). Contrary to what their designers, managers, and sellers say, profit opportunities do not necessarily justify the exposure taken by the funds themselves and by the end-investors (see Chapter 4).

A factual and documented evaluation of risk versus reward is the basis of every investment. Yet, banks, brokers, special alternative investment vehicles (SAIVs), and hedge funds are demanding, in the name of alternative investments, that investors in effect abdicate the responsibility of managing their money. They would not ask this with more classical investments in equity and debt.

What many end-investors fail to appreciate is that the amount of leverage connected to alternative investments is high. To manage the impact of leveraged instruments competently, it is necessary to employ not only competent people (who are in short supply), but also advanced technology able to provide instant ad hoc access to intraday, reliable information on risk and return. Powerful mathematical models are also necessary for

- analysis;
- experimentation; and
- risk control.

Risk is related to the volatility of the future value of a position due to market changes. Foretelling these changes is an art, not a science, and forecasters often fail in their assumptions. Particularly difficult is to factor-in the effects of uncertain and unlikely events. That's why in banking and in trading we impose *limits*. But private investors don't have that culture, let alone the knowledge, on how to establish limits and follow up on them.

'The difference between genius and stupidity,' Winston Churchill once said, 'is that genius has limits.' In trading and in banking we need high technology to compute the right limits and exercise timely control. Not only the end-investors, but also many of the entities specialising in alternative investments are not known to be technology leaders.

Some of the hedge funds that call themselves alternative investments experts are too small to be able to claim technological leadership, not to mention rigorous risk control. Others are too oriented towards making a double-digit profit and, because of gearing, end up paying scant attention to the preservation of the assets of end-investors. This is not meant to be a critique but a statement of facts.

> 'Hedge funds may not be technology leaders,' said one of the reviewers, 'but this equally applies to many traditional mutual funds, which often have access to much less sophisticated technology. We need to make it clear that the risks are the risks of strategy vs experience, rather than whatever name the fund is called.'

The statement about mutual funds is true, and it can be extended to the whole of the banking industry. In its time, Bankers Trust was a technology leader, the old UBS (prior to its merger with Swiss Bank Corporation) was a technology leader, and so were Citibank, StateStreet and other like institutions. These, however, were and continue being a minority, while the risk assumed with complex financial instruments is so much greater when the technology is not state of the art.

I would agree to the reviewer's comments about the importance of strategy and experience (more on this later), but would also most definitely add *risk control policy* as a basic prerequisite to survival. Unfortunately, in the general case, the risk control policies are wanting. As for past experience, while it is precious it is by no means a miracle maker. An example is the legendary hedge fund manager Julian Robertson Jr who, undone by bad bets on old-economy stocks and wrong foreign exchange guesses, closed his Tiger Management hedge fund including its flagship, Jaguar fund, and five other entities.

At his peak in 1989, Robertson had $23 billion under management at Tiger, which ran six different investment pools. But a combination of investment losses and heavy withdrawals had left that hedge fund a shadow of its former self. In a March 2000 letter, Robertson told partners that he had already liquidated Tiger's portfolio and was ready to immediately return up to 75 per cent of some $6 billion in investments to stakeholders in cash. Revered for his long-term record as an investor, Robertson appears to have succumbed to the rapid change in world financial markets.

> The Tiger fund's fate answers the reviewer's comment that 'he has looked closely at one long-short equity hedge fund whose manager has had 16 very successful years of long-only experience and knows his subject well,' adding that 'All this is to say that hedge funds can be run sensibly and can have advantages...'

But what about the huge risks being assumed? In the last analysis, whose money is on the block? Figure 1.2 answers this query. As the reader can appreciate, the merchandising of risk reached a point where a little more than 50 per cent of the inventoried exposure hits on the head of private individuals.

Given the risks associated with navigating the uncharted territory of financial markets speculation, a lack of technology makes matters worse. With strategies such as *shorting* and the *macromarkets* falling behind in risk and return, information can be deadly. Leveraging magnifies the traders' and investors' curve of greed and fear (see Chapter 7). What most end-investors fail to appreciate is that the risks connected with these deals are very different from those of classical stock market volatility. In principle, without risk no high yield can be obtained, but strategies such as shorting and the macromarkets do not have good metrics to measure assumed exposure, and steadily compare risk and return in a meaningful sense.

'...traders mastering the macro markets,' said a reviewer. 'You are making a comment with respect to investment managers, how are traders relevant?'

This remark is infantile. The role played by traders is very, very relevant because trading and traders are the motors behind hedge funds. Organisations are made of people. Alternative investments are based on trading. Going short, long-short, event-driven, market neutral, macro-markets, all these are components of a trader's toolbox.

Indeed, this emphasis on trading is one of the main differences between mutual funds who basically have a buy-and-hold strategy, and hedge funds who must always be on a buy-and-sell alert. That is also why high technology is so much more important with hedge funds than with mutual funds.

Beyond this, as far as transparency and embedded risks are concerned, the shares of most alternative investments vehicles are not traded daily, but only at the issuer's choice: once a month, once a quarter, or even further out. The risk associated with the lack of transparency with respect to prices, management practices, and assumed exposure is one of the reasons why, until recently, alternative investments were the preserve of a small and wealthy financial community that could easily afford the losses.

With the *fund of funds* schemes (see Section 6) marketed by many banks to their retail clients, new ways have opened up to place consumers' money in these higher risk instruments, often with an artificial entry-and-exit strategy which works at prices set by the alternative investments managers themselves. Therefore, both investors and managers need to understand where these risks lie. This is what the book seeks to do.

3. A definition of alternative investments terminology

The term *end-investor* is used to identify the ultimate investors of alternative investments. I use the term to differentiate those (people and companies) purchasing alternative investment instruments from those originating and selling them – typically hedge funds, banks (acting as *aggregators of risk*), SAIVs and other *merchandisers of risk*.

One of the reviewers particularly did not like the reference to the 'merchandisers of risk' and 'aggregators of risk', which he found unnecessarily pejorative. He thought that it was possible to provide these people with value neutral labels.

I don't think that these terms are pejorative. Neither is risk something unwanted. Paraphrasing what Dr John von Neumann once said about *errors, risk* is not an extraneous and misdirected accident but an integral part of investing.

- The question is not whether or not to take risks, but how well can we manage the risks which we are taking.
- Provided they know how to identify and control risk, an aggregator of risk and a merchandiser of risk can be an honourable profession like any other.

Quite to the contrary, *if* this aggregator does not know how to manage the risks he takes and/or covers them under a blanket of secrecy, *then* he is very unfair to his customers, the end-investors. Sooner or later he is going to go bankrupt, taking his investors down with him. That is what the LTCM, Enron, Tyco, WorldCom, Global Crossing, and so many other stories are all about.

Let's now look into strategies. Classically, investors take long positions in assets. By contrast, in a *long/short strategy* portfolio managers take long and short positions to gain quick advantage of market fluctuations. Theoretically, this helps to reduce market risk. Traders will go long on a security if they think it will go up, and short if they believe it will go down.

Short sellers trade in the market by borrowing stock and selling it, hoping to buy it back at a lower price. A portfolio manager may short overvalued securities as a hedge for long portfolios, in anticipation of bearish trends in the market, on rumours that certain events will happen, or following dramatic events (such as the World Trade Center and Pentagon attacks on September 11, 2001).

A *macromarkets* strategy requires the portfolio manager to anticipate changes in global markets that can result from shifts in economic policy, or other reasons, affecting interest rates, exchange rates, or energy prices. 'Macro is the three-dimensional equivalent of asset allocation,' says George Soros. The problem is that persons trained to think in a three-dimensional way are very rare.

Typically, macro approaches employ leverage, with the portfolio manager taking positions in stocks, bonds, currencies, and other financial instruments. Macromarkets can suffer a depression as it happened in 1994, 1997, and 1998; and the bankruptcy of Enron does not suggest that many traders really master the macromarkets.

Market-neutral strategies attempt to minimise, if not completely neutralise, market risk (which is often an illusion). They do so by using offsetting long/short positions and arbitrage of various securities, including equities, debt, convertibles, and bond futures. But they also leverage to enhance returns, which sometimes magnifies losses.

In theory, *market-neutral* products such as Alternative Performance Units and Units on Best International Managers, can offset fluctuations in equity and bond returns thanks to their low correlation with traditional types of investments. In practice, this is very difficult to achieve and what end-investors are told is smoke and mirrors.

Private equity, too, is a type of alternative investment and private placements have been included in the definition which was given in the Introduction. But they are far from being risk-free.[2] Quite to the contrary, banks, big and small, have lost lots of money with private equity, particularly in a down market. (Private equity and its risks are discussed in Chapter 4.) Curiously, it is after these losses have been incurred that repackaged private equity deals start showing in the alternative investments landscape.

Another negative aspect of private equity is that it tends to correlate with exchange-traded equity, albeit at a higher volatility level. Therefore it does not satisfy the prerequisites for diversification advertised by originators and merchandisers of alternative investments. Up to a point, the same is true of real estate property. Look at the correlation between equity prices and real estate prices in Japan during the 1990s.

Also in theory, *capital-protected* alternatives, such as currency products, open up opportunities to capitalise on short-term trends. While it is true that such short-term opportunities exist, it is equally true that the adage 'capital-protected' is an euphemism. These investments are very risky. Investors should not be misled by the implication of 'protection'. As with another misnomer: Collateralized Mortgage Obligations (CMOs) there is no collateral to cover the losses of the end-investor.

One of the reviewers challenged the statement about risk implications.

The answer to this disbelief is that it is enough to look at the bankruptcy of Orange County at the end of 1994.[3] It is indeed ironic that so much money was lost by a treasurer whose traditional job – like that of an investment advisor – is to reduce the risks encountered by the organisation for which he works, rather than increase them.

Robert Citron, the treasurer of Orange County, and his people who once had $7.5 billion in real money to invest, leveraged it to $22 billion, and lost $2.1 billion with CMOs and other derivative instruments. After the bankruptcy they tried hard to appear as financial innocents. The court took a different view of Citron's personal responsibility. There are no financial innocents in business, but there are illiterates in terms of risk – and these should keep themselves out of complex investments.

An *event-driven* strategy is based on a different type of gamble. Its sense is that returns are driven by specific events rather than market trends. This sort of trading is thought to generate a targeted return, over a defined time period, by using investments that may include private equity, real estate, the result of mergers and acquisitions and/or risk arbitrage. It also uses distressed securities created by bankruptcies, liquidations, or financial restructuring.

Emerging growth and *emerging markets* investments are two totally different concepts – except that they have in common a good deal of uncertainty. Investing in *emerging growth* usually targets emerging industries; this is a strategy focusing on specific high-growth sectors or equity types: for instance, technology stocks, equity in biotechnology firms, small caps, initial public offers (IPOs), and so on. Internet equity has been an emerging growth type with which investors have made, and then lost, fortunes.

Investments in *emerging markets* address equities in the so-called 'developing countries', which may offer greater potential for profits but also have significant downside risk. Look at Argentina and Turkey, among others. More exposure is involved in investments in emerging markets than those in industrialised nations, because when expectations are not met or there is a panic, foreign investors leave the market in a single rush.

> 'Event-driven strategy, emerging growth, emerging markets. These comments would also apply to emerging market investment funds, perhaps we should make this point,' said one of the reviewers.

That is a point to which I would be quite happy to subscribe. Also, to better explain to the layman what lies behind complex and obscure financial instruments which are now offered to end-investors – private individuals, pension funds, and other institutional entities – the reader will find in the Appendix to this chapter an excellent allegory by Richard Geiger on the *Dead Mule and the Old Country Farmer*.

4. Back to basics: investing in the financial markets

As alternative investments are part and parcel of financial markets, prior to talking of their impact and their risks, it is wise to briefly examine how financial markets operate and to take a closer look at the instruments which they use. Foremost is the fact that they are constantly on the move. Whether the trend is positive or negative, investors are always moving in and out of positions.

There are many ways of classifying financial markets, their behaviour, and their instruments. Each way illustrates some essential features, for instance, whether the transaction taking place relates to:

- the first purchase of the issue, hence a *primary* market; or
- a trade between holders of securities, carried out in *secondary* markets.

There are two classes of secondary markets for financial instruments:

- organised exchanges; and
- over the counter (OTC).

With the first alternative, buyers and sellers of securities meet in regulated exchanges to conduct trades. Increasingly, however, open outcry is being replaced by electronic networks. Whether transactions are carried out in a central brick-and-mortar location or by means of networks, exchange-based trading is monitored and regulated by a government supervisory authority, such as the Securities and Exchange Commission (SEC) in the United States and the Financial Services Authority (FSA) in the United Kingdom.

By contrast, in an OTC market, dealers of different institutions, often based at widely separated locations, trade new instruments or positions out of an inventory of securities owned by their institution. Usually, these traders are ready to buy and sell securities OTC to anyone who is willing to accept their price and pay cash.

Financial markets can also be grouped according to the original maturity of the traded instrument or contract. A classification according to this criterion distinguishes between an original maturity of less than one year and one of more than one year, though in some countries, for example France and Italy, the short term is taken to be six months or less. The way of sorting out financial products according to timing leads to the distinction between the *money market* and the *capital market*.

Besides timing, the money market differs from other financial markets because it is typically a wholesale interbank market where transactions are, generally, large. Also, reserve banks and financial systems, such as the Eurosystem, can influence contractual conditions in the money market through their monetary policy and other operations. For instance, reserve banks can alter the refinancing conditions affecting credit institutions in their area of authority. This impacts on the way credit institutions and other market participants transact in the money market.

Similarly, reserve banks can influence the capital market in the area under their jurisdiction, through successive changes in interest rates. When the central bank eases, money becomes cheaper, its velocity of circulation accelerates,[4] and (all things being equal) the capital market booms. The inverse is true when reserve banks tighten, because reserve banks are increasing the discount interest rate or are demanding more in terms of reserve requirements by commercial banks.

Regulated financial institutions and non-banks

Usually, reserve banks have authority only over credit institutions, also known as monetary financial institutions (MFIs). However, finance to the public and private sectors of the economy is provided not only by MFIs, but also by other intermediaries. These are often called *financial auxiliaries*, comprising all companies that are principally engaged in activities closely related to classical financial intermediation, but which are not registered as financial intermediators. Examples are insurance, savings and loans (building societies), securities brokers, pensions funds, mutual funds, and hedge funds.

A distinction between MFIs and financial auxiliaries (or *non-banks*) is very important because, among other reasons, it says a lot about who is supervising and regulating them. All of the main supervisors in the United States: The Federal Reserve, Office of the Controller of the Currency (OCC), and Federal Deposit Insurance Corporation (FDIC), address themselves to the banking industry, and most specifically to deposit-taking credit institutions. So does the FSA in the United Kingdom.

There are a vast number of corporations which are involved in pseudo-banking functions. Enron has been one of them: *The Economist* described Enron as a hedge fund with a gas pipeline. Many non-banks are better managed and more reliable than Enron, but they still escape regulation. General Electric, for instance, is not a bank. Yet, GE Capital, its financial arm, represents nearly 50 per cent of GE's business and 60 per cent of its profits. Neither is General Motors a bank, but it owns and operates General Motors Assurance Corporation (GMAC) which is a huge financial entity.

For any practical purpose, GE Capital, GMAC and a myriad of other similar companies which are non-banks are unsupervised. The same is true of hedge funds (see Section 6). Yet, they undertake a great deal of financial transactions and take plenty of risks. Hedge funds form part of the non-regulated non-banks industry which some consider to be the weakest link in the modern economy.

Classification by financial instruments

Still another common, but also important, classification of financial companies and markets is based on the financial instruments in which they deal. The main distinction is between:

- equity;
- debt; and
- derivatives.

Among other issues, this three-way dichotomy describes responsibilities and their associated liabilities. Equity does not have to be repaid until liquidation, at which point the company may be bankrupt. By contrast, debt is a financial claim which (usually) has to be repaid. This is done in specified amounts at a set interest rate. Compared to classical equity and debt instruments, the value of derivatives (see Chapter 6) comes from underlying prices of securities, interest rates, foreign exchange rates, market indices, or commodity prices.

The concept behind derivatives and their contracts dates back to antiquity, but until the 1970s financial products based on derivatives were exceptions. Today, derivatives make up a vast market, and over the short decades they developed as customised instruments and market movers. Their underlying security may be found

- either within a certain class, such as equities, or
- by combining different categories of assets.

Derivatives are innovative products and their markets are central to the functioning of the financial system, but excesses involve high risk and can destabilise a company's, an economy's, or, in our global market, the world's financial balance:

- On the positive side, derivatives help to improve the pricing, assist in reallocation of financial risks and, when the hypotheses are right, lead to profits.
- On the negative side, derivatives are highly leveraged instruments transacted mostly OTC. They escape regulation, their contracts are non-transparent, and their market is illiquid.

In the 1980s, a decade after the derivatives market began evolving, the amounts at stake were still small and regulators allowed the banks to write the transactions and their results off-balance sheet (OBS).[5] But as this market boomed and large banks became exposed to the tune of trillions of dollars, in notional principal amounts, the regulators stepped in.

By the late 1980s, they brought all derivatives transactions within the broader perspective of the capital adequacy requirements.

New capital adequacy requirements

From 2006, financial institutions must address all three pillars of the New Capital Adequacy Framework by the Basle Committee.

Pillar 1: Capital adequacy
Pillar 2: Supervisory action
Pillar 3: Market discipline

This is true of credit risk, market risk, and operational risk,[6] which is the loss resulting from inadequate or failed internal processes – including people and systems – or from external events other than credit risk and market risk.

Note that the criteria being used with all three main types of risk are neither purely quantitative, nor purely qualitative. This is shown in Figure 1.3,

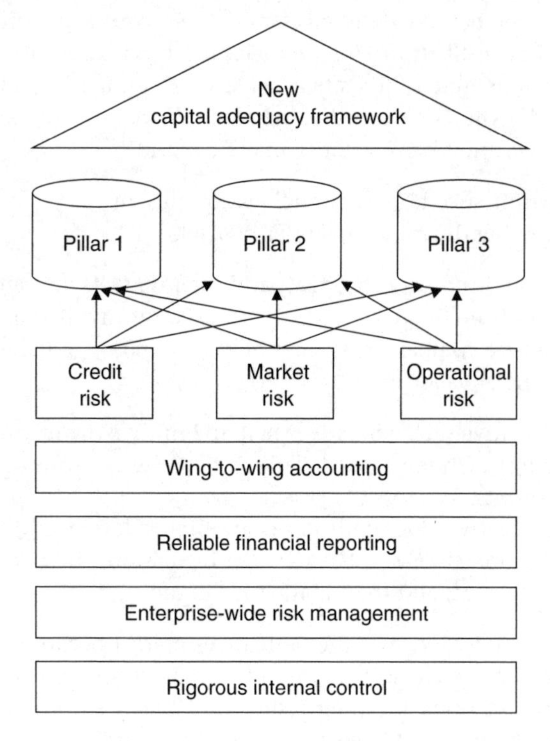

Figure 1.3 The control structure underpinning the new capital adequacy by the Basle committee.

which gives an appreciation of capital allocation requirements in the function of risk measurements, monitoring, and control. In the case of qualifiable operational risks, a key role is played by Pillar 2 and Pillar 3.

In my opinion, all financial transactions, including alternative investments, should satisfy the requirements established by the three pillars. This is fundamental to both market confidence and market discipline. As the financial crisis of 2000–2 has shown, the time for half-measures and postponement has passed.

All this is very pertinent to alternative investments because banks and traders dealing in them, as well as their clients, are exposed to high degrees of risk. They hope to benefit from the positives, but the negative cannot be avoided. Often, the end-investor (whether a private individual institutional investor or other company) experiences an inordinate amount of exposure lured by the promise of a wonderful future.

5. The participants in alternative investments

To better appreciate the effect of multiple leveraging which characterises alternative investments deals, it is advisable to think of the different layers composing the structure of intermediaries between the instrument and the end-investor. Figure 1.4 suggests this structure consists of at least four layers, each with its own risks:

- At the bottom of the chain are the derivative instruments, many of them novel and complex.

These are designed and inventoried by movers and shakers, the hedge funds in the next layer. Note that the contents of alternative investments portfolios are not audited, even by an Arthur Andersen auditor.

- Next to the bottom of the chain are the hedge funds, which take on the crude risk.

The small number of funds that work with a bank as portfolio managers of alternative investments are behind what is known as the *multimanager* concept (see Chapter 5). The existence of multimanagers gives the next layer its reason of being.

- Above the hedge funds stands the *aggregator of risk*, with its stable of 10 or 20 entities, each weighting a variable share of its portfolio.

Many of the claims about liquidity, security, and high returns (see Chapter 2) come from the aggregator of risk. As for the control of exposure, commercial banks that are in this business say: 'We monitor daily'. Chapters 2 and 3 examine the shaky grounds of this claim.

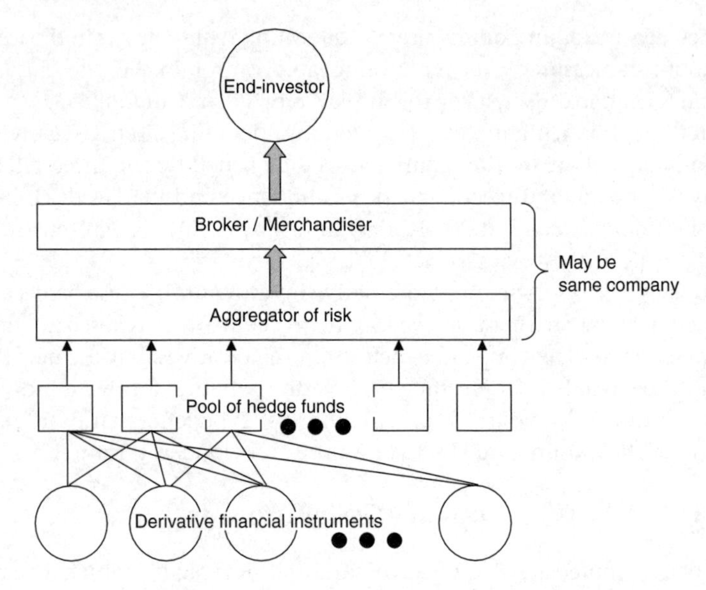

Figure 1.4 The multilayer structure between leveraged instruments and the end-investor.

- At the top of the layered structure is the broker, or SAIV, which sells the alternative investment instrument to the client, the end-investor who is assuming the *full risk*.

Typically, those at the bottom of the chain are independent entities trading for their own account. They pass their risks to the aggregator, who transfers them to the broker, and from there they go to the end-investor. The aggregator of the hedge funds and the broker may be two different companies, or they may be two different divisions of the same firm. The SAIV is usually an independent business unit which does both jobs: aggregation of risk and sales. In either one of these cases:

- The aggregator of risk and the broker would try to offload the risk on their customers. At the core of their business is *distribution*.
- The hedge fund would use different strategies to leverage itself: macromarkets, emerging markets, commodities, equity long/shorts, event-driven solutions, debt gearing, and so on.

Because too many players in the hedge funds industry target the same instruments, markets, and end-investors, some strategies are becoming less effective. Among the other aftermaths, heightened demand for financial instruments used by hedge funds (largely based on hopes) has narrowed spreads and diminished their profits. Unavoidably, this led to more risk taking.

Absolute power corrupts absolutely

> One of the points a couple of reviewers have made is that this text does not give the readers the credit to be able to make up their own minds about the subject of alternative investments and their risks. It is telling them up front what the author's opinion is, and goes on to prove it.

There are several ways of answering this argument. One of them is that all 17 books on alternative investments already in the market praise them as the right deal at the right time – which is wrong. Investors are being overfed with the merits of shrewed pieces of dealmaking. It is high time that they hear a contrarian opinion, so that they can *really* make up their own mind.

The second answer is based on the extensive research which has gone into this book. Its contents present many opinions, not just the author's own. In fact, my own opinion has been shaped by the research findings which can be summed up in one short sentence: *'Be very, very careful with alternative investments. You may end up regretting your decision.'*

The third and more brutal answer is that secrecy, lack of transparency, leverage and complexity – all of them characteristic of alternative investments – are very bad counsellors. Winston Churchill once said that power corrupts and absolute power corrupts absolutely. Money is power. Therefore,

- Absolute power over money leads to a wave of corruption and malfeasance.
- The old days of 'your word is your bond' are more a part of the past than of current business practice.

This is fully documented by the well-known cases of absolute irresponsibility at the CEO and board level in the 2001–2 timeframe. Just look at the grand larceny that took place at the investor's expense, with the result that business confidence has taken leave and virtue has been dethroned by greed.

Don't follow the herd. You will get burned

Precisely because the reader should make up his or her mind after carefully evaluating different, often conflicting viewpoints, the strategy chosen for this book is to warn the reader before he gets depressed because he lost his assets. Basically, the contrarian spirit says: 'Never follow conventional wisdom in the market,' including investment drives which masquerade as being conventional.

To go counter 'this' of 'that' instrument, particularly one which is aggressively promoted by the merchandisers of risk, means that you have to learn how to think for yourself. The problem is that most people and companies don't want to take up the effort to do so. They prefer being the followers of a trend, but by taking this track they do not appreciate that even riding the wave requires thinking.

If one wants to go in for alternative investments, he or she should examine them not as a trend but individually. A rigorous evaluation must definitely pay a great amount of attention to risk and limits to exposure, as well as to the practice of doing stress tests regularly.[7] Don't be afraid to uncover huge amount of risks through stress testing. This is the best way to learn something about the unknown which surrounds you with alternative investments.

In conclusion, the complexity of the layering arrangements in the origination and merchandising of risk, outlined in this section, is often as ill appreciated by the end-investor as concepts of leverage and illiquidity. A basic question I ask in my seminars, for instance, is: 'Do you know exactly what you are buying when you are 30 per cent short, 50 per cent long and 20 per cent market-neutral?' Many financial experts come to these seminars but none of those exposed to this query gave me a reply that really made sense.

6. Hedge funds and the lack of regulation

Commercial and investment banks work with ten, twenty or more hedge funds, allocating anywhere from two to ten per cent of the money in a portfolio they offer to the investor. Theoretically, and only theoretically, exposure is diversified, because the different funds do not assume the same risks. This sort of amalgam of credit risks and market risks taken by the different funds, which may well be unrelated to one another is packaged together and marketed as a *Fund of Funds*. With respect to the product mix in a fund of funds, Chapter 5 gives some examples of the types of financial instruments being used and their weight in a managed fund.

The first *fund of funds* was launched in 1969 by Leveraged Capital; George Soros followed with Quantum. Today, practically every major financial institution is becoming involved. Noteworthy is the domicile of funds of funds. The British Virgin Islands lead with 29 per cent, followed by the State of Delaware with 26 per cent, Bermuda with 15 per cent, Cayman Islands with 8 per cent, the balance being in Netherlands Antilles, Bahamas, Illinois, Florida and elsewhere.[8]

> 'We need to make the explicit point that the reason why most hedge funds cannot operate onshore is because they are heavily restricted (rules about shorting etc),' said one of the reviewers. 'That is why the domicile is noteworthy.'

Regulation and compliance to regulation is necessary to keep a sense of balance between risk and return. Traditionally secretive, hedge funds face big pressure from regulators and investors for more disclosure. That the activities of hedge funds should be regulated, and therefore restricted, is a self-evident truth. Why should banks be regulated and closely supervised while hedge funds are not?

As the *Economist* aptly noted in a recent issue: 'Hedge funds and other highly leveraged institutions are regulated lightly in most countries, and not at all in America. A proposal by a presidential working party for tougher regulation of hedge funds, prompted by the collapse of Long-Term Capital Management, was unexpectedly blocked in Congress.'[9]

This total lack of supervision decreases the transparency and increases the risks taken by hedge funds; therefore also by funds of funds and end-investors. Indeed, this is one of the reasons why I am very negative in terms of the way hedge funds are looking at risk control. *If* supervision was useless, *then* the taxpayer should not be asked to pay the costs for FSA, SEC, the Fed, FDIC, or OCC. But it is valuable – and every entity should be subject to supervision and compliance.

Ways and means of supervision should be polyvalent because there are different types of funds. The main classes are: open-end, close-end, close-end secondary market only, open-end with secondary market, and open-end with no secondary market. Other characteristics differentiating between different versions of funds are subscriptions, minimum size of investment, redemptions, and the client population which they address.

The merchandisers of risk appeal to both equity and fixed income investors. Since derivatives are versatile financial instruments, hedge funds and funds of funds have created leveraged bonds. Their target is pension funds and other institutions, as well as private investors, who are conservative and keep more than 60 per cent of their wealth in fixed income instruments. Of course, leveraged bonds are totally different instruments from classical bonds, because they have a high risk profile.

Today, in Europe at least, the majority of pension funds are primarily bond investors. An estimated 80–85 per cent of them are not yet hedge funds clients. Some, however, are having second thoughts. In February 2002, a conference held in London[10] revealed that 64 per cent of pension funds managers believed that hedge funds could help reduce their portfolio risk (!!!) – presumably through diversification into uncorrelated investments. The keyword in this statement is *presumably*. To my judgement it is the wrong presumption.

- Alternative investments are derivatives based on assets and liabilities, not the real assets themselves.
- Because they are leveraged, as their underliers go up or down, they will also follow in the same direction – only much faster.

> 'These two statements are not necessarily valid,' said a reviewer with reference to the above bullets. 'Many hedge funds would claim (with performance to back it up) that they reduce volatility (the most common measure of risk) i.e. they are less risky. (Hence) we cannot generalise about them.'

That derivative instruments are less volatile than their underlier is something which turns economic theory on its head. It's voodoo economics as people in America used to say about Reaganomics in the 1980s. Hedge fund managers should not be making such statements, because the value of their stock drops in the market. The same is true of pension fund managers.

As for past 'performance to back-up' silly statements, no doubt the reviewer knows that past performance is no guarantee of future performance. This is even more true when the supervision of institutions is nil or minimal, and in many cases creative accounting practices have taken the driver's seat.

Pension funds managers, mutual funds (unit trusts) managers, other institutional investors and high net worth individuals should be worried about this lack of hedge funds' transparency and the opaque correlation to which reference has been made. Indeed, some of them are concerned not only about *transparency*, but also about management *tools*, ability to *control risk* and market *liquidity*. None of these is self-evident, and each of these issues poses a special problem.

- With alternative investments transparency is at bare minimum (see Chapters 2 and 9).
- Tools are still in their infancy, though some are coming along, the best one being *stress testing* (see Chapter 8).[11]

- The ability to control risk is as much a function of management intent and resolution, as it is of available tools (see Chapters 3 and 9).
- Liquidity with alternative investments is at bare bottom and there is no guarantee that the central banks or the IMF will be willing or able to bail banks out.

> 'Liquidity,' said one of the reviewers, 'depends on the fund. It was certainly true of LTCM but not for all hedge funds.'

The answer of course is that practically all hedge funds are illiquid because of the goals which they pursue, and the strategies which they follow. When they promise their investors 20 or 30 per cent returns per year, they cannot afford to be otherwise than fully invested. In the money market, they will only get a low one-digit interest per year. Over and above full investment comes high leverage (more about this later).

One can understand how pension fund managers and other institutional investors are bewildered by the barrage of calls they receive inviting them to consider individual hedge fund or fund of funds. This is not surprising. What is surprising is that many managers have made the transition to 'hedge funds thinking' without appreciating that the required skills to keep it running are a scarce commodity.

Record inflows are chasing too few of the better known funds, straining the performance of existing managers. As an article in *Business Week* was to comment, the hedge funds industry suffers from a dearth of talent.[12] Increased demand from investors and financial institutions is luring inexperienced entrants into hedge fund management with potentially catastrophic results.

It is all very well to say 'go for a manager with a track record'. But there are not that many well performing, stable funds among those that are rarely accessible, and one should never forget that past performance is no guarantee of future performance. Furthermore, if every institutional holder moves to hedge funds because of the search for diversification, low returns in the bond markets, or any other reason, the alternative investments' business runs the risk of becoming another emerging markets' boom and bust.

7. The role of hedge funds in alternative investments

Alternative investments policies and practices have been followed by the better known hedge funds since the 1980s. Quantum and Tiger Management, for example, pursued a policy that combined leverage with geopolitical conditions. They verified valuations through the use of models and information obtained from academic and industrial experts. They also looked for catalysts to unlock the value they had identified.

Quantum and Tiger had many imitators, some of which eventually brought new tools to the investment game. Today, though no two hedge funds have exactly the same product mix in their portfolio or go after precisely the same goals (see Chapter 5), their strategies tend to be similar, that is:

- they use derivatives, portfolio leverage, and equity shorting rather than pure hedging;
- their macro securities portfolio includes fixed income, currency and financial futures;
- the percentage of long/short equities and macro strategies in their portfolio identifies the risk strategy which they have chosen; and
- the amount of leveraging they are after, as well as the elasticity in expanding the leveraging ratio.

During the 1980s and 1990s (as well as today), leveraging was practiced not only through huge loans from banks and institutional investors, but also by taking advantage of broader market opportunities by means of derivatives in equity and debt securities, currencies, interest rates, stock market indices, and certain key commodities. Investments have taken place in spot and forward markets, as well as through futures, options and other derivative financial instruments.

These instruments are in steady evolution, but what really differentiates the alternative investments (and hedge funds) of today from those of yesterday is that they address themselves not just to institutional investors willing to risk their money for higher returns, but also to private investors, both wealthy and retail. There is an argument that individuals invest their own money at their own peril, and it is the involvement of institutional investors, and pension funds in particular, in high risk investments which should be closely monitored.

This argument is correct only up to a point. While every measure should be taken to assure that pension funds safeguard their corpus – and the same is true of not-for-profits foundations and endowments[13] – there is no reason why the general public should be defrauded of its assets. Neither is there any reason why hedge funds should not be regulated in a way similar to that of brokers and commercial banks.

- Theoretically, alternative investments address themselves to wealthy individuals.

- Yet practically, they are sold to everybody willing to sign the investment disclaimer.

Business Week had described the shaky ground of investments in the 2000–2 timeframe, and what it means to the growing class of private investors, and to the economy as a whole. The advice by *Business Week* that private investors 'must learn to gauge risk and manage it'[14] is great, but it necessarily means that the institutional, as well as the average investor must learn the nuts and bolts of risk management or would find himself or herself at a loss in identifying the true risk of hedge fund and fund of funds investments.

Let me add that the reference to the 'average investor' includes people and companies who do not quite understand the risks they are taking with leveraged instruments that bet, rightly or wrongly, on the market's direction and other unpredictable events (see Chapter 2). To press this issue of exposure, and link it to a likely return, I will examine the infrastructure supporting the new 'wonder deals' before looking at the factors propelling alternative investments.

The impact of hedge funds on financial markets

The end-investor may be offered an alternative investment by the bank where he has his deposits, by a broker, or by a SAIV. No matter who is the selling party, the way to bet is that behind this offer stand one or more hedge funds trying to increase their returns in an uncertain and volatile financial environment.

There are between 4,000 and 6,000 hedge funds worldwide (experts are not sure of their exact number) with an estimated US$500 billion currently under management. Around 80 per cent of that money is in the hands of the 400 larger entities. Hedge fund executives argue that while US$500 billion sounds like a lot of money, it is trifling compared with the worldwide equity market of around US$25 to US$28 trillion.

To respond to this argument let's recall that, as opposed to credit institutions, hedge funds are highly leveraged. This does not mean that credit institutions are not leveraged. Their leveraging can be computed through the level of reserve requirements implied by regulators. Commercial banks leveraging is, in principle, a mid-one-digit factor.

By contrast, the leverage factor of many hedge funds is well above 50, or 5,000 per cent. Taking just 40 as a reference level, this would mean US$500 billion $\times$ 40 = US$20 trillion. This is above the total current capitalisation of US markets by an impressive margin. Heavily geared hedge funds must therefore be considered financial market movers rather than small market players.

'It may be true that the larger funds have a leverage factor above 50, but it is not true of all funds,' said one of the reviewers. 'We need some degree of quantification here. What is the leverage of the average fund, what is the worse case, what is the best.'

Since this reviewer works with hedge funds he should have known that the answer to his query can only be found in 'cloud 9'. The reason is secrecy and lack of transparency. Hedge funds are so secretive nothing transpires in terms of any individual hedge funds gearing figures, except hearsay manipulated the way it fits the hedge funds best. What is generally known in the market is that:

- Current trend sees to it that the average leverage factor increases over time, along with the stakes.
- LTCM had a leverage of 350 when it crashed. Even if this is an extreme value, the fact it can be done did not get lost among hedge funds.

Neither is there a 'best' leverage figure. Every hedge fund makes its own decision on that matter. The rule is that the higher the gearing, the greater the amount of assumed risk. Indeed the reviewer himself reached this conclusion when he stated:

> **Markets are markets. They are difficult things to read, no matter what "expert" you claim to be**. We should not damn the hedge funds industry particularly for failing to read the markets.

Every banker, every trader, every investor and evidently every hedge fund manager should have the bold letters of this statement before his eyes during working hour – and in his mind the rest of the time. The statement made by the reviewer is absolutely correct. And it is also the reason why investors should not use too much leverage. The bold letters of this statement are a warning against taking high risks.

A different reviewer agreed with the message in this text about the risks in general – lack of transparency, problems with valuation, and so on. He added, however, that most hedge funds instruments are bought by professional investors, institutions and high net worth people and 'it is quite clear that funds of funds put together by banks, SAIVs etc. are not suitable for Aunt Agatha.'

Leaving aside the fact that alternative investments are now marketed retail, it is wrong to assume that professional investors have a first class risk management system. They don't. As for the 'Aunt Agathas', in the 1990s they have burned themselves very badly by becoming 'names' in the Lloyds Syndicates. Some did it for greed, others for prestige. It cannot be excluded that they would repeat the experience with alternative investments.

Every institution is exposed to mismanagement of risk

That many hedge funds, mutual funds, and pension funds are behind in risk control is not written as a pejorative reference but as a statement of facts. Even the best known investment banks are not always tier-1 in risk management. A *Business Week* article credited Jon S. Corzine then CEO of Goldman Sachs for getting the Wall Street institution (founded by Marcus Goldman in 1896) back on track. Corzine, the article said, took the helm in September 1994 when Goldman had been derailed by huge trading losses and bad management decisions. He quickly

- refocused the firm on client relationships;
- installed risk control; and
- tightened the management structure.

A new risk management system and rigorous internal control assured that the CEO was again in charge, *Business Week* suggested.[15] If in one of the best investment banks in the world risk controls are in disarray, guess about what happens in the average hedge fund.

> Therefore, a third reviewer was right when she made the comment 'Being able to manage/reduce risk is going to be a critical issue with alternative investments, particularly for institutional investors.'

The reviewer then asked to elaborate on risk management in this text. How to exercise prudential risk management in a complex portfolio like that of hedge funds must be the subject of a series of books, not of a paragraph or of a chapter. As a basic advice, however, nobody – including institutional investors – should assume risks he

- does not fully understand;
- is not able to see through their consequences; and
- cannot steadily measure and control.

As a second advice, beware of volatility because volatility and risk correlate (see Chapter 2). Gearing significantly increases volatility. Yet, the aggregators and merchandisers of risk suggest that alternative investments have a negligible impact on the volatility of the overall market, and that they cannot be held responsible for the growing market uncertainty.

Disregard of basic market facts and over-optimistic statements on alternative opportunities in capital markets and other instruments by the hedge funds, the banks, the brokers, and the SAIVs, are means used to convince investors that the macromarkets, long/short deals, and market-neutral investments both:

- keep risk under lock and key; and
- still have the potential to grow.

I would argue that almost the opposite is true with both statements. As far as exposure is concerned, nobody knows the direction the market will take. One experiment I undertook between January 2000 and February 2002 was to speak to many experts: analysts, quants, investment advisors, asset managers, hedge fund executives. When I ask the question of market direction, I made a point to write down their answer – and then check it in the light of subsequent developments. The hit rate has been 30 per cent.

Even 50 per cent failures in prediction can be an unmitigated disaster with high gearing, and many of these people were dealing with leveraged investments. The best directional advice was that by J.P. Morgan to a Harvard graduate who once asked the great master if the stock market will go up or down: 'It will fluctuate, young man, it will fluctuate,' Morgan said.

Finally, an answer to the second of the above two bullets must pay due attention to the available options. Merrill Lynch has been a vendor of alternative investments for many years, promoting several funds and funds of funds. However, on 1 July 2002, this investment bank found the courage to write the following in its US Strategy Update:

> Cash has now outperformed the S&P 500 for the time period spanning the last 55 months (December 1997 to July 2002). The bull market in cash continues.[16]

Add to the S&P reference made by Merrill Lynch all hedge funds and any other alternative investment vehicle, and you have a perfect quotation summarising in a nutshell the message Chapter 1 brings to the reader.

Appendix: the dead mule and the old country farmer*

At last, someone must put the risks being taken in layman's terms! Back to basics, the Enron, WorldCom, and alternative investments cases can be expressed in a simple form so that everyone can understand.

* This story is one of the most beautiful orphans of the Internet. I got it from Alain Bernard, who received it from Rich Geiger.

An old country farmer with serious financial problems bought a mule from another old country farmer for $100, who agreed to deliver the mule the next day. However, the next day the seller drove up and said, 'Sorry, but I have some bad news: The mule died.'

'Well, then, just give me my money back,' said the buyer. 'Can't do that. I went and spent it already,' answered the seller. 'OK, then. Just unload the mule.' 'What ya gonna do with a dead mule?' 'I'm going to raffle him off.' 'You can't raffle off a dead mule!' 'Sure I can. I just won't tell anybody he's dead.'

A month later the two old country farmers met and the one who sold the mule asked: 'Whatever happened with that dead mule?' 'I raffled him off just like I said I would. I sold 500 tickets at $2 a piece and made a profit of $898.' 'Didn't anyone complain?' 'Just the guy who won. So I gave him his two dollars back.'

2
Are Alternative Investments Inherently Risky?

1. Introduction

The golden rule in investments is the higher the leverage, the greater the amount of risk assumed and (hopefully) profits gained.

Unlike most end-investors, traders know from experience that leveraged positions are risky because the market can turn against them, and that they can also lose their company in the process. Exposure is so much higher when going short, because there is absolutely no yardstick on how high or how low the market can go.

Neither are price/earnings (P/E) ratios what they used to be. During the internet boom, the high fliers were companies such as Amazon.com, making huge losses. Over a surprisingly long period, its stock could go only one way: Up. But those that bet that there were no upper limits to the price of internet companies paid dearly for it.

Whole nations have been bankrupted by leverage. Japan repeated in the 1980s the same mistakes it had made in the Second World War through military overgearing. Twelve years down the line, after Japan's growth curve bent in 1990, the country is still unlikely to see a sustained recovery in its economy and in its stock market. In such environments, the only strategy that makes sense is that of a long-term horizon, and this only by investors who

- are not leveraged;
- are in control of their exposure; and
- are also prepared to take a risk.

Nobody can escape the aftermath of overgearing. The first year of the new millennium became one of global financial crises as analysts, bankers, and investors realised that in 2000 financial assets reached

US$400 trillion while the world's GDP stood at US$30 trillion. Although hedge funds seem to be the most geared entities of the 'new economy', the whole global economy itself has been leveraged about 13 times over.

This has an evident impact on capitalisation and on the potential for lost wealth. Mary Meeker, a Morgan Stanley analyst, estimated that US$727 billion in wealth was lost by the fall in the market value of about 362 internet companies between December 1999 and mid-July 2001. Though non-technology firms also suffered, she characterises the prevailing situation as a difficult 'third inning' of a technology cycle that should eventually rebound.[1]

Eventually yes, but nobody knows really when. Therefore, many banks are building up their defences. For example, in early September 2001, Crédit Suisse stopped dealing in margin accounts. Merrill Lynch has not dealt in risky commodity futures since early 1999. Meeker has adapted an aphorism from the Depression to describe the danger created by investors' trauma. The 'biggest risk we all face,' she summed up, 'is not being willing to continue to take risks'.

Because they are largely contrarians, hedge funds continue taking risks (which is good for the economy) but now, through risk aggregators, (in a process described in Chapter 1) these risks are being passed on to end-investors. The claims being made with alternative investments are questionable, while the risks being taken are real. Arguments in favour of alternative investments include:

- 'Above average reward with limited exposure', a smoke and mirrors argument;
- 'Low volatility and high liquidity', another mirage. Exactly the opposite is true (see next section);
- 'Benefits derived from diversifications' an argument which avoids mentioning the risk of high leverage; and
- 'Very low market risk and credit risk', a false pretention. Both credit risk and market risk are significant.

My experience has been that a great deal of the risks with alternative investments are ignored. These include:

- operational risk (such as legal risk and technological risk discussed in Chapter 3);
- reputational risk, which is very often downplayed;
- risks resulting from lack of transparency;
- exposure due to the lack of regulation for certain types of financial entities (see Chapter 1).

> 'This comes over as very biased,' said one of the reviewers.

I disagree with this statement, because these risks are present and real; therefore investors and traders should face them. But, I agree with the second statement of the reviewer: 'These risks are faced by everybody, not just the hedge funds, funds of funds, SAIVs, and their alternative investment instruments.' The question then is: 'How well are banks, hedge funds, institutional investors and other investors controlling the risks they are taking?'

2. Identifying the risks of alternative investments

Everybody working in finance and in any other walk of life, except the bureaucracy, takes risks. At the same time, it is only normal that entities that assume more risks because of the instruments they use and their leverage, are more exposed than others. Derivatives are more risky than the products from which they are derived, and alternative investments are more risky than classical investments.

> '(You) need explaining the advantages of alternative investments,' the same reviewer continued.

This statement touches a sensitive cord. I don't march by orders, and I don't make my heels click. To put it bluntly, had I found in my research factual and documented evidence about advantages connected to alternative investments, I would have been most happy to outline them in this text.

The reader does not need to worry about missing an outline of such 'advantages' in this book. Surely, he or she gets plenty of sales literature and offers about the 'benefits' to be derived from alternative investments some time in the future. By contrast, what this book does is to discuss the *risks*, elaborate on them, and provide investors and managers the opportunity to assess them in the context of their own investment portfolio goals.

To begin with, one way to appreciate how much risk the end-investor assumes with funds of funds and special alternative investment vehicles (SAIVs) is to focus on the effects of volatility and liquidity. Market illiquidity and market volatility correlate among themselves, and with highly leveraged trading.

Illiquidity and volatility magnify the risks

A great deal of alternative investments positions, and trading associated with them, involve instruments which are not only inherently geared but also volatile and materially affected by unpredictable factors. It is in their illiquidity and volatility that the essence of the risks of alternative investments lies. Because of this (1) relatively small price movements may produce a large profit or loss; and (2) capital losses are magnified by the fact that hedge funds and SAIVs enter into borrowing arrangements for leveraging their proprietary trading, over and above the gearing they do through derivatives.

What investors of alternative investments should appreciate is that while volatility creates profit potential, it also amplifies the risks associated with trading. The combination of these two factors: leverage and volatility, can subject the value of the investment portfolio to sharp fluctuations, both positive and negative. A frequently applied rule of thumb is that:

- when the market falls by 10 per cent it is a correction;
- when it falls by 20 per cent, it is a bear market.

Looking at the market trend from mid-2000 to mid-2002, we see that all of the major stock indices were clearly in negative territory (except perhaps China's). Globalisation is not a one-way street (see Chapter 3).

A principal risk in the speculative dealing of hedge funds and risk aggregators is the volatility of market prices regarding the instruments being traded. The profitability of alternative investments depends, to a significant degree, on the asset manager's ability to forecast price movements correctly. If he or she fails to predict the direction of market changes, substantial losses could result. These are paid for by the end-investor. End-investors must understand that:

- in general, futures trading and other derivatives deals are *risk transfer* activities; and
- for every gain there is an equal and offsetting loss, rather than a participation over time in general economic growth.

This zero sum game is particularly true in shorting and in speculation, while long positions tend to gain from growth in the economy which – in the long run – is not zero sum. Growth in economic activity has been one of the pillars of capital markets.

To benefit from growth associated to capital markets, investors must heed the advice of Amadeo Giannini, the founder of the Bank of America. He was telling his clients, his friends, and his employees to

Table 2.1 Order of magnitude annual return and volatility with alternative investment strategies

	Annual return (in %)	**Volatility (in %)**
Long/short equity	20	13
Macropolicies	15	8
Event-driven	15	6
Emerging markets	14	16
Equity market neutral	11	3
Convertible arbitrage	10	4
Fixed income arbitrage	6	5
Short selling	−3	20

invest in the stock market, but never to borrow money to speculate. If equities turned sour, Giannini prodded his friends to sit on their investment and wait for the upturn. Only a long-term investor who is not leveraged can heed this advice.

The type of capital investments Amadeo Giannini was speaking about was linear. This is not today's investment style. Even so, the great California banker was always on alert for risk. On 14 March 1928, way before the crash, he issued a press release warning investors to pay off their debts and get out of the market. 'We want them to own their own shares outright,' he said. 'We don't want them held as security of loans.'[2]

The linear type of investing is not the present-day policy, but this does not mean one should become careless about risk. The practice of mixing different strategies, including a variety of instruments to create a highly leveraged portfolio, known as *multi-style,*[3] can be especially dangerous. Based on real statistics, Table 2.1 indicates that losses can be hefty, not only due to the amount of leverage. Just as difficult is finding the proper algorithm to balance risk, as well as to locate and train the right personnel able to screen, execute, and follow-up on such trades. I discuss the perils of this strategy in Chapter 5.

Are alternative investments liquid financial products?

The average alternative investments' customer may not recognise it, but the exposure he or she is taking with highly leveraged instruments can eventually consume all of the capital put at risk. Part of the reason for accepting such high levels of risk can be explained by greed, or at least an aggressive attitude towards the seesaw of risk and reward. The other part is explained by the expectations of investors being raised, with respect to year-to-year profitability of their assets. Banks and hedge funds selling alternative investments commonly claim that:

> The target market audience includes investors who want to obtain above average risk-adjusted returns.

This is a misstatement. What the investors are offered are *not risk-adjusted* returns, but a situation where 'risk is king', paving the way to the total loss of the capital invested. This misstatement is often accompanied by the following declaration:

> Alternative investments include selling borrowed assets, because shorting can outperform in both bull and bear markets.

This, too, is incorrect. These misstatements feed on the fact that very few end-investors understand what 'going short' means, let alone the risks involved in doing so. Moreover, the assumption that shorting can outperform in both bull and bear markets is inaccurate; in bull markets it can be deadly. Another statement commonly found in an alternative investment prospectus (this one from a well-known commercial bank, not a hedge fund) is:

> The financial instruments being offered are liquid investment products.

As I never tire of repeating in my seminars on risk management, exactly the opposite is true. Most derivatives are traded over the counter and, in almost all cases, they are illiquid. Only incidentally they might be liquid, and when this happens it will not last long. In fact, illiquidity is the alter ego of leverage, as I describe in this chapter.

'This is biased,' said a reviewer.

I disagree. Quite to the contrary, it is objective. Biased is the negation of a statement based on thirty-five years of experience in banking, as well as on the opinion of many cognisant investors and traders.

'You say there is a role for hedge funds in a modern economy, but never stipulate what this is and what the benefits are,' said another reviewer.

Unlike the avalanche of remarks made in Chapter 1, which are baseless, this one has a point. On the whole, I am not an enthusiast of hedge funds, because of the risks embedded in them that have not yet been tested as is the case with the banking industry. Also because hedge funds escape supervision. Yet, in a modern economy there is a role for them.

- For the most part, they act as contrarians and therefore, though they themselves are illiquid, they bring liquidity to the market.
- They are also active in both long and short trades which, in any other case than of a deeply bear market, might act as a stabilising influence.

It is essentially the high gearing of hedge funds (see Chapter 1) that creates an inordinate amount of systemic risk, augmented by the lack of prudential supervision. Soros is right when he states: 'The international financial system is in danger of breaking down.... There is practically no recognition that financial markets, particularly the international financial markets are inherently unstable.... We are talking about boom/bust processes.'[4]

Prudential supervision at the level of the international financial system is not going to produce miracles, but it can help as the fly wheel keeping the bust process – systemic risk – more or less at bay. It can as well set some standards for alternative investments in connection to:

- maximum allowed exposure;
- mandatory liquidity level; and
- the policy on redemptions.

As things stand today, the hedge funds' control over redemption period works against the end-investor. Hedge funds control redemption uncertainty through restrictive redemption provisions, which are detailed in their offering memorandum. They commonly require a lock-up period, which can vary between six months and two or three years after an initial investment is made, and a 30 to 60 days' redemption notice. The latter clause:

- mitigates the adverse impact of unexpected withdrawals; and
- helps the hedge fund manage the calculation of net asset value (NAV).

If there were no other reasons why hedge funds are typically illiquid, and I have presented plenty of them, including the experts criteria of liquidity (see Chapter 1), stringent redemption periods would have seen to it that *alternative investments are illiquid as far as end-investors are concerned*. The prospectus given to the end-investor may state otherwise, but the absence of immediate liquidity is a fact.

Liquidity, transparency, and supervision

Trading in public stock exchanges still has three major advantages over alternative investments: *liquidity, transparency,* and *supervision*. Stocks, particularly stocks of companies traded in the Group of Ten countries, are more or less liquid assets, even if their price fluctuates. This is not true of derivatives, which are typically traded OTC, and of many other products with which hedge funds are engaged.

'Derivatives are not necessarily traded over the counter,' said a reviewer.

Here, I am afraid, we are playing with words. This is the kind of statement by the merchandisers of risk to which I particularly object, because it is made to misguide the unsophisticated end-investor. Not only, by large majority, derivatives are traded OTC, as Tables 2.2 and 2.3 show, but also the more exotic – and therefore the more risky derivatives – are strictly traded OTC.

These percentages between OTC and exchange-based derivatives represent a real-life situation. They are based on actual numbers from one of the major European commercial banks. Gross volume of buy and sell contracts is combined. The percentages include unsettled spot transactions in

Table 2.2 Notional principal amounts in derivatives OTC versus exchange-traded

Instrument	OTC (in %)	Exchange-traded (in %)
Currency products	41.0	1.0
Interest-rate products	30.0	21.0
Equity derivatives	5.0	0.5
Precious metals/commodities	1.1	0.4
Total	**77.1**	**22.9**

Table 2.3 Notional principal amounts by taxonomy of derivative instruments

Instrument	OTC (in %)	Exchange-traded (in %)	Total
Currency products	41.0	1.0	**42.0**
Interest-rate products	30.0	21.0	**51.0**
Equity derivatives	5.0	0.5	**5.5**
Precious metals and other commodities	1.1	0.4	**1.5**

notional principal amounts. As the reader can easily see, OTC trades are 335 per cent more important than exchanged-traded instruments.

To appreciate the risk embedded in illiquid derivative instruments it is appropriate to recall that the amount of cumulative exposure increases 25 to 30 per cent per year. When two derivatives dealers – Bank of New England and Drexel Burnham – failed, the damage was successfully walled off, because in notional principal amounts the exposure of their companies was relatively trivial. Each had 'only' $30 to $36 billion of contracts outstanding when the crash came.

With the exception of LTCM, the derivatives industry has so far not been tested by a giant failure. This would have been the case if serious problems affected one of the mammoth banks with trillions in notional principal derivatives exposure. The derivatives portfolio of JP Morgan Chase was at that level of $24 trillion on 31 March 2001. Figures for 2002 are not yet available, but the market believes this exposure would not be far from $30 trillion.

It does not take much to understand why derivatives are primarily OTC trades. The power of this financial instrument is precisely that it is flexible. If we keep the risk out of the picture for a moment, the major contribution of derivatives is that they can be tailored to meet the investor's goals, drives, and wishes – and this is done through bilateral agreements. Typically, instruments traded in established exchanges are standardised – not custom made.

3. Risks resulting from diversification and from absolute returns

At the root of alternative investment strategies is the fact that, with globalisation, the equity markets around the world correlate, and something similar can be said about the bond markets. There used to be a time when the stock exchanges in New York, London, Frankfurt, Hong Kong and Tokyo moved, at least some of the time, in opposite directions. Therefore, investing in two of them that were negatively correlated, or uncorrelated, provided a certain degree of diversification.

For any practical purpose, what is stated in the preceding paragraph is no longer the case. The markets for equities and debt around the world tend to correlate. Information spreads fast and networks accelerate the execution of trades, news coverage, and the propagation of market shocks. Because of these factors, today the major stock exchanges usually move in unison. They directly influence one another, with New York more or less establishing the mood.

The fact that stock exchanges around the globe are considerably correlated means that diversification through equity investments is no longer possible to the same degree, if at all. Therefore, investors are drawn to the message put forward by those selling alternative investments, that they bring high returns and are uncorrelated. These are of course two different issues:

- The one does not necessarily imply the other.
- Neither are they telling much about risk and return resulting from diversification.

Such facts contradict what is said by many merchandisers of risk through alternative investments who describe their vehicle as 'the billion dollar sure thing', using the argument of diversification – across investments, across funds, across strategies – to substantiate their claims.

A globally diversified portfolio using long/short and macro strategies seems attractive, but, it is also very risky, and the results may not be commensurate with the assumed exposure. Even *if* the risk aggregator seeks to deliver enhanced returns, and says that he diversifies between investment styles and markets, he does not do away with exposure. In fact, because of leveraging he is assuming more of it.[5]

> 'Correct, higher reward means higher risk,' said one of the reviewers, 'But you need to introduce this in a less negative way, rather than saying that people who are greedy get burned.'

This comment surprises me, because the paragraph in question did not speak of greed. What it said is that diversification through alternative investments is no penicillin. Beyond this, even a diversified portfolio can get burned. Table 2.4 shows the contents of a diversified investment portfolio, which includes both derivatives risk and more classical credit risk/market risk. The warning about the risk of exposure wins thumbs up.

The careful reader will notice that all ten examples in Table 2.4 are of the bread-and-butter derivatives type. There are no exotics where the risks will be much higher. A typical hedge fund portfolio today may include plenty of much more sophisticated derivatives instruments than those written in this table.

Notice also that those instruments with OBS risk may have only credit risk, or market risk, or both. Two basic criteria underpin this classification. The first is the amount of accounting loss the financial institution,

Table 2.4 Some financial instruments with OBS of accounting loss; only issuer[a] OBS risk is involved, no holder OBS risk

Instrument	OBS risk	Credit risk	Market risk
1. Repurchase agreements:			
Accounting for as a borrowing by issuer	No		
Accounting for as a sale by issuer	Yes	Yes	Yes
2. Put option on stock (premium paid up front):			
Covered option	Yes	Yes	
Naked option	Yes	Yes	
3. Put option on interest rate contracts (premium paid up front):			
Covered option	Yes	Yes	Yes
Naked option	Yes	Yes	Yes
4. Call option on stock, foreign currency, or interest rate contracts (premium paid up front):			
Covered option	Yes	Yes	
Naked option	Yes	Yes	
5. Loan commitments:			
Fixed rate	Yes	Yes	Yes
Variable rate	Yes	Yes	Yes
6. Interest rate caps	Yes	Yes	
7. Interest rate floors	Yes	Yes	
8. Financial Guarantees	Yes	Yes	
9. Note issuance facilities at floating rates	Yes	Yes	
10. Letters of credit and standby letters of credit at floating rates	Yes	Yes	

[a] Issuers refer to both the trust and the sponsor.

industrial entity, or end-investor would incur if:

- any party to the deal involving a given financial instrument failed to perform according to the terms of the contract; and
- the collateral or other security for the amount due proved to be of little or no value.

The second criterion regards the soundness of collateral or other security to support financial trades. Practically all collateral is subject to credit risk and market risk. Therefore, risks must be assessed in terms of the position held by each entity involved in a financial deal. In this list, swaps, forwards, and futures are two-sided transactions. Therefore, the holder and issuer categories are not applicable in a separate sense. The OBS risk regards *both counterparties*.

Whether we talk of the examples in Table 2.4, an equity index, debt instrument, commodities or their derivatives, the greater the instrument's complexity, the more risky it becomes. In spite of a manager's strategy of going long and going short, alternative investments will by no means be always profitable during downward cycles in stock and bond prices. Their performance may or may not be similar to that of the general financial markets.

- During certain periods, the results they obtain might be correlated to more traditional portfolio holdings, providing little if any diversification.
- Alternatively, geared instruments can easily lose more in adverse markets, and gain less in favourable markets, than the stock and bond assets underlying the derivatives.

Executives of SAIVs whom I questioned on this matter have not been able to convince me that their offerings provide sufficient diversification to traditional portfolio holding. Nothing guarantees they *will* be successful in the future, or be able to avoid substantial losses.

Two comments were made by the reviewer: 'Nothing they said convinced you...' and 'Guarantees is a very strong word – hopefully no one ever suggested that there was a guarantee.'

First things first. To be convinced, I need proofs. These were not forthcoming; mostly I was told orally rather than being shown audited documents. As for 'guarantees', the fact of mainly presenting to the prospective client of alternative investments some statistics on what is said to be past performance – while we all know that the past in financial business is no prognosticator of the future (see Chapter 1) – is implicitly if not explicitly trying to convince the potential end-investor that alternative investment would have significant positive returns.

Objective information which tells the prospect about both *potential returns* and *potential losses* is so much more vital than this sort of one-sided presentation. Potential end-investors must be told explicitly that alternative investment strategies involve risks that are materially different from those characterising classical investments. Examples of some of those risks are:

- investing in other highly leveraged entities over which the fund has no control;
- investing in entities which are significantly less liquid than the originator of the alternative investment;
- investing in managed accounts, which potentially exposes the investor to huge losses;
- fiduciary risks connected to the management of third-party capital.

Neither is the multi-manager concept a sort of financial cure-all as the funds of funds seem to be saying. A number of geared fund managers does not necessarily average out risk; it compounds it. Seeking out value and growth with concentration on 'strong stock-picking' (a frequent fake argument) is in no way different from regular investment practice. It is hardly worthy of an extra risk premium and fat fees, as will become clear to the reader in the discussion on multi-management of leveraged deals in Chapter 5.

This can be stated in conclusion: There are major risks with many types of leveraged instruments, and sometimes 'diversification' essentially means higher expected returns and potentially booming losses, rather than the reduction of exposure. Examples are collateralised mortgage obligations (CMOs), securitised subprime credit, unlisted securities, private equity, securitised catastrophe insurance, and junk bonds (see Chapter 4).

4. Lies associated with liquidity, high returns, and other propaganda

Many fund managers have an absolute return orientation, and they usually seek performance that is generally not correlated to the world's equity markets. This is not something reserved for long/short, macro strategies and global emerging markets. What is, however, particular to all geared instruments, and therefore to alternative investments, is their sensitivity and exposure to the illiquidity of markets.

The reviewers made the following comments:

- Not every fund manager has an absolute return orientation, some have an index orientation.
- Not all geared instruments have in common sensitivity and exposure to the liquidity of markets.
- Lots of smaller company investments on recognised stock markets can be largely illiquid too.

The statements in the first and third bullets are correct, except that an index orientation does not mean there is no risk. Indices go down along with the equities they represent, and the more leveraged the position the greater the downturn; except also that the average investor will be very much ill-adjusted to lend money to small and frail companies. That is the gamble of private placements (see Chapter 1). Hedge funds specialising in small caps and in private equity would surely appreciate the reviewer's message in his third bullet.

But, I take exception to the reviewer's second statement which I consider to be a lie. Geared instruments have a high sensitivity to the liquidity of markets. Hedge funds try to counteract this through diversification, but diversification has its own risks as we have just seen.

Market liquidity and illiquidity are also characterised by cycles. From time to time, certain markets where hedge funds are trading may become particularly illiquid and/or impose dealing restrictions which make it difficult or impossible to liquidate positions, or even acquire new positions. Market illiquidity not only eliminates profit opportunities and makes it impossible to protect against further losses, but it can also lead the fund to bankruptcy, as with LTCM.

Execution typically becomes difficult in thinly traded markets. Although funds attempt to participate only in markets meeting certain minimum liquidity criteria, their orders are not always executed at or near the desired price in all markets, and generally the resulting alternative investments have less liquidity than other investments.

These are facts carefully kept close to the hedge funds, SAIVs, and other leveraged entities chest, so as not to scare end-investors. What amounts to an implicit lie is that end-investors are not told by the merchandisers of risk that lack of liquidity can lead to significant losses with exiting positions, as it becomes difficult to value the inventory, and execute changes in the composition of one's assets.

'This is true, but it is not restricted to hedge funds,' said a reviewer.

I fully agree with this statement. Did I ever say that hedge funds and funds of funds are the only entities misinforming their clients and prospects?

The principle is that one buys and sells in a given market when it is feasible to do so under prevailing conditions. But it is not always possible to execute an order, or to close out an open position; in particular, to act on a predetermined market price. Daily price fluctuation may upset the best laid plans, and limits are established in certain contracts by US and other exchanges.

- When the market price of a futures contract reaches its daily price volatility limit, no trade can be executed at prices outside such limit.
- Dealers may, accordingly, be locked into an adverse price movement and lose considerably more than the initial margin deposited to establish the position.

Lack of liquidity can be a huge disadvantage, both in the realisation of the prices which are quoted by hedge funds and other leveraged operators, and in the execution of orders at desired value levels. Lack of liquidity also increases the risk that the hedge fund or SAIV, will be required to liquidate positions at a notable disadvantage because of its inability to raise margin collateral from other sources.

> 'Lack of liquidity also applies to mutual funds facing redemptions,' said a reviewer. 'This is an issue of the *strategy* involved, rather than the name of the investment or the fund.'

The reviewer is definitely right in this statement, provided we all appreciate that the risk of market illiquidity is materially heightened by the use of leverage and the possibility that margin calls will need to be met in declining or disrupted market conditions, let alone in the case of panic.

The message the reader should retain from this discussion is that the limited liquidity of some of the assets in the portfolio adds to the risks. There is no secondary market for most alternative investment shares, and the majority of hedge funds and SAIVs do not intend to permit a secondary market to develop. This accounts for the frequent appearance of a clause that shareholders may redeem some or all of their shares at the end of a given period subject to the conditions set by the fund under 'Purchase and Redemption of Shares'.

- Once the money is locked in, there is no way to take it out,
- Redemptions require the consent of the aggregator of risk and its merchandiser, which is not easy to obtain.

> 'Secondary market, volatility, illiquidity. This is very biased towards the worst case scenario where the investor cannot retrieve money,' said a reviewer.

A worst case scenario is a legitimate, objective, and crucial way of evaluating risks (see also Chapter 8 on stress testing). Rather than considering it to be biased, hedge funds should proactively use expert systems and human judgements to do worst case scenarios every day. 'If you know yourself and know your opponent, you don't have to be afraid of the outcome of a thousand battles,' said Sun Tzu at about 500 BC.[6]

Investors should further realise that due to the volatile nature of markets in which hedge funds and SAIVs trade and invest, the net asset value of shares, when redeemed, may vary substantially from their net asset value on the date a redemption request is submitted. In addition, these entities generally have broad authority to:

- suspend redemption; and
- reset the valuation of shares.

This is synonymous with saying investors must make a long-term commitment to the alternative investment sector in order to have a reasonable expectation of achieving certain profit objectives. Such a commitment entails making substantial payments over time to the hedge fund in the form of management, incentive fees and bonuses, and must be factored into an investor's expectation of return.

In their prospectus, hedge funds, risk aggregators and brokers/merchandisers say that no holder of redeemable participating investor shares can lose more than the amount of his or her investment plus any undistributed profits, and dividends declared and redemption requests received but as yet unpaid. This may be true. However, what is not being said is that such an amount of money can be quite substantial.

- Many investors today put 1, 2 or even 5 per cent of their total assets in alternative investments; and
- Even more deceiving is the fact that otherwise serious banks now advise their clients to put 20 per cent of their assets into illiquid alternative investments.

This is clearly *capital at high risk*, and credit institutions which give that advice (there are several) should be ashamed for doing so. That end-investors should feel comfortable with 20 per cent toxic waste in their investment portfolio is one of the bigger lies told in connection to alternative investments.

> 'Marconi also turned out to be pretty risky – alternative investments are not the sole risky products, and you need to put this into perspective,' said a reviewer.

Not only Marconi but also many other firms have turned belly up in the 2000 to 2002 timeframe because of overleverage, mismanagement, and plain CEO malfeasance. For instance, as of mid-2002, the whole telecommunications industry is in a coma. Interestingly enough, this happened because of imprudently large loans and overcapacity. WorldCom, Global Crossing, Marconi, Lucent, Alcatel, Ericsson and so many other carriers as well as telecommunications equipment firms, make ideal case studies because they demonstrate that real life finally catches up with creative accounting and other lies. They have tried to push too hard at a time when their luck had run out.

5. An interesting meeting with one of the better managed hedge funds

Learning how to work with hedge funds, and most particularly how to exercise effective risk control, is tantamount to adapting to 'turn of the millennium' realities. Therefore, this text rather than being 'against' hedge funds, as some of the reviewers tend to believe, is a contribution to their risk control – the Achilles heel of the majority of them (see also Chapter 3). My fundamental message to all investors and potential investors in hedge funds is to:

- meet with the correct people;
- ask the right questions;
- carefully examine risk control and worst case scenarios;
- ensure you are satisfied with the answers.

> 'Your fundamental message,' said one of the reviewers, 'this is what most end-users do, except with funds of funds products.'

Here precisely is where end-investors, and the funds of funds marketing the alternative investments, can be mistaken. The reason is a human weakness which lead people to believe in myths, even if they are too good to be true. Few investors follow the advice of these four bullets in their investments – and they particularly forget when they need it the most, as in the case of funds of funds products.

Even if confronted with totally different conditions than those in the past, the majority of people feel comfortable in the world they already know, which under the new setting is the wrong location. This does not permit them to act meaningfully within the new perspectives, or to ask the questions which are right for the new type of investments rather than for the old.

Because organisations are made of people, to understand how an entity and the environment within which it works operates, as well as what it might be doing in the months and years to come, it is necessary to meet the people who are at the controls, understand how they think and see how they decide. In late October 2001, I met with Tim Tacchi and Henry Bedford, co-chief executives of TT International, a London-based hedge fund.

'One of the most important decisions in investment is whether you are pessimistic or bullish about the market's prospects,' said Tim Tacchi. Chances are the net asset value (NAV) allocation in equities will be around 20 per cent if the fund manager is pessimistic, and 80 per cent if he is bullish. Among the factors which enter into this evaluation are:

- the fund manager's own appreciation of market sentiment;
- macroeconomic criteria;
- trends in market behaviour; and
- the securities themselves.

As nearly every investor appreciates, technology stocks and utilities stocks are two fundamentally different investment propositions. A significant question with equities is that of hidden liabilities, as Tacchi pointed out. Other criteria, too, are important. Value selection needs milestones, as well as triggers to release the value.

TT International also invests in the macromarkets, particularly by taking position in currencies. Trading in currencies and interest rates are *not* intended as a hedge. At TT, macromarket trading is its own independent profit centre, to which that part of NAV is allocated that is not in equities or in cash and liquid instruments. The latter include liquid government securities, futures, options, and money market futures contracts.

Macrotrading occurs not only in foreign exchange products, but also in government securities, emerging market exposure, as well as other products and permutations of different instruments. Henry Bedford said he was agnostic about strengths and weaknesses of the euro, but he saw a tactical opportunity to shorten it: TT used to be 80 per cent long in euro/dollar, but Bedford re-positioned himself 30 per cent short. In the week following our October 2001 meeting, the market rewarded that position.

How is this hedge fund computing its NAV? The competitive valuation of equities is straightforward: based on earnings, cash flow, EBITDA, return on assets, and return on equity. The search is for asset and franchise value. Global comparisons are made, if appropriate.

Equities investment is largely in medium-term positions, not for trading. The catalysts in equity investment decisions are:

- management of change;
- realisation of hidden value;
- regulatory changes; and
- accounting standards used by the firm.

The choices made by the asset managers are verified by industry specialists and academic experts acting as external consultants. Price action is closely followed because it can signal opportunities. Fund managers are ready to take advantages of medium-term trends, which is the essence of directional trading.

Though the equities portfolio of TT may include 25 or 30 positions, it is four or five of these positions that will really contribute to the P&L. Nobody can anticipate from the beginning which will be 'pluses' and which will be 'minuses'. A comment was made during the meeting that value investing and growth investing have similarities. A sound approach towards any stock is to take 5 to 10 year cash flow, and then add a residual value. Also, it is wise to look into longer term prospects. Is the big bear market in telecoms/media/technology (TMT) over? 'There are some very undervalued stocks around, but not all of them are appealing', said Tacchi.

The TT example relates highly to alternative investments, indeed it is at the core of any prudential approach to the hedge funds business. To careful hedge fund managers, the TMT stocks are not appealing, because while many TMT companies lost 90 per cent or more of their market value in 2000–2 they may still have plenty to lose. By contrast, hedge funds managers with a huge risk appetite find TMT stock appealing because they believe the market would turn around and they would regain the 90 per cent of value they have lost.

Here, in a nutshell, is how the logic behind equity asset management at TT works, which is prudent logic. If an investor wishes to pay a premium for growth stocks, how does he make a choice? Vodafone has a high multiple to Novo, the pharmaceutical company, but its earnings are no better. Vodafone has no free cash flow and financial history suggests that the stock of phone companies does not rise until they have free cash flow. The quality of management evidently plays a crucial role in equity picking. Hence the need to meet periodically with company managers to estimate their:

- personal capabilities;
- decision-making processes;

- products and R&D;
- inventories; and
- marketing effectiveness.

Correctly, TT considers the sophistication of information technology used by the firms in which it invests as being important (see also Chapter 3), but it is one of the decision-making variables not the whole story. Reference was made during the meeting to a well-known insurance company which has obsolete information technology but a huge domestic market and tremendous margins in life and non-life insurance. 'Almost obscene margins', said one of the partners. This is crucial because when you are picking equities you want to have:

- visibility of earning; and
- transparency of accounts.

You also want to be in a market which has the potential to move ahead. Even if the Nasdaq, and to a lesser extent the Dow Jones, were battered, as of late 2001 the United States was still a better place to make money, Tacchi suggested. If things improve, the United Kingdom will be one of the growth markets. Improving fundamentals saw to it that TT International changed its equity strategy from 20 per cent to between 30 and 35 per cent of assets in equity investments.

Tacchi and Bedford did not fail to point out that external events can influence most significantly the course of the market. Before September 11 2001, the US. economy was nosediving, because of a drop in consumer confidence. After September 11, careful market watchers saw that the direct effect of the terrorist action has been minor, and it was *not* long lasting. Even the much maligned internet index bounced back, as shown in Figure 2.1. In fact, as Tim Tacchi pointed out, from an economic point of view September 11 was a 'plus' for the United States' economy, although some industries need to consolidate faster – airlines and banking being examples.

Nowhere during the one and a half hour meeting was there any reference to multi-styles and the list of risky vehicles shown in Chapter 1, which characterises the investments made by some other funds (see also the discussion on multi-styles in Chapter 5). In fact, the input I have received suggests that the equity investment policy followed by TT could have been that of a well-managed mutual fund, but, as we will see in Chapter 4, mutual funds fatigue makes the hedge fund label more sexy.

> 'Your point about TT goes to the route of the issue,' said one of the reviewers. 'Mutual funds and hedge funds are not that far apart, it all depends on the management of them.'

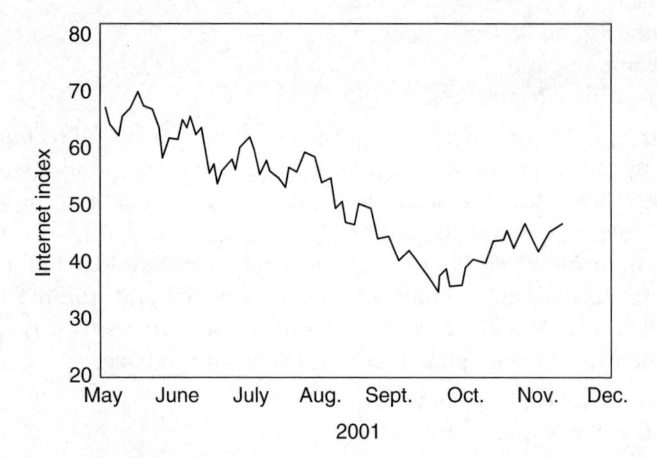

Figure 2.1 Turnaround of the USA Today Internet Index after September 11, 2001.

The answer is less than 50 per cent 'yes', and more than 50 per cent 'no'. Mutual funds and hedge funds are not very far apart in the sense they both seek to make money through some type of investment. But they are quite apart in terms of the strategies they follow and the risks they assume. In both types of funds, of course, the quality of management makes a great deal of difference, as explained in Section 7 on operational risk.

6. Everything changes, including the market and its performers

Given that TT has performed well in the past, is this a guarantee for the future? As I never tire of repeating, a short but focused answer to such a query is that past performance is not a prognosticator of future events or results. Any investment, even one very well crafted, can turn sour. Companies which are thought to be well-managed turn belly-up. For recent examples, look at Enron, WorldCom, Global Crossing, Kmart – but also at Lucent Technologies, Nortel, Ericsson, Vodafone, AT&T and (to a lesser extent) Ford.

The FSA makes a similar point. It has recently suggested that, despite extensive research, it has been unable to find any evidence that funds that outperformed in the past are any more likely than other funds in the sector to continue doing so in the future. FSA researchers have examined whether past investment performance repeats itself.

Their conclusion has been that:

- Repeated good performance, if there is any, is small in size and effect, as well as shortlived.
- By contrast, there is evidence of some persistency for smaller, poorly performing funds, but even this remains low in terms of degree.

The lesson to retain from the FSA comments is that the tendency to draw conclusions from past performance is not rational, even if investors hope that this information can help them to 'understand' what the prospects for their money might be. Investors should, therefore, be wary of alternative investments salesmen making that sort of pitch to conclude a contract.

Part of the FSA research goal was to investigate whether or not the authorities should allow fund management outfits to use performance figures in their advertising. Although the investigators suggested allowing this practice to continue at least for the time being, they advised FSA to find ways of tightening the rules – specifically because of the danger of misleading consumers. The operational risk is that any presentation of past performance information could inspire speculation about expected returns. Nowhere is this danger greater than with multi-styles.

The wave of failures and malpractices which hit the American business landscape from December 2001 onwards: Enron, Global Crossing, Andersen, Tyco, Xerox, WorldCom, and a long list of others, may help regulators pass legislation which permits the prosecution of chief executives when their luck in creative accounting and unlawful loans to themselves and their buddies has run out. We are not yet there. But new financial reporting requirements are developing. The frame of reference shown in Figure 2.2 is an example from accounting for derivative instruments with SFAS 133, by FASB, in the background.

A lot of homework needed for tax liability

Another issue investors must appreciate with alternative investments, related to that above, is the risks associated with lack of regulation of hedge funds, and its opposite: the risks of regulation (particularly taxation liability) being imposed on investments. Take the issue of taxation first: there is a possibility of alternative investments becoming subject to taxation on certain types of income, particularly in certain jurisdictions. Investors should specifically consider the nature and scope of tax exposure.

Hedge funds and SAIVs say that they structure their trading and operations so as to avoid any significant income tax liability. However, the

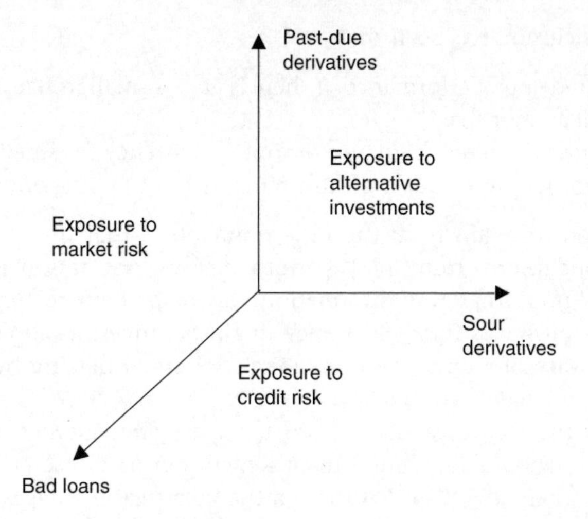

Figure 2.2 The developing new shape of reporting requirements in the United States.

internal revenue authority at the end-investor's place of residence could disagree on this issue. If income taxes were imposed on any component of the alternative investments' income, the result would be a reduction in the effective rate of return realised by investors well beyond what might have been shown in the prospectus. A situation could occur in which:

- the income derived from an alternative investment is taxed;
- but the loss of capital is not tax-deductible, as it comes from exotic instruments that tax authorities consider a gamble.

A guaranteed principal is one of the options

I cannot emphasise too strongly that to a significant degree alternative investments is very speculative and involves a high level of risk. Investors must be prepared to lose all of the funds which they invest. Therefore, they should not put at risk money they need for their business, their ongoing financial requirements, or money that they would like to keep as an asset.

> 'Perhaps this is a bit strong,' said one of the reviewers. 'Unless you are putting gold coins under your mattress (and even that is not entirely safe) capital is always at risk, fundamentally.'

I would not advise hiding money in one's mattress, like French peasants do, but there are plenty of risk-free investments – albeit at lower rate of return. Examples are US Treasuries, British Gilts, German Bunds, and debt instruments issued by other Group of Ten nations.

Also safe are bank deposits guaranteed by the state or by a state agency. In the UK, the level is a low £20,000, but in the US it is $100,000 per personal account. In the go-go 1980s when the savings and loans (building societies) were thirsty for money, they were paying high interest rates. What many people did was to put $100,000 to half a dozen or more S&L. They obtained a good interest rate, and benefited from full safety for their money at the taxpayer's expense.

I don't necessarily advise putting big chunks of money in this passive sort of investing, but it is always an option. What I do advise however is to avoid doing 'tax optimisation', as Dennis Kozlowski tried to and paid dearly for it. That's an interesting case study.

The June 2002 indictment came from Robert Morgenthau, New York's district attorney, and it alleged that Kozlowski – till then Tyco's boss – evaded $1 million in New York state taxes when buying fine art to decorate his Fifth Avenue apartment. According to Morgenthau, Koslowski who was paid more than $30 million in 2001, is alleged to have had these paintings shipped out of New York State to avoid sales tax, then covertly re-imported them.[7]

While what will be the case in terms of taxation connected to alternative investments is still uncertain, the likelihood of major losses increases as new instruments – like private equity – are added to the instruments, and hedge funds continue being unregulated. Lack of transparency exacerbates this. Under the guide of *portfolio confidentiality* investors do not have access to, and are not provided information on, the composition of the hedge fund's or the risk aggregator's portfolio, or any position thereof.

7. An introduction to operational risk for alternative investments

Successful approaches to operational risk management are based on clear distinction between credit risk, market risk, and operational risk, even if these three major classes of exposure tend to overlap as we have seen in Chapter 1. One of the difficulties in handling operational risk is that it has so many aspects which are heterogeneous to one another.

Operational risk is present not only in hedge funds, funds of funds and SAIVs but in any business for that matter. One of the basic requirements with the identification and follow-up of operational risk is to account for the migration from credit risk and market risk to operational risk, as is the case with collateral.[8]

As a general rule, the lack of proper logical classification of operational risk results in significant difficulty in understanding and measuring it. Ideally, proper identification and classification must see to it that defined risks are mutually exclusive and comprehensively exhaustive. This is indeed a challenging mission because many operational risks are cross functional and usually overlapping among themselves.

Because most alternative investments offered by commercial banks, SAIVs, and other entities to their clients rest on a mixture of products from 10 to 20 hedge funds, the operational risks being encountered are well beyond those of a single entity. The reason is the prevailing variety of procedures, supporting system solutions, and possibly incompatible financial strategies. Lack of standardisation engenders a great lot of operational risk.

> 'Multimanager environment. This may apply to funds of funds, but not to most hedge funds,' said a reviewer.

This statement is correct as long as we talk of a single hedge fund. My reference focuses on multimanager solutions, funds of funds, and SAIVs which are more closely associated to alternative investments and their merchandising to private people.

The New Capital Adequacy Framework by the Basle Committee on Banking Supervision has made operational risk one of its focal points, but it does not address multimanager environments. Basle has presented five different methods for operational risk control, as well as a standard list that includes seven classes:

- Internal fraud
- External fraud
- Employment practices, and workplace safety
- Clients, products and business practices
- Damage to physical assets
- Business disruptions and systems failures
- Execution, delivery, procurement, management.

These operational risks correspond to the business lines shown in Table 2.5. Each of the operational risks in reference can be broken down to further detail. There are as well operational risks associated with:

- Business concentration
- Insider trading

Table 2.5 Matrix of standard business lines and standard operating risks

Operating risk Business line	**Internal fraud**	**External fraud**	**Employment and workplace safety**	**Clients, products, business practices**	**Damage to physical assets**	**Business disruption, system failures**	**Execution, delivery, process management**
Corporate finance							
Trading & sales							
Retail Banking							
Other commercial banking							
Payments & settlements							
Custody & agency services							
Asset management							
Retail brokerage							

- Repeated litigation
- Legislative changes
- Wanting compliance methods
- Development and use of models
- Taxation.

Mismanagement is a major operational risk

A major operational risk not shown in the Basle list is *mismanagement*, which is a high impact risk that can turn an investment, indeed, the whole organisation, on its head. Associated with management risk is the absence of internal control which often has dire consequences.[9]

Internal control is not only concerned with the company's internal matters but also with external issues, such as mishandling or misinforming the firm's customers. Some excellent examples on the perils of customer misinformation have been provided by 'The Value of Trust', an article by *The Economist.*[10]

Starting with the reference to the $100 million penalty paid in May 2002 in an off-court settlement with the New York General Attorney's Office by Merrill Lynch, because of misinforming some of its clients on the worth of certain dot-coms, this article brings into perspective the fact that other well-known institutions too – like Morgan Stanley and Citigroup – are now facing growing public scrutiny.

'Countless private lawsuits are pending against financial services firms that seem likely to drag on for years and may result in huge payouts,' says *The Economist*, further adding that:

- 'For a financial firm to go to trial over such matters is to risk bankruptcy,' and
- 'The laws in the area are sufficiently untested for them to prefer not to present their case to a judge.'

Therefore, far from being against hedge funds – as it has been accused by some pros – this book may well prove to be their best friend because

- it makes evident the pitfalls;
- explains the measures needed for risk control; and
- calls for exercising great caution.

Beware of operational risks in a sales pitch

One of the pitfalls which might not strike the untrained eye is the sales pitch by the originators of alternative investments, the aggregators of risk, and the brokers/merchandisers. In a significant number of cases, this pitch is covert. It is largely made orally during the meetings, while lawyers have seen to it that the material handed out to end-investors (unaware of the risks they would be assuming) writes exactly the opposite of what the salesman says:

> 'This document does not constitute an offer to sell, or a solicitation of an offer to purchase any securities.'

On face value, this statement is contradictory because the sales pitch of the alternative investments salesperson and the documents handed out during the marketing meeting are indivisible. As it has been my personal case on several occasions, the sales pitch and handouts address the same investor. The reason of the prospectus folder, glossy prints and tricky graphs is to make the oral arguments by the salesmen more convincing.

This red herring marketing strategy bases its hopes on the notion that people don't like to read. They only like to hear the good news, and therefore they are prone to believe anything they are told. Even those who read the alternative investments document may miss the fact that legal experts have inserted curious statements in fine print.

Happenings like the example I have given are failures of the institution's internal control. They are operational risks that can end up by being very costly to the enterprise, if an investor tests them in court. Other types of operational risk are also prevalent.

A close call, which resulted from deficient internal control, has been the case of liquidity problems that affected Salomon Brothers at the time of its Treasury bond scandal in 1991. Salomon had more than $600 billion in derivative contracts on its books – still small fry compared to today's amounts, but a big number at that time.

The need to control operational risk

To a significant extent, financial institutions can identify and capture a good deal of operational risk by using information available in the backoffice and in databases. A good way to improve operational risk control is to:

- avoid providing incentives for hard sales;
- understand backoffice performance within the organisation;
- co-involve senior management in clarifying responsibilities; and
- obtain a commitment on operational risk awareness, monitoring and measurement.

Some organisations have one person dedicated to operational risk per business line, steadily reviewing current practices to identify weak links and other reasons leading to operational risk. They also see to it that *new product* approval observes operational risk issues, and hold an annual operational risk review in coordination with the corporate operational risk office. This is a policy hedge funds, funds of funds, and SAIVs will be well advised to follow.

Multimanager environments, as that which is characteristic of most alternative investments, must be more attentive to operational risks than other, more linear solutions. The policies which I recommend to companies as the best way to address operational risk are:

- Investigate your strengths and weaknesses
- Strengthen management supervision
- Train all personnel in operational risk control
- Study emerging best practices
- Develop and use advanced measurement methods.

Much can be learned by what has been accomplished in the past by top tier financial institutions. For instance, Goldman Sachs' ability to mobilise people for difficult projects stems from the large amount of time it spent:

- Recruiting;
- Evaluating; and
- Managing human resources.

Goldman Sachs has an elaborate annual review process, including an interactive audit which involves open review of best and worst performers. This began in the 1980s, as John Weinberg, then Goldman's co-chief, called on:

- the partner with the best results; and
- the partner with the worst results.

To discuss in front of the other partners how and why each delivered so different results. In one session, the partner in risk arbitrage got up in front of his peers to explain why he had lost $20 million that month. Weinberg felt that the people who owned the firm deserved an explanation of how the firm was doing.[11]

Other general advice for operational risk control is to undertake risk mitigation through insurance, develop contingency plans, provide consistency in operational risk control, and target as a priority those operational risks that have the greater punch. For the latter should be provided incentives, through a system of merits and demerits, able to keep operational risk under lock and key.

3
Globalisation, Legal Risk, Reputational Risk, and Technology Risk

1. Introduction

As Chapters 1 and 2 have documented, *alternative investments* involve high risk assumed by *hedge funds*, repackaged by *aggregators*, and sold by *merchandisers* to consumers, institutional investors, and other entities. The size of the exposure taken over by end-investors changes with every strategy – and often with every transaction.

Globalisation makes the estimation of risk imbedded in alternative investments much more complex, because of the number of unknowns it brings into the picture (see Section 2), including the likelihood of reversals. 'Everybody talks about the global financial markets as if they were irreversible. But this is a misconception', suggests George Soros. '(This) involves a false analogy with a technological innovation like the internal combustion engine.'[1]

Credit risks, market risks, and operational risks taken in a global landscape make it so much more difficult to calculate exposure, whether the investor deals directly with the hedge fund(s) or through banks, brokers, and SAIVs. This statement is just as valid of technology risk, legal risk, reputational risk, and other risks – for instance, management risk discussed in Chapter 2.

> 'Much of this chapter is directed as much towards hedge funds as it is to investors. The text needs to make this clear, and perhaps outline what risks managers within hedge funds need to consider on the one side, and what investors need to consider on the other, with respect to legal, technological risk etc.,' said one of the reviewers.

The reviewer has a good point, provided one does not forget that hedge funds, SAIVs, banks and their investors face very similar risks. The difference lies in the way they control them. The previous two chapters have emphasised the risk to investors, particularly those who assume most of the exposure – a subject to which we will return many times in the following chapters. The present chapter is devoted to analysing the risks, primarily faced by the banks, brokers, and SAIVs who have become involved in the merchandising of alternative investments.

One of the interesting aftermaths of alternative investments has been that investors now need to apply the same level of research to choosing a broker as they do to purchasing a stock. As Section 3 shows, end-investors are becoming more vigilant than in the past, are more actively seeking accountability on the part of their asset managers, and are providing judicial incentive for some reappraisal of the risks associated with investments at large and to alternative investments in particular.

The aggregators of risk and their brokers/merchandisers can fall subject to serious legal difficulties, even where their lawyers craft documents and prospects given to clients in a way that appears to make their originators bullet-proof. The risk to a financial institution is not waived by forming an independent business unit as a fully or partly owned subsidiary, and delegating to that unit the aggregation of risk and/or the marketing of alternative investments.

Low technology can add to the woes, as shown in Sections 6 and 7. By contrast, fairly sophisticated analytical software and on-line data mining may be employed not only to track exposure but also to target cross-selling opportunities. High technology enables a credit institution to cater more precisely to its clients, and to tune its products and services to their needs. Generally, however, computer programs presently used for client profiling and the control of exposure are old technology and cannot handle client needs (and sorrows) as they develop.

This chapter documents that brand-name risk, technology risk, and legal risk are an integral part of any investment offer, and of every supplier–client relationship. None can be ignored. The prevention and/or resolution of conflicts that might arise in these three areas is only 10 per cent analytics; the remaining 90 per cent is policies adopted by senior management and the board as well as the will to see them through.

2. Deregulation and globalisation propel the alternative investments

Deregulation and globalisation are two of the forces propelling the alternative investments paradigm. Deregulation has permitted greater freedom in choosing investment vehicles, while globalisation has made it increasingly difficult to establish clear regional preferences as stock markets have become more closely correlated to one another. Globalisation has also tremendously enlarged the investment community, particularly in connection with the wealth effect that today characterises many countries: both industrial and emerging.

Another factor propelling the growth in alternative investments is market psychology; most specifically, herd mentality. The analysis of past market cycles shows that positive and negative sentiment spreads fast, and alert traders as well as asset managers try to capitalise on movements taking place in both directions. Some succeed, others fail. Misjudgement about where the market is going can turn into a torrent of red ink. When this happens, individuals and institutional investors exposed in alternative investments will be the parties who pay the debacle.

A sudden market turnaround on a highly geared hedge fund, fund of funds, SAIV, or other entity can have a dramatic aftermath – and it comes at an unexpected moment. For ten days, after the terrorist attack at the New York twin towers and the Pentagon, of September 11, 2001, the US (and other western) stockmarkets nosedived. Many traders surfed on the big negative wave. Then, as we saw in Chapter 2, suddenly the market turned around.

With many of the 4,000 to 6,000 hedge funds going short, economic losses can be massive. The explosion in the number of hedge funds and the diversity of their strategies makes an individual or institutional investor's choice and evaluation of asset managers and their bets both extremely important and very, very difficult. In contrast to traditional investments, the evaluation of performance of alternative investment managers is most demanding because of:

- lack of transparency;
- inherent complexity of deals;
- difficulty of pricing inventoried positions;
- scant information on the status of current exposure; and
- (usually) illiquid instruments and markets.

One of the reviewers said that transparency does vary between funds. That's true. Another reviewer added that he knew a hedge fund manager whose fund is regulated deliberately.

I would have been most happy to see that this becomes a general policy – which it is not. One swallow does not bring the spring. However, I would not buy two other statements made by reviewers concerning hedge funds and alternative investment instruments. These stated that:

- instruments are not always illiquid; and
- it is not necessarily difficult to price inventoried positions.

The thoughts underpinning both bullets are wrong. While the definition of an illiquid instrument varies across different participants, among most experts the prevailing concept of whether an instrument is illiquid is that there exists:

- no market-marker, or just one market-marker;
- no price change for five consecutive business days;
- inability to sell a position in one week at 1/3 daily volume; and
- inability to sell the instrument at its current value within seven days.

Applying these criteria, we come to the conclusion that all alternative investments are illiquid. That's what experts with no conflict of interest on this issue are saying, and I think they are right.

A different way of looking into instrument illiquidity is that *if* the portfolio primarily contains OTC financial products, *then* the investments are illiquid, because it is most unlikely that the seller can get fair value. (The Financial Accounting Standards Board (FASB) defines fair value as the price a willing seller can obtain from a willing buyer in an open market, under other than gire-sale conditions).

Also, as institutions steadily move from bread-and-butter derivatives to exotics and do so in growing numbers, not only do the portfolio's contents become more illiquid but also they cannot be priced in a reliable way. (See in Chapter 2 the discussion on OTC trades.)

The reviewer who said 'He knows of a hedge fund which will have daily net asset values (NAVs) published' would be well advised to examine closely the numbers.

When Long-Term Capital Management (LTCM) crashed in late September 1998, and UBS lost $1.2 billion with it, its director of risk management revealed that the bank's daily value at risk (VAR) included a vague estimate of intrinsic value communicated by LTCM once per month.[2] Even that seems to have been a guestimate having to do more with wishful thinking than with market facts.

Another comment by a reviewer which left me thirsty is that 'Some in the hedge funds industry are making an effort to change, and will do more so as institutional investors come on board.' I would have been much more comfortable had I read that:

- Every single hedge fund, fund of funds, and SAIV is making a factual and documented effort towards transparency, and
- Institutional and other investors become proactive, requiring to see the change in hedge funds culture before voting with their money.

The message conveyed by both bullets is important because, as already noted, deregulation and globalisation propel alternative investments. The difficulty is compounded by the fact that there is little agreement across the participants in the alternative investments landscape in defining rigorous risk control rules, let alone complying with or performing to specific benchmarks of prudential risk management.

3. End-investor activism and legal risk

End-investor activism and legal risk correlate. Therefore, it is in the interest of hedge funds, aggregators of risk, SAIVs, and other merchandisers of alternative investments to seek protection under the three pillars of the New Capital Adequacy Framework, of the Basle Committee on Banking Supervision, briefly discussed in Chapter 2. The lack of capital adequacy, absence of rigorous supervision and non-existence of transparency in the reporting of financial institutions:

- masks lax management;
- induces hyper-aggressive risk-taking; and
- promotes an inordinate amount of leverage.

Under these conditions, the law of unintended consequences comes into play, while at the same time the courts are getting tougher and cases which in the past might not have been sanctioned are sanctioned today. Globalisation increases the legal risks taken by an institution. Crédit Suisse, for example, was penalised by Indian regulators because of shorting. Shorting is illegal in India, and it matters little if it is legal in Switzerland where Crédit Suisse is based.

Conflicts of interest can lead straight into legal risk. In mid-July 2001, Merrill Lynch agreed to pay US$400,000 to settle a claim by a former client to whom its Internet analyst recommended a stock in which it had a conflict of interest. The former client had sought to recover investment losses of US$800,000, including those involving a stock that was not part of the settlement, and had requested US$10 million in punitive damages. Merrill Lynch had to pay about $400,000 altogether.

This is an interesting example because what has happened applies hand-in-glove with alternative investments. According to an arbitration claim filed with the New York Stock Exchange, the Internet analyst had recommended shares of Infospace, and another employee cited his research to persuade the client to hold the stock as its value fell precipitously.

The conflict of interest, the claim said, was the relationship of Merrill Lynch as financial adviser to another Internet company, Go2Net, that was later acquired by Infospace. The broker had issued a report, recommending Infospace without mention of Go2Net. Following the settlement, Merrill Lynch moved to bar its analysts from investing in the firms they cover. Other major investment banks in New York followed suit.

- There are plenty of conflicts of interest that analysts face even without owning shares in the companies whose profitability and viability they cover.
- There are also plenty of conflicts of interest confronting commercial banks and investment banks when they offer alternative investments to their clients.

It is always wise to account for *reputational risk*, particularly when the developing jurisprudence is unfriendly to misrepresentation of facts or the exploitation of end-investors' ignorance about the exposure they are assuming. The heavy hand of the law on investment banks was first felt in 1995 following the meltdown of Orange County (California) in December 1994. Since then, it has been relentless, whether the cases concern tobacco companies or financial institutions.

- Legal risk and *brand name risk* are difficult to control when the effects of assets disintegration come into the public eye.
- Therefore, measures taken to keep them under steady surveillance must be proactive, not reactive.

Brand name risk and reputational risk are practically synonymous: brand name risk is the reputational risk associated with the brand name of the institution and its product at 'this' point in time. These are risks that every financial institution faces where somebody knowingly, or unwittingly, abuses the regulations or the confidence of companies and consumers.

In the era of globalisation, reputational risk increases dramatically, as shown by the aforementioned example of an executive of Crédit Suisse responsible for its operations in India, who broke Indian law by selling short Indian securities. This might have been done without intention of non-compliance because in the United States and most of Europe, there is nothing illegal in selling short. Both personal accountability and company accountability increase as globalisation:

- brings to the foreground huge differences in cultures, rules and regulations;
- it is making compliance much more complex than in the past; and
- risks tarnishing reputations even in the absence of intentional wrong-doing.

Today, dissatisfied clients who lose because of false or misleading assertions about returns and the security of their capital, are more likely than ever to sue – either individually or through class actions. The spectre of litigation is by no means academic; financial institutions should be aware of its potential adverse impact and take proactive steps to mitigate this.

Unilever provides an example. On 15 October 2001, pension-fund trustees for Unilever began an action against Merrill Lynch investment managers for negligence. They sought £130 million ($190 million) in damages for the alleged mismanagement of their £1 billion ($1.45 billion) pension fund, claiming that the extent of the underperformance at Mercury Asset Management amounted to negligence in that:

- The contractually agreed performance target was to beat the benchmark by one percentage point.
- But between January 1997 and March 1998, Mercury underperformed the benchmark by one percentage point.

In its defence, Merrill Lynch claimed that neither performance target nor floor was guaranteed, and nobody should have assumed that the fund would never perform outside the range in a given period. Still, without admitting guilt, the investment bank settled this case off-court. This judicial test of underperformance will most likely be followed by other legal tests to judge whether an asset manager:

- took excessive risks when responsible for pension-fund assets and other property;

- failed to diversify sufficiently or to deliver on benchmarks; or
- was stopped by his superiors when investment decisions diverged greatly from house policy.

Arguments about underperformance usually arise when the equity markets are in a tailspin. Firms that are active managers of money are taking major risks to come up with double-digit profits. When they do not show extraordinary results, at best their assets under management shrink and at worst the clients bring court action.

In 2000–1, the United Kingdom's 20 biggest fund-management firms lost 14 per cent of institutional assets under management, while costs climbed as new computers were installed and staff hired. Loss of clients and rocketing costs can lead a company to disaster. Attrition of the client base greatly affects the bottomline. Banks must build into their P&L the impact of unsound premises made to their clientele. A recent study found that a 1 per cent attrition in customer base has a 7 per cent impact on the bottomline.

In conclusion, a sound business principle is that a financial institution must be extremely careful about what it says to its clients. Reputation takes a lifetime to build and it can be destroyed in one hour. Short-term profits should never blind management about the risk of attrition of the client base. Being fair in client handling makes sense for any individual company, and for assets managers in particular.

4. Banks, special alternative investment vehicles, and brand name risk

For a number of reasons, financial institutions have adopted the practice of creating new, fully owned entities to design and market alternative investments. Typically, these independent business units address themselves to the overall market or focus only on a specific segment of it; but the responsibility stays with the parent company.

For instance, in June 2001, UBS Asset Management and UBS Warburg jointly launched a new business unit for alternative financial instruments to manage the market of pension funds and other selected investors. The brand name of this independent business unit is O'Connor. (O'Connor was originally a self-standing Chicago-based entity specialising in derivative financial instruments, prior to being bought, about 10 years ago, by Swiss Bank Corp., which itself merged with the old UBS to form the new UBS.) Today, O'Connor integrates global research, investment, and distribution capabilities with trading and derivatives expertise.

Its mission is to:

- provide financial products with (what is thought to be) risk-adjusted returns; and
- ensure that these instruments have a low correlation to traditional investments.

O'Connor is an example of a SAIV which we mentioned in Chapter 1. There are plenty of them, some better known than others. Though no two SAIVs are exactly the same, they do feature several common characteristics which, more or less, underpin all independent business units designed to promote alternative investments. However, without proper regulation and control, SAIVs have the ability to affect the reputation of their parent companies. Dissatisfied clients losing because of false claims about high returns and capital security, will most likely sue both the daughter company and the parent.

As far as potential brand name damage is concerned, it matters little that the aggregation of risk and its merchandising is done through SAIVs or the parent company. What counts is that the responsibility is indivisible. This responsibility is increased by the fact that there are no material regulatory limitations on alternative investments. Hedge funds, banks, brokers and SAIVs – as well as their senior managers – are accountable for:

- the choices they make;
- the clients with whom they trade; and
- the instruments and vehicles they use to do so.

Brand name risk sees to it that some financial institutions choose to keep out of alternative investments altogether. Their board is concerned by the fact that there are potential conflicts of interest if their institution is acting as the hedge funds' prime broker. Conflicts of interest may also derive from the fact a bank is tracking and rating another institution's performance.

Morgan Stanley says it will not act as prime broker for a fund which it is tracking (most likely) because it does not want to take on reputational risk and/or be liable for damages. What particularly concerns self-respecting institutions is the position they may find themselves during periods of severe market turbulence.

In June 2002, a similar reputational argument developed in connection to recommendations made by financial analysts in terms of buying, holding, or selling specific equities. The old rule of the marketplace has been *caveat emptor*, or buyer aware. But on 3 June a US Supreme Court ruling in favour of a SEC action against a broker, stated that the securities markets regulation of 1936:

> Sought to substitute a philosophy of full disclosure for the philosophy of caveat emptor, and this to achieve a high standard of business ethics in the securities industry.

Alternative investments are not immune to this Supreme Court decision which constitutes a major piece of jurisprudence. Suddenly, according to the courts, caveat emptor does not go far enough. Analysts – and therefore banks, brokers, and SAIVs employing them – have a legal duty to care for their retail customers.

The risks to reputation following from the instrument's design, sales techniques, or documentation and technological laxity must be properly studied and appreciated by all funds, funds of funds, and banks promoting alternative investments. At the same time, all investors should become aware of the legal clauses attached to alternative investments.

The hedge funds, SAIVs, and commercial banks that sell leveraged, illiquid and non-transparent financial products to companies, pension funds, charities, and the public often fail to explain the amount of risk assumed by entering into such deals. The sale of alternative investments capitalises on the fact that the majority of the Group of Ten countries do not have in place legislation to regulate what could be described as new types of Ponzi games.[3] Only in the United States and Canada are such investments subject to some closer supervision and therefore, most offerings carefully include a warning, often in fine print:

> Neither this document nor any copy hereof may be sent or taken or transmitted into the United States or Canada or distributed, directly or indirectly, in the United States or Canada to any U.S. or Canadian person. Any failure to comply with this restriction may constitute a violation of U.S. securities law.

There is an irony in this statement because most of the 4,000 to 6,000 hedge funds in existence today are located in the United States and in off-shores not far from continental US. The sales pitch by the originators of alternative investments, the aggregators of risk and the brokers/merchandisers is, in a significant number of cases, covert, as it has been explained in Chapter 2 in connection to operational risk. For example, the offer for an alternative investment I received a short time ago states:

> [This] is an investment product which is not governed by Swiss investment fund legislation. Therefore, the investor does not get the specific protection of Swiss Investment Fund Law.
>
> As a consequence, prior to the placing of an order in the Units, the investor should make him-/herself aware of the specific risk of this product.

The salesman from a Swiss bank who approached me argued that this was an 'unmissable business opportunity', simultaneously featuring very high returns and preservation of assets. I studied the documents, which indicated that there were factual errors in the offer; and the fine print (above) stated this 'investment' was outside the letter of Swiss Law.

Investors need to be aware both of the risk of leveraging, and the specific risk of individual alternative investment products. Salesmen may not be ready or able to answer focused queries. As a first step to identifying specific risks, I asked the banker who made me that offer about credit risk. His response was: 'Don't you consider our bank to be creditworthy?' Yes, but the salesman also said that his bank *did not* guarantee the capital he wanted me to invest in this scam.

5. No investment policy should leave aside reputational risk

'The road to *invest*ments today passes from *invest*igation,' said a senior financial analyst. This is what Enron, WorldCom, Xerox, Tyco, Global Crossing, Qwest and so many other recent cases prove. It's an old Wall Street adage that there is nothing like a bull market to bring out the crooks – and a bear market to begin to catch them.

Crooks are not the only reason for investment nightmares. Due to the challenges facing investors with regard to definition, choice, performance and measurement of risks associated to alternative investments, today more than ever, the global market tends to move according to the herd instinct. This sees to it that many investors seek cover under a general trend and they are unable or unwilling to make independent decisions.

When in the mid to late 1990s the Dow Jones, Nasdaq, and the European stock markets rose quickly, highly leveraged hedge funds were behind them, hiding among other investors but acting as a major force in propelling the market's rise. Then, as the equity markets tanked, hedge fund managers who did not go short fast enough lost money. Choosing the right fund with a risk strategy in conformity with an

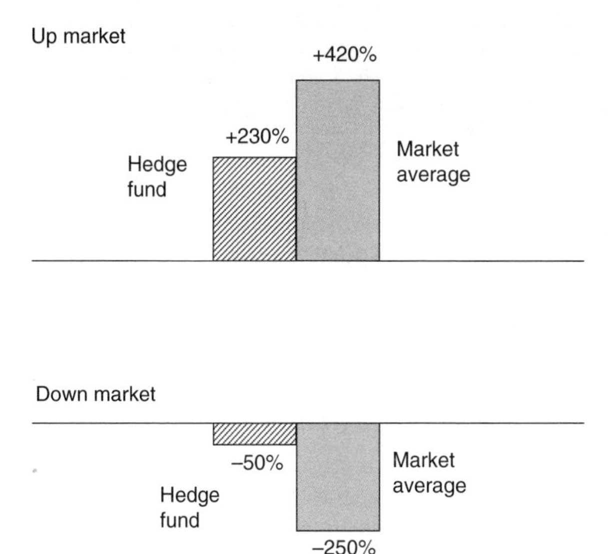

Figure 3.1 Leverage and shorting can alter the overall returns.

investor's expectations was (and is) therefore critical; but it is not an exact science by any means.

As Chapter 1 brought to the reader's attention, those in favour of alternative investments usually claim that with their diversified and generally market-neutral strategies, hedge funds contribute to reducing the high volatility of a traditional portfolio. Yet, it is by no means true that hedge funds always outperform. This is shown in Figure 3.1, based on statistics from one of the funds. The results throw up some interesting points:

- In the rising market, gains were only 55 per cent of the market average despite high leverage and, therefore, risk.
- In the falling market, however, losses were a fraction of those suffered by other investment entities because of shorting.

In a *shorting strategy*, the portfolio manager will sell short the equity of companies believed to have stock prices which reflect unrealistic earnings expectations, have used creative accounting to overstate earnings, or encounter fundamental problems that could adversely impact revenues, earnings, cash flow and other crucial criteria such as self-confidence and stability of management. Enron provides a cogent example.

> 'Enron is perhaps not one of the best examples. It was a one-off exposed fraud. In any case, it is not a good argument, because every fund manager knows that he will make mistakes,' said one of the reviewers.

This was written in the wake of the WorldCom fraud, which was conveniently forgotten. Neither did the pension fund manager who made the comment take account of the indictment of Tyco's CEO by the New York Attorney General and the reputation of other people and companies which had become damaged good because of tricky dealings. Yet, all of them loomed in the background.

The cover-up is worse than the crime

Failure to bring to the foreground crucial issues like misleading information, meaningless statistics, and the likelihood of reputational damage amounts to a minor cover-up. And there is an old saying that 'the cover-up is worse than the crime'.

Risks are not being swamped by denying their existence. For instance, denying the existence of risks embedded in the *multi-layer* structure used for assuming, aggregating, packaging and reselling damaged goods. From a longer term perspective, the practice of credit institutions to employ a pool of hedge funds which administer geared and illiquid financial paper is, at best, questionable – even if in the short term this has been good business for banks and brokers who sell alternative investments. From hedge funds to brokers all these parties:

- have secured for themselves guaranteed income, from sales of instruments they bring to the market;
- receive a substantial management fee for running these investments, which is non-transparent, subtracted from returns; and
- get a performance fee of 20 per cent (even up to 30 per cent) of the paper profits – but in real money.

The capital which floods into alternative investments from a variety of investors swells the hedge fund cash flows. In the first quarter of 2001, net inflows to hedge funds totalled nearly US$7 billion, bouncing back to levels last seen before the crash of LTCM in September 1998. Some of the experts I have been talking to see this rush to find a home for capital, even an uncertain home, as the result of a two-year-long stock market blues. To a large extent, the cash flow to hedge funds has gone into equity long/short deals (see Chapter 5 for percentages).

- The bets are large and the policy is that of trying to get in and out of the market fast.
- That's what arbitrageurs are doing, but making a profit on small movements in value requires large bets.

Market risk may be king, but credit risk is an ambitious spouse. By late 2001, there were fears that some brokers may be close to, or may even have breached, capital adequacy requirements in a manner that is unsettling regulators. This situation did not get better in 2002 as huge profits previously acquired by investment banks shrank to bare levels.

> 'The trick is to be right 53 per cent of the time consistently. That is what investors should be looking for in fund managers, some of them achieve it,' said another reviewer.

This 53 per cent puzzles me. Why not 55 per cent, or better 60 per cent. Mistakes are unavoidable, but they should be the exception not the rule. When we talk of exceptions we typically mean less than 5 per cent. Even a broken watch is right twice per day.

No investment professional should disregard the fact that even a 60 per cent hit rate is extremely generous to the risk taker. Neither is the suggested '53 per cent' saying anything about the size of the deals. It may be that one of them which failed was so big as to wipe out the fund. This sort of ratio targeting is, to my judgement, the way to make a small fortune if one starts with a big one.

Risk takers can lose track of their priorities

> A reviewer said: 'The point that you make (about shorting) is actually an endorsement of hedge funds, as shorting did enable them to mitigate loss. (You) need to expand on this idea which will also help explain why hedge funds exist.'

I do hope hedge funds do not exist because of shorting, though the opposite may be true. Short selling is a very dangerous exercise particularly so, as it is the very same reviewer who has said 'markets ... are difficult things to read, no matter what "expert" you claim to be.'

Often, a portfolio manager also takes short positions on the basis of earnings warnings, other news and rumours, as well as other events, such as the September 11, 2001 attack on the World Trade Center in New York. When he or she speculates, it is imperative to watch out for news and events that demand adapting rapidly to changing market conditions.

Short of this, his reputation suffers. Traders are opportunistic in the use of leveraged short positions, focusing intently on companies that have:

- Downward earnings revisions
- Deteriorating fundamentals
- Peak profit margins
- Increasing competition, or
- Early stages of a technical weakness.

The reputation of a good trader also depends on the criteria he or she uses. Different criteria are used with a long strategy, a strategy which is typical of classical investment. The portfolio manager will invest in companies he believes to be undervalued because their fundamentals are not fully reflected in the stock price. Alternatively, these entities may present minimal investment risk because they, or the industry to which they belong, are currently out of favour with investors. This means searching for entities that have:

- a product or service dominant in the market;
- an edge in their economic sector or industry;
- current and potential market leadership, and earnings growth;
- first-class management teams and other human resources.

All these factors come into play when risk takers set their priorities. Whether one is going long or short, the two lists just mentioned reflect the objectives followed when carrying out company valuations. Whichever may be the strategy a trader, asset manager, or investor chooses, upholding his or her reputation requires:

- very clear goals;
- an enormous amount of concentration;
- first-class benchmarks; and
- technology which is ahead of the curve.

Leaving aside the fact that a large proportion of the 4,000 to 6,000 hedge funds in existence are staffed by two or three persons equipped with a couple of PCs, even bigger entities are not renown for satisfying the prerequisites posed by these bullets. Some valid human resources do exist in certain cases, but they are not infinite. Worst of all, risk management is very often run by the risk takers, a story already familiar from LTCM. All too often, the executive who takes the risks is also responsible for controlling the exposure, as John Law demonstrated in 1720 with the bankruptcy of Banque Royale and the Mississippi Bubble.

6. Hedge funds and credit institutions should care about legal risk

Lets return to the discussion in Section 4 and the salesman's statement: 'Don't you consider our bank to be trustworthy?' Leaving aside the fact that this bank had an A+ credit rating not a AAA, as the discussion with the salesman progressed, I wanted to know more about the creditworthiness of the ten hedge funds this senior representative of a credit institution (a senior vice president) said were to be the alternative investment's managers.

The banker – who also doubled as director of research – answered that there were now not 10 but 20 hedge funds and, 'if one of them fails all it means is a 5 per cent risk.' This contradicted another paragraph in fine print in the bank's document which stated:

> An investment in [this instrument] entails a high degree of risk and is suitable only for sophisticated investors for whom an investment does not represent a complete investment program and who understand and are capable of bearing the risks of [such] investment.
>
> There can be no assurance that [this instrument] will be able to achieve its investment objective or that investors will receive a return of their capital, and investment results may vary substantially on a monthly, quarterly or annual basis.

Few investors are truly aware that the objective of such and similar carefully crafted clauses by legal counsels is to excuse the issuer for very poor results with alternative investments, which were supposed to outperform the market. The portfolio description of another offer I received stated:

> The Technology Long/Short Portfolio seeks to gain exposure to the technology sector by investing in technology specialists with proven money management skills who have the ability to take long and short positions. These funds capitalise on both the *winners* and the *losers* in the dynamic technology industry.

But the investment review which followed the aforementioned short description was not so upbeat:

> Only five of our twelve managers posted a profit in February (2001). While we are never happy about losing money, the losses were modest in comparison to the 22% loss of the Nasdaq.

> The largest losses came from a few managers who increased their long exposure in the second half of February thinking we had hit a short-term bottom. Most managers, however, maintained their conservative stances and are well positioned for any trouble ahead.

What this statement does not say is that such losses are typically leveraged. The information about losses also contrasted with the euphoric account I was told orally by the same party: 'The portfolio's first month of investing was a profitable one.'

Any alternative investment can become a drag

The investor constantly needs to keep in mind two basic principles which have already been discussed: First, with investments the past is not a prognosticator of the future. The past is past. Any investment which behaved beautifully last season can become a drag in the next. Successful banking practice depends on knowledge, experience, flair, and ethics – and all of them have to be present in every transaction.

Second, as I have already mentioned, one of the reviewers, who comes from the hedge funds industry, aptly said: 'Markets are markets. They are difficult to read, no matter what "expert" you claim to be.' Awareness of the fact nobody truly knows the market's whims, its gyrations, and its timing:

- Will make investors aware of dangers, and
- It will help to significantly reduce risk.

By contrast, risk, particularly legal risk, zooms when the lack of transparency with respect to alternative investments allows their originators and vendors to make exaggerated claims orally, which are then contradicted by the written documentation. Claims such as, 'we have subjected each of the funds in which we invest to an extremely thorough examination, and our analysis has uncovered some completely new and unique findings...' sound hollow, yet this precise wording comes from one of the best known European banks.

Such silly statements need to be carefully scrutinised by senior management, followed by disciplined action. I have heard that sort of arguments often enough to be immune to it, but other investors have not.

The aggregators of risk and brokers of securities based on highly leveraged deals should *not* do what this sales pitch suggests, for the simple reason that such trades, the banks frontending and the hedge funds behind them, are exposed to growing legal risks. Lack of transparency magnifies reputational issues and their aftermath.

- *If*, for instance, the bank which acts as aggregator of risk uses a Russian salad of 20 hedge funds;
- *Then* this entity and its customers are exposed to 20 foggy deals involving leveraged, illiquid instruments which escape supervision and thorough examination by any serious standard.

Another unsubstantiated and dangerous claim is one sometimes made by risk aggregators that they have subjected each of the funds in which they invest to thorough examination, and they are satisfied that the invested assets are 'secure'. The implication of this statement is that the findings are positive, though the aggregator typically fails to be precise about how or why, and for good reason. No asset is secure in finance; particularly so if it is highly geared and the deals behind it are both not transparent and unregulated.

The lack of regulation with alternative investments increases the potential exposure of investors, as well as the reputational risk assumed by banks. Since strategies utilised by hedge funds, SAIVs, and the aggregators of risk involve borrowed money and substantial leverage, not only the clients, but also these entities and their counterparties are at risk – specifically at risk from litigation. Companies involved in alternative investments need to provide their managers and traders with legal protection, which is a costly business as we will see below.

Paying for legal protection

An alternative investment company's by-laws, which are binding on all its stakeholders, generally provide that every director, secretary and other officer shall be indemnified against any liabilities incurred by any act or omission made in the discharge of his or her duties. The amount of any such indemnity shall attach as a lien on the property of the company and have priority over all other shareholder claims.

The hedge fund's, SAIV's, or other risky entity's by-laws may however stipulate that no director, secretary or other officer shall be liable for any loss, damage or misfortune arising out of their own acts or omissions, unless it occurs as a result of fraud or dishonesty on their part. This is a significant disincentive for investors and shareholders thinking of suing the company, no matter how serious the company's omission or commission has been.

Clauses concerning trading, sales, advisory and management obligations are also carefully drafted, particularly those clauses which guarantee to indemnify and hold harmless their partners, officers, directors, employees and agents from and against any and all losses, damages, penalties, actions, liabilities, obligations, suits, judgements or other disbursements of any kind. Expenses listed as being the obligation of shareholders include:

- Attorneys' fees,
- Settlement fees, and
- Other costs incurred in connection with the defence of any actual or threatened action or proceeding, which may be imposed on, incurred by or asserted against any indemnified person.

This is an overgenerous, frequently used clause, the only limitation being that such losses resulted from mistakes of judgement, acts, or omissions by any indemnified person – if it reasonably believed his or her conduct was in, or not opposed to, the best interests of the SAIV, the bank, or the hedge fund; or, in the case of a criminal proceedings, provided that the indemnified person had reasonable cause to believe that his or her actions or omissions were lawful.

The broad nature of these clauses amounts to an abolition of negligence. Legal protection at the fund's expenses might even involve, in some circumstances, a second layer of employees, agents, or delegates selected, engaged, or retained by the indemnified person with 'reasonable care'.

Protection risks are legal risks which can be of significant dimension, as hedge funds and SAIVs delegate a high level of dealing discretion to internal traders, and place a substantial amount of assets with unaffiliated traders over which they have no control. Through these loosely coupled deals, as well as the usually prevailing internal delegation of trading authority, the investor's assets are subject to the risk of:

- Trader fraud
- Violation of trading policies; or
- Simply bad judgement.

To appreciate the potential amount of legal risk, the reader should keep in mind that funds of funds, SAIVs, banks and hedge funds effectively trade any instrument permitted by law and delegate the execution of trading and investment strategies to independent sub-contractors and agents. Furthermore, they are not required to adhere to any particular trading or investment system or approach, nor are they supervised by the government.

7. The need for high technology by alternative investment vehicles

One method by which fund managers can provide a modicum of risk management with their highly leveraged funds is through the careful and professional employment of the latest technology. Whether by the

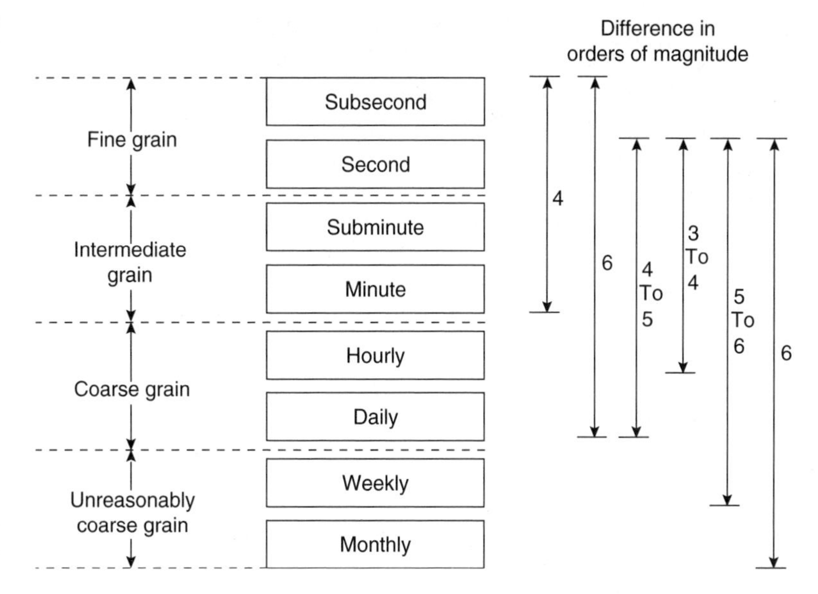

Figure 3.2 There are orders of magnitude in difference between fine grain and coarse grain information.

parent company or by the daughter, fine-grain tracking of gains and losses is essential as risk and return can vary substantially intraday, not just week-to-week or month-to-month. By fine grain, or tick-by-tick, I mean subsecond speed in:

- Data capture
- Database mining
- Computation, and
- Response to events.

The concept underpinning this process is known as *high frequency financial data* (HFFD).[4] As Figure 3.2 demonstrates, there are six orders of magnitude difference between subsecond fine grain and the coarse grain daily reporting systems which are available today among the better-managed hedge funds and SAIVs. Notice also that in the majority of cases financial reporting is a monthly event or worse.

One of the reviewers who does not seem to buy the need for high tech said: 'HFFD ... I read an article recently (the Economist or FT, I'm not sure) which suggested that daily reporting systems also have their own risks, particularly that of encouraging short-term, extreme decisions, rather than allowing a pattern to develop ...'

This is like the argument about who is responsible for car accidents: The auto or the driver behind the wheel. The motor vehicle may have perfect brakes but if the driver speeds and does not use his brakes, the crash is inevitable. It is not intraday reporting that crashes a firm, it is the lack of internal control and plenty of mismanagement.

This sort of argumentation that interactive, intraday financial reporting serves precious little, is the excuse found by low tech companies to justify – to themselves and to others – their regrettable condition. As such, it makes sad reading because in any and every financial institution low technology is part of the problem, not of the solution.

'Perhaps we can discuss more the virtues of different approaches to financial reporting,' asked the reviewer.

I am happy to oblige. In the palaeolithic time of technology, in which many institutions still live, balance sheets were prepared once per year with a couple of months of delay after the closing of the year. Now companies quoted in the New York Stock Exchange or in Nasdaq have by law to compute and report their assets and liabilities quarterly. SEC regulations ask for it. Quarterly reporting is necessary, but not enough.

Whether the balance sheet is established yearly or quarterly, by the time it is available, it is obsolete. Therefore, it helps precious little in steering the hand of management and in informing investors. Factors behind the need for a real-time balance sheet framework are:

- the ability to have intraday valuation of gains and losses;
- close watch over exposure, to enable timely countermeasures; and
- sustenance of a leadership position in a highly dynamic market.

Some institutions have obtained this position of leadership. The Boston-based State Street Bank, for example, is able to produce a *virtual balance sheet* within less than 30 minutes, and the next goal is 5 minutes. This is doable with advanced technology provided senior management has the will and the know-how to get commendable results, and the technologists are able to produce and sustain intraday solutions.

To begin with, a virtual balance sheet permits us to map assets and liabilities with 96 per cent or better accuracy, which is plenty for a real-time management information system. To appreciate the importance of interactive computational finance we must keep in perspective that at any minute, the hedge fund (or the bank's independent business unit) which speculates, can implode.

- Analytical risk management models run in real-time are not just the best way to face the challenges posed by this amount of risk-taking. They are the only way.
- Such models have to be developed and supported by hedge funds, SAIVs, banks, and brokers acting as aggregators and merchandisers of risk – and they should be made available to end-investors.

The query posed by the hedge fund executive who reviewed this text documents that importance of HFFD is not yet widely appreciated in the financial industry. Yet, while back in the late 1990s the emphasis was on average volume trade on a daily basis, today investment specialists have to look at intraday effective spreads and volumes of all the instruments in which they deal, to optimise the way they trade. This underpins the need for HFFD.

The use of high technology is a basic responsibility of risk-takers- and by extension of hedge funds, funds of funds and SAIVs. In their large majority, the ultimate users of alternative investments do not have the skills and technology to use HFFD, or to develop rigorous risk models by themselves, let alone to conduct stress tests (see Chapter 8). Unfortunately, quite often this is also true of the creators and aggregators of financial instruments that involve excessive risk.

The better managed funds specialising in alternative investments often employ a computer-based statistical approach, including a proprietary database of prices, volume, volatilities, open interest and various other market statistics. This is absolutely necessary to the development and monitoring of their trading strategies, but it is not sufficient for risk management. While market charting is welcome, the rather classical way in which it is employed is not the answer to the challenges I have been outlining. A much better method is the steady use of:

- Tests of hypotheses,
- Experimental design,[5]
- Agent technology,[6] and
- Stress testing procedures (see Chapter 8).

The better-run funds develop their own computer programs to search for patterns in data. These help to analyse and evaluate trading strategies which permit to exploit those patterns. Their trading decisions reflect a combination of methods able to effectively support the trading discretion and experience of their specialists. In this way, speculative moves and decisions leading to them are assisted by evaluation methods which can be modified from time to time, though there is no guarantee that they precisely reflect market movements.

Traders in these funds are free to use their discretion about whether or not to follow the trading signals or parameters generated by models and turn them into trading strategies. It is evident that decisions not to trade in certain markets or not to make certain trades indicated by computer-based systems may materially affect performance. Still, models or no models, the final decisions have to be made by people who bear responsibility for any losses incurred with leveraged investments – but the use of high technology is also instrumental in risk control.

8. Technological leadership and end-investors

Technological backwater can be deadly because the exposure taken with derivative instruments continues to mount. Figure 3.3 presents 20 years of statistics on the ever-growing outstanding volume of American agency mortgage backed securities. There is plenty of toxic waste in these two trillion dollars, and it has found itself into the portfolio of insurance companies, mutual funds, pension funds, and individual investors.

In its most generalised aspect, quantitative research is not new, and it is presently used by all sorts of investments companies. Fund managers, particularly equity specialists, employ quantitative methods to cope with increasingly global and complex trading strategies. A great deal of the work in quantitative analysis has been done on the fixed-income side and was mainly derivatives-related, but the use of modelling for cash and equities has been evolving as the investment horizon broadens.

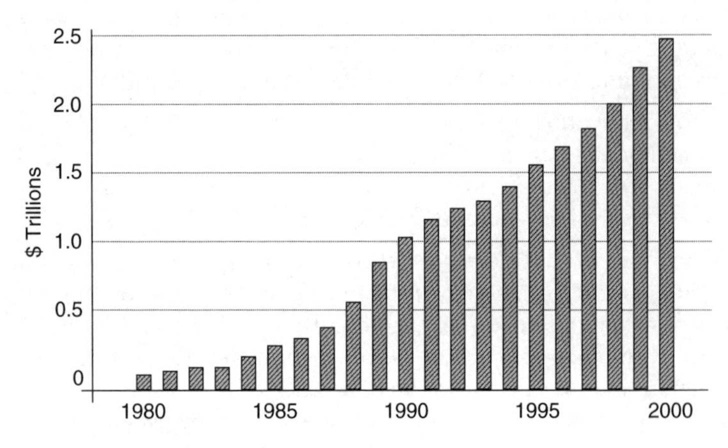

Figure 3.3 The ever growing oustanding volume of American agency mortgage backed securities in the US.

- Financial institutions wanting to gain the upper ground go well beyond classical quantitative approaches.
- They develop innovative, advanced software, do so very rapidly, and keep on sharpening their edge.

The evolution of the market makes this kind of policy mandatory. As a general trend, partly because of globalisation and partly because of the euro, instead of just investing in 40 or 50 domestic stocks, European equity analysts are now looking at 500 large caps and perhaps 2,000 medium and small caps. Rocket scientists help fund managers to answer queries about why part of their portfolio is performing and why another part is not.[7] The leaders use high technology because:

- Over the last few years the markets have become much more sophisticated; and
- There are now many more factors affecting performance than just the rise and fall of interest rates or a company's financial results.

Also, in the more traditional investment lines, fund managers are under pressure to perform, therefore they want a more objective and systematic approach to select stocks, construct portfolios and steadily evaluate their investment. Advanced quantitative tools can help asset managers to identify exposure to various macroeconomic and microeconomic factors, as well as experiment on different investment styles. The more leveraged and more risky is the investment, the higher is the level of sophistication necessary with models and technology.

What end-investors must appreciate is that a bank, hedge fund, or any other entity is not a technology leader simply because it says so. It takes a great deal of effort to be at the forefront of technology, and this involves:

- Policies,
- Goals,
- Skills, and
- Capital investments.

Sometimes, companies come up against what is known as *algorithmic insufficiency*. This term was coined in the early 1990s by the Japanese government when it financed a large project known as Real World Computing (RWC).[8] The goal of RWC has been to develop much more powerful algorithms and heuristics, able to deal with the *complexity* of our current financial and technological systems.

- This project led nowhere, in terms of deliverables, because of misdirection; hence algorithmic insufficiency remains a bottleneck.

- The fact that insufficiency in analytics has not yet been resolved, has a negative impact on the study of complex deals such as alternative investments.

Apart from the analysis of business opportunity, and its inverse: growing exposure, fund managers need powerful algorithms and heuristics to help themselves with specific evaluations. One of the biggest challenges that rocket scientists face today is the non-linear impact of volatility and liquidity.[9] In the past, the effect was spread more or less evenly throughout all industrial sectors and company equities, but this is no more the case.

Today, the impact of high volatility and on- and off-market liquidity is concentrated on the higher risk deals such as going short and going long at the same time, as well as in trading the macromarkets – two types of deals which, as we have seen, underpin alternative investments. Since 1997, much greater volatility seems to be concentrated in a few sectors, and fund managers have to adopt a very systematic, process-driven approach to their choice of leveraged assets and the evaluation of their inventoried positions:

- They must look at risk and return on an *intraday* basis rather than just once a month; and
- They should cost analyse every transaction, including as a cost factor the longer term risk being assumed.

It is not surprising, therefore, that during the last few years *transaction cost analysis* (TCA) has become one of the vital tools, particularly for stocks which present significant challenges. As Pareto's law would suggest, 80 to 90 per cent of equities offer no major problems. It is the less liquid but more lucrative ones that contribute most to trading costs and risks. Market-impact cost models help fund managers:

- to pinpoint the problem cases; and
- steer accordingly their alternative investment strategies.

Another vital method in modern finance concerns the concept and tools associated with *confidence intervals*. Figure 3.4 gives an example. By itself, the mean (or expected value) is no longer a significant statistic. For example, two world wars in the twentieth century added less than 10 per cent to the mortality figures over that timeframe. As an average, this 10 per cent does not look extreme, but neither does it make war a normal phenomenon. The mean is just the first momentum of a distribution. We must also know the second, third, and fourth momentum.[10]

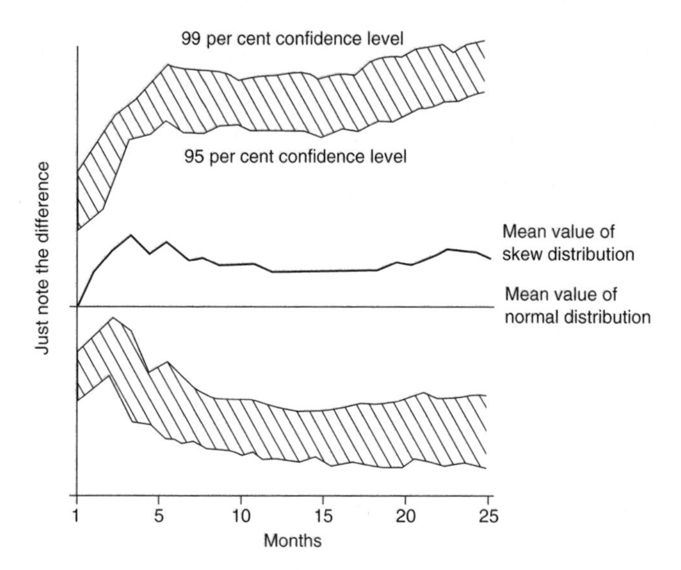

Figure 3.4 Expected value of exposure and 95 per cent, 99 per cent confidence intervals.

In conclusion, whenever we estimate risks we must evaluate our level of confidence with respect to our statistics, as well as in regard to our estimates and projections. What is the level of exceptions we are willing to admit, and therefore what are the tolerances? Figure 3.4 explains this concept in a nutshell by comparing the

- mean, or expected value;
- 95 per cent confidence level, with 5 per cent exceptions;
- 99 per cent confidence level, with 1 per cent exceptions.

Even if we are confronted by algorithmic insufficiency, we have tools which permit fund managers to take a more rigorous approach to their investment policies than is generally the case. The more risky is the instrument the more those responsible for managing it must be focusing on methods and tools that help them be more effective in their trading and portfolio performance – and, above all, in safeguarding their company's and their clients' assets.

4
The Financial Risks Taken with Alternative Investments

1. Introduction

Hedge funds have strategies, and there are plenty of them. The most important, such as macromarkets, going short, market neutral, private equity, structured approaches, emerging industries, emerging countries have been introduced in Chapter 1. We will look at the way in which they are implemented in this chapter and in Chapters 5 and 6.

Some of these trading strategies have been practised for years but not to the extent that they are today. In the early twentieth century, for example, what are now called securitised products were known as *Straus bonds*, after Simon W. Straus who invented them in 1909. Straus's real estate bond was a security with a senior claim on a building, and their inventor became a financier of skyscrapers.[1] Slowly, however, their quality degraded because in the gathering prosperity of the 1920s lending standards softened and there were many defaults.

- Without saying anything to his investors, Simon W. Straus invented the junk bond business.
- He, and his imitators, found out that new buyers of doubtful bonds can be created by intensive merchandising.
- As the creditworthiness of the Straus bonds degraded, each new wave of investors in effect paid the preceding wave.

This was the first try of alternative investments on record. Other, much more recent alternative investment strategies are debt instruments like credit derivatives and catastrophe insurance derivatives: the CATs and superCATs (see Section 8). Two things that all these off-balance sheet instruments have in common is leveraging and the fact that they base themselves on somebody else's liabilities.[2]

'This is unnecessarily negative in tone,' one of the reviewers said.

Most likely what is meant by this comment is that telling the truth is a negative. Everybody has to be always upbeat about new and untested instruments which try to find their way into the mainstream, no matter what the assumed risk is. This sort of thinking is very tricky and it is absolutely unacceptable. My opinion is quite different: with new and untested instruments we have to be more careful than ever.

Rather than hiding the exposure which is associated to alternative investments, this chapter looks through a magnifying glass at risk and return embedded in alternative investments instruments based on emerging markets, emerging companies, securitised products, private equity, structured approaches, other debt-based products, and insurance derivatives. As with all alternative investments, these must offer a much higher yield than traditional vehicles, for investors to assume a greater amount of risk.

'They do give higher yield because of greater risk. Yet nowhere do you provide us with a risk/reward assessment, which we really do need,' said a reviewer.

When the reviewer wrote this commentary, he probably had not read the rest of the chapter, nor Chapter 5. Had he done so, he would have seen that his wish was fulfilled – albeit in what he considers to be a negative way in regard to risk/reward, because these are the facts. The facts cannot be changed in order to please the risk aggregators and merchandisers.

What a serious investor who contemplates entering into this sort of deal should keep in mind, is that *all* types of investments – and particularly those exposed the most – must be examined not only for risk and reward but also for *extra risk* and *extra reward*. Are the added basis points or increased returns enough to compensate the investor for extra risks being taken? This is the key question which this chapter addresses.

2. Alternative investments and mutual funds fatigue

Dynamic markets incite companies to take more risk, often without knowing exactly the exposure they are assuming. Since stockmarkets began to decline in late March 2000, the signs of mutual fund fatigue have been almost everywhere. Contrary to traders, investors have been rather patient. It took another two years to build up a trend to redemptions.

Mutual funds fatigue has been a change in investment culture because not that long ago, mutual funds (unit trusts) were the most popular, if not the most outright cost-effective way to build a diversified equity portfolio. Part of the reason for the change lies in the fact that:

- With networks, on-line investors could achieve reasonable diversification at less long-term expense than if they bought mutual funds.
- A fund charges management expenses year after year, as do the different banks selling alternative investments and the many hedge funds working with them.

Indexing, which substituted a computer and a stock index for an individual stockpicker, attracted more attention, as did fairly inexpensive on-line investing – with about 12 million accounts. By early 2000, internet-based brokers and day traders seemed to have the upper hand (though many day traders went out of business with Nasdaq's blues). Where individual investors seemed to need help was in risk-taking. That's where hedge funds found their niche.

Hedge funds and mutual funds contrast sharply in their policies. The performance of mutual funds correlates with that of the markets. They do not borrow to gear-up on bullish expectations and do not massively sell short securities with poor prospects. Also, they rarely use derivatives. In contrast, hedge funds are very active short sellers and derivatives players. They usually:

- do not suffer from the problem of dead-weight investments
- do not often manage against a benchmark, and
- do not have to buy a stock to minimise a tracking error or because the stock is in a benchmark.

> 'The main difference is that hedge funds nearly always look for absolute performance rather than try to beat an index, even if the index is going down,' said one reviewer.

True enough, but as the careful reader will recall from the previous chapters, another reviewer made precisely the opposite comment. Each reviewer is right from his viewpoint, but awfully wrong from the other party's point of view. *That's what makes the market*, as I learned early enough on Wall Street.

Back to the hedge funds versus mutual funds issue, many analysts now believe that the drive behind the mutual funds industry has largely been exhausted. After growing so fast for so long, mutual funds presently feature about US$7 trillion in assets, and (redemptions aside) signs are that they are tapering off. Experts point to factors that help explain the shrinking flow of cash into mutual funds:

- investors are now spending some of their money, which has helped the boom in the consumer economy; and
- stockmarket jitters have made many people nervous about putting more money into equities.

Hedge funds have come to the foreground by convincing investors that they have more dynamic strategies than standard mutual funds. For example, they offer high leverage, with all this means in risk and return; investments in multiple asset classes; simultaneous long and short positions; a vulture kind of HI-ILDA3 attitude (some call themselves vulture funds); and plenty of promises about future gains. They also emphasise that:

- their portfolio managers have a substantial amount of their own capital at stake, and
- they tend to be reinvesting the money they receive as incentive rewards when the fund's profits rise.

The power of big mutual funds became a negative factor

The demise of mutual funds may also be the result of investors becoming more uncomfortable about the growing power of big mutual funds, which buy and sell billions of dollars of shares, influencing the market in upswings and downswings. In personal meetings, it was clear that several equity traders believed the large price moves by technology stocks in the late 1990s, when the Nasdaq raced ahead of itself, were caused at least in part by the 'marking up' of portfolios.

Publicly, mutual fund officials deny that they try to push up stock prices to improve performance or engage in window-dressing. Privately, however, a few fund managers admit they suspected or had heard that some of their competitors engaged in such practices, but said they were not widespread. Critics suggest mutual funds are well aware of such practices, if they are not themselves the motors behind this trend.

Recently, certain experts have proposed a more fundamental reason for the stock market's wild swings: individual investors' irrepressible search for the new and untried has dimmed the attraction of mutual funds which, in the longer run, acted as the fly wheel. Now, alternative investments' targets have emerged, and their proponents suggest that they are now acting as stabilisers of the economy. It is difficult to see how this can be substantiated, as

- they are highly leveraged;
- lack transparency; and
- run after glamorous derivatives products.

In the United States and the United Kingdom pension funds have been long-term investors in business with a fairly positive investment outlook. They are not only an accepted but also a welcome part of the financial industry, as protectors of the savings of millions of working individuals, and an engine behind the drive for shareholder value. But sometimes, pension funds and other institutional investors spend money on projects that have not been adequately researched, let alone proved in regard to their profitability.

In the late 1990s, at the height of IPOs, pension funds financed venture capital firms and made a profit. University endowments and other not-for-profits organisations did the same.[3] The reader should not confuse venture capital firms with hedge funds, even if both engender greater risks than mutual funds.

What makes venture capital a different species

Venture capital firms have a productive and constructive role to play in the economy. They provide the money for start-ups, many of which will fail but some will become the motors of tomorrow's knowledge economy. One of the advantages the American economy has over the European is that it is much more venture capital oriented.

Venture capital firms are not the favoured investment vehicles in a bear market. Through June 2002 the give-backs have totalled at least $3 billion. And that's a fraction of what's to come, observers say.[4] Venture capital firms may end up returning about $50 billion to investors in 2002 and 2003 – yet, contrary to alternative investments, these companies have a productive role in the economy.

Some people tend to confuse venture capital with private equity. My reference to venture capital is primarily focused to the financing of start-ups. By contrast, under private equity I will include mezzanine financing, distressed firms, buyouts, and middle market private firms (more about private equity in Section 5).

Generally, venture capital outfits are much more transparent and, in their way, less complex than hedge funds, funds of funds, and their alternative investments. In the go-go years of IPO, venture capital firms might have been seen as an alternative investment strategy. Yet, the financing of venture capital firms and of hedge funds does not at all entail the same frame of mind, neither does it represent the same risks.

> 'Venture capital investing is not always transparent, and if they go wrong, you can't get your money out,' said a reviewer from a hedge fund.

There is no doubt that venture capital firms can go wrong. Everybody can go wrong. Financing research and development (R&D) is not for the faint hearted. From my industrial experience I can confirm that 80 per cent of R&D projects lead nowhere, 15 per cent just arrive, and 5 per cent become blockbusters covering all other losses and leaving a good profit. (Compare this to the curious goal of '53 per cent being right' advanced by another reviewer from the hedge funds.)

The R&D paradigm is supreme with venture capital outfits because that's precisely what they are doing: they search for, screen, select and finance brilliant young brains with a terrific idea. Provided it is not overdone, and therefore becomes subject to the law of averages, venture capital investing is:

- *transparent*, because it targets specific entities and their products;
- *productive*, because it helps the most imaginative elements of society to come up with new products;
- *controllable*, because financing comes at stages and design reviews give the green light for the next instalment.[5]

It is all a matter of degree and of careful evaluation, based on facts. By contrast, alternative investments the way they are practised today by the merchandisers of risk:

- are non-transparent;
- do not contribute to industrial production; and
- are non-controllable.

Yet, both credit institutions and investors like pension funds, who should be very careful in their fiduciary duties, are now pouring big money in these vehicles. They are also lending to hedge funds and even contributing to their capital. Understandably, regulators are feeling nervous as pension funds and insurance companies put themselves at such risk.

3. Emerging companies and emerging markets

If one looks into the vocabulary of the mid-1990s he will not find the term *emerging companies*; it is more recent than that. Sometimes, the term emerging companies is confused with venture capital financing. That's wrong because the two are quite distinct.

- Emerging companies are essentially an industry sector, like dotcoms, and
- Their financing is mezzanine and other sorts of private equity (more on this later).

Emerging companies have been a favourite of day traders, many of whom were burned. Even individual investors who have gone through a broker, acting on 'expert advice', saw their wealth disappear overnight. Table 4.1 shows eight real-life examples of alternative investment returns of 'emerging companies', covering little more than a year (7 June 2000 to 27 July 2001).

Table 4.1 How the 'experts'' stock picks fared in the short span of 1 year and 50 days. Eight examples with emerging industries

Company	Type of business	Price 7 June 2000 (in $)	Price 27 July 2001 (in $)	Lost capitalisation (in %)
Integrated Information Systems (IISX)	Software	7.50	1.01	86.5
Latitude Communications (LATD)	Communications software	10.38	1.60	84.6
Mobile Data Solutions (MDSI)	Wireless communications	14.44	2.55	82.4
Adept Technology (ADTK)	Automation hardware, software	46.63	8.54	81.7
Hall Kinion & Associates (HAKI)	Technology staffing	35.31	6.89	80.5
IMPCO Technologies (IMCO)	Alternative fuels	40.31	26.60	78.9
Ceridian (CEN)	Information technology	22.56	17.75	21.4
Boston Scientific (BSX)	Medical devices	22.44	18.15	19.2

> 'By day traders, you mean end-users?' asked one of the reviewers.

That a hedge fund executive would ask this kind of question is, to say the least, curious. The evident answer is that end-users and day traders are two different species and they belong to quite different lots. What the reviewer calls 'end-users' are investors. By contrast, day traders are 99 per cent traders and may be 1 per cent investors.

> Another reviewer was to suggest he did not believe that hedge funds as a whole were big in this area or emerging companies and he asked for statistics showing exposure, to decide whether this is a realistic risk or not.

These are two different issues merged into one query. The examples in Table 4.1 (which were available to the reviewer) document that emerging companies are indeed a real risk. Another even more famous catacomb of capital is that of the money investors put in dotcoms; it would be redundant to elaborate on their fate.

As for the part of the query regarding 'statistics' about hedge funds investment in emerging industries, sorry about this but it is laughing matter. Right from page 1 of this book, the argument about hedge funds, funds of funds, SAIVs – and therefore alternative investments – is that they are so dangerous in *capital at risk* terms because:

- they are very secretive;
- they are not transparent; and
- they are not subject to prudential supervision.

Financial statistics which are worthy enough to be read and reported come from two sources: They are compiled by the supervisors, like the Basle Committee on Banking Supervision is doing for commercial banks;[6] and they are published by the financial entities themselves. With hedge funds, nothing of that sort is forthcoming. (Incidentally, precisely the same query is posed by the reviewers a couple more times, as we will see in Chapter 7.)

Emerging markets is another domain in which hedge funds and the aggregators of risk try to capitalise. However, emerging markets are not alien to mutual funds. Like all volatile investments, these markets offer investors large sums in losses and gains. In 2000–2, investment returns from emerging markets were bad and asset managers, including mutual funds and hedge funds, were hit.

Many international funds, which invest in all types of foreign stocks, and taking on significant emerging-markets stakes, failed to understand the amount of exposure they were assuming. Investors cannot afford to be complacent or stand still. But do they understand the risks they are taking?

Some of them did, at least on paper. Real profits is another matter. Let's recall that all emerging markets funds tanked in 1997 with the meltdown of the Asian 'tigers'; an experience repeated in 1998 with the Russian bankruptcy, as well as on so many other occasions. This does not mean investors should never go for emerging markets (previously known as underdeveloped countries, then as countries in process of development). Investors should however appreciate that what makes these markets tick *is* foreign capital which:

- rushes in when everything goes well; and
- rushes out with the first signs of distress, let alone panic.

> 'Diversified foreign stock funds have bounced in 2002,' said one of the reviewers.

Globalisation sees to it that capital rushes in and out of a country in search for a comfortable home. An estimated 40 per cent of the money invested in the US equities in the late 1990s was foreign money. This was one of the big reasons behind the strength of the dollar, and when in early to mid-2002 such capital started to move out of the US, the dollar and the euro reached parity (on 15 July 2002).

Because globalisation sees to it that foreign investments can be attractive, a number of large, diversified foreign-stock funds, have at least one dollar out of every seven invested in emerging markets. But their track record of these stocks is not very encouraging, as can be seen in Table 4.2.

In the 2001–2 timeframe, Turkey has tanked, Poland has been on the brink, the Czech Republic is in a coma, confidence in Argentina has evaporated, Indonesia is beset by separatist movements and an unstable government, and currency woes have threatened Brazil. Other emerging countries are also struggling, with falling exchange rates, rising unemployment, social unrest and a foreseeable end to the era of very cheap labour.

Table 4.2 emphasises the risks taken with emerging countries in real terms. While it is worrying that highly paid hedge fund professionals

Table 4.2 Examples with alternative investment returns in emerging countries – 1 August 2000 to 31 December 2001

Investment fund	**Assets in $ millions**	**Per cent of assets in emerging markets**	**Returns over a 12-month period (%)**
Pilgrim International Value A	1266	15.0	−12.8
Nations International Value Inv A	469	16.9	−11.6
Alliance Worldwide Priv A	248	30.0	−31.1
William Blair International Growth N	161	21.7	−21.5
BlackRock International Small Cap Equity	100	15.6	−29.3
Tocqueville International Value	82	33.2	−14.6

make such investment mistakes, banks also have made similar errors by providing loans to emerging markets without appropriate risk and return analysis. Among the more glaring examples is the battering two major Spanish banks received with the bankruptcy of Argentina at the end of 2001. Several Italian and American banks also found themselves in distress in the same country, for the same reason.

In conclusion, whether we talk of handouts in loans, emerging companies, emerging countries, or any other alternative investments, lack of management control, particularly with respect to risks, leads to regrettable results. Many hedge funds managers might work late, but they don't work smart.

4. Securitised subprime credit and junk bonds

Since the late 1990s, a new investment paradigm has been promoted. Higher risk securitisation consists of buying up a lot of bonds in, for example, telecommunications, healthcare, and other distressed companies, and packaging them into securities for sale. The ingenuity has been in the fact that each new securitised instrument is offering investors a range of risk options even if many or all of the underlying bonds carry junk ratings.[7]

For instance, investors that are generally risk averse are being sold manicured investment-grade slices giving them first claim on cash from the bonds, but at lower interest rates. Others can take a bigger gamble, buying slices with junk ratings but paying higher rates. There are even investors who buy the riskiest, non-investment grade slice, offering interest rates of 20 per cent or more, known as 'toxic waste' in the market.

Private investors, pension funds, insurance companies and many others have entered the fray. Yet, it is no secret that some of those assuming the risks of junk bond securitisations have been casualties. American Express is an example. Flush with money from insurance and annuities premiums paid by its customers, it plunged into this high-risk market. Not only did the company buy plenty of securities from other issuers, but it also began packaging its own securitised junk bonds for sale through other investment firms, keeping some of the highest risk (and highest interest) slices for its own account.

Experts on Wall Street believe American Express entered into these alternative investment securities in about 60 separate deals, including 12 created internally in exchange for management fees. This was a company that had plenty of experience of losses resulting from dubious financial instruments. In 1989, Shearson Lehman Hutton Holdings, a subsidiary of Amex, suffered megadollar losses on loans partially backed by junk bonds.

Other issuers, too, did not miss the collateralised opportunities. Since the mid-1990s, about US$175 billion in junk bond collateralised obligations have been issued, underwritten by investment banks such as Morgan Stanley, Goldman Sachs, and Credit Suisse First Boston. Exactly how much of that has already been lost is unknown, but analysts estimate that real losses and paper losses to investors such as hedge funds and insurance companies exceed several billion dollars.

Risks originating from businesses that fail because of management, overleveraging, and/or overexposure now dominate the investment landscape. Originators include US corporate household names such as Pacific Gas & Electric (PG&E), Enron, Global Crossing, Exodus, Polaroid, Bethlehem Steel, Regal Cinemas, Federal Mogul, and more. The first ten months of 2001 saw 32 bankruptcies of companies with liabilities of over US$1 billion, which is more than the whole period of 1989–91, the low point of the previous cycle.

'The biggest bankruptcy of all' has now become almost an annual event. In 2000, P&G collapsed with US$26 billion in liabilities. In 2001 this honour went to Enron. In July 2002, while this text was written, WorldCom was at the brink and analysts said this was going to be the biggest US bankruptcy ever. Indeed, the amount of big bankruptcies is alarming. So is the rate of default of junk bonds, which in 2001 approached the all-time peak of 10.3 per cent, set in 1991.

Defaults have their own volatility to be taken into account. They had been pretty stable between 1993 and 1998, at below 2 per cent of outstanding issues; then they started to rise and in the first nine months of 2001, companies with liabilities totalling US$170 billion declared bankruptcy. The last three months of 2001 and the first semester of 2002 saw many other major bankruptcies. What worries most analysts about the 2000/2001 type of credit risk is that:

- the problems are more widespread; and
- they are not confined to particular companies that took on too much debt.

Whole industry sectors such as telecommunications, airlines, hotel business, movie theatres, nursing homes, steel and others are in trouble. Interest rates do not reflect credit risk anxiety. Because of easing by the Fed, interest rates are currently low, though banks are tightening their lending standards as credit risk increases and there is growing uncertainty about how to value a firm in today's fast-changing economy.

One of the peculiar aspects of 2001 and 2002 has been that financial institutions and other entities had trouble quantifying their exposure to junk bonds and hedge funds. One example is in the area of securitising subprime credit. On 27 July 2001, the Federal Deposit Insurance Corporation (FDIC) seized Superior Bank FSB in Oakbrook Terrace, Illinois, in a bailout that could cost US$500 million.

- Superior Bank specialised in inferior subprime loans.
- It failed because it became overexposed in this sort of lending and became insolvent.

In the past, central banks have bailed out the large credit institutions which were in distress, because they are afraid of systemic risk. This occurred with Continental Illinois and Bank of New England in America; and Crédit Lyonnais in France (among several others). But the small and medium-sized banks are allowed to descend to the abyss.

Even the fire brigade of the central bank, however, has its limits. Leading economists today worry about many large banks failing at the same time, thereby creating a climate of market panic and depriving the central banks of the possibility to intervene.

The Superior case is by no means a one-off, neither is a distressed economy the only reason for bank failures. Even in the boom years of the late 1990s, more than a dozen non-bank subprime lenders in the United States went bankrupt after they had overvalued their loans. After the fall of Superior, the FDIC said it would be closely tracking 150 banks that have sizeable subprime portfolios. Critics suggest that banks are being irresponsible by lending so much to debt-strapped consumers with a history of not paying their bills. In June 2001 a record one-in-ten subprime-mortgage borrowers was in arrears by 60 days or more. Moreover:

- More than 6 per cent of all US subprime loans are seriously delinquent, since they have not been paid for over three months; and
- In 2001, over US$160 billion in mortgage loans, the bulk of subprime lending, was advanced to borrowers with imperfect credit; this is 540 per cent up from US$30 billion in 1995.

Junk bonds, like alternative investments, have entered the retail trade. Consumers with doubtful credit histories took out about US$100 billion in credit-card and auto loans in 2000 in the United States alone. Most of this business was carried out by banks such as Citigroup, JP Morgan Chase, and Bank of America. Banks seem to be happy to extend subprime loans as they earn more profit (when things go well), because they carry interest rates as much as 150 to 600 basis points higher than traditional loans. The downside, of course, is that losses are also much higher than on traditional loans.

One of the risks analysts see in connection to soaring subprime loans, and the resulting heavy losses because of the depressed economic climate of 2000–2, is that banks may be tempted to securitise them. They may offer them to consumers and institutional investors as alternative investments, without properly emphasising the amount of credit risk. It should not be forgotten that:

- Individual investors are not good at making credit-risk decisions; and
- Some institutional investors seem to be as risk-hungry as individuals looking for a quick return.

If this were not the case, successive junk bond meltdowns in the late 1980s and in the early part of the twenty-first century would not have been seen. One of the reasons for the higher credit failure of junk bonds in 2001 was that during 1996–2000, large numbers of junk bonds were issued by the telecoms industry to finance expansion plans and takeovers. According to Moody's Investors Service, during the first quarter of 2001, 93 US companies defaulted on US$35 billion of junk bonds, a record volume. On 23 July 2001, the *Wall Street Journal* reported that:

- The recovery rate for junk bonds was 12 cents on the dollar.
- This is less than half the 25 cents on the dollar in 1999–2000.

These are ominous statistics because the US market for junk bonds is valued at US$690 billion, a huge amount, even if it represents only 7 per cent of the US$10 trillion market of all US corporate and treasury bonds. The risk is that a massive junk bond failure could bring down with it the larger bond market, particularly so if coupled with bond and loan failures by Latin American and other emerging countries.

Beyond the foreign debt of sovereigns and of global companies looms the liabilities encapsulated within derivatives trades, numbered in trillions. The largest portion of the derivatives bubble is within the largest banks and other big financial institutions – US, European and Japanese. The question is how to structure a rigorous global test which accounts for the compound effect on investors, individual banks, national economies, and the global economy. This should include the unprecedented current level of leveraging and all major risk factors: junk bonds, subprime lending, sovereign debt, derivatives, and other alternative investments.

5. Private equity and unlisted securities

Another strategy followed by alternative investments, is private equity. The careful reader will recall that I have included four main chapters in the private equities definition: mezzanine financing, distressed firms, buyouts, and middle market private firms. These are the subject of our discussion in the present section.

Entities specialising in private equity overwhelmingly invest in unlisted companies, taking an active hand in managing their investments over the medium term to increase their value, and exiting them in a manner to maximise capital gain. They seek both majority and minority equity interest in established and emerging unlisted companies, either by risking their own capital, or through sponsored investment funds.

> 'This is unnecessarily negative in tone,' said one of the reviewers, adding that 'It is true that lots of private equity investments – as with TMT and lots of others – have plummeted recently, but markets are markets. Nothing is safe.'

The 'unnecessarily negative' flag attached to anything that does not promote alternative investments has been used so very often that I really became immune to it. It is the author's responsibility to inform the reader about the risks. The reader, if he chooses, may disregard the warning. This is something he or she is absolutely free to do, at his or her own peril.

As for the second half of the remark, the reviewer aptly answers his own argument through the statement: 'Markets are markets. Nothing is safe' – or almost so. Since nothing is safe, it is wise to be prudent about everything. To be ignorant about the huge risks associated with alternative investments is like having been in a cave for 20 years.

Back to the private equity discussion, although the main focus of such investments is late-stage financing, such as management buyouts, expansion, or replacement capital, many private equity companies allocate a minority of their portfolio to early-stage investments in industries with significant growth potential. For instance, in the late 1990s, their preference has been technology and telecommunications. Some of the opinions regarding private equity can be summed up as follows:

- Private equity still offers investment opportunities but only on a very selective basis (which should always be the case);
- Investors need to be more careful when considering private equity funds as the pitfalls have increased;
- The market saw significant changes during 1998–2002. Because of big losses the focus is now on common sense investing.

With the fall of Nasdaq, enthusiasm for internet companies has waned. Much money was invested at the top of the bull market, at levels that will not be seen again for some time. In the past, start-ups and other companies assumed funding would always be available at higher valuations. This is no longer the case. The early sharp increase of valuations has been followed by a sharp decline of the internet sector. The leveraging and deleveraging of some of the better known technology stocks is depicted in Figure 4.1.

There have been winners and losers with private equity investments. By the end of 2001, the spread of returns offered by the top quartile funds compared with low quartile funds had increased. The selection of investment opportunities and fund managers has, therefore, become even more critical. Investors want to see a return to core values and basic valuation metrics, and, although there are still private equity investors around, the easy and spectacular profits are no longer there. Figure 4.2 depicts the sources of capital commitment to private equity in 1998, when this kind of financing was on the rise.

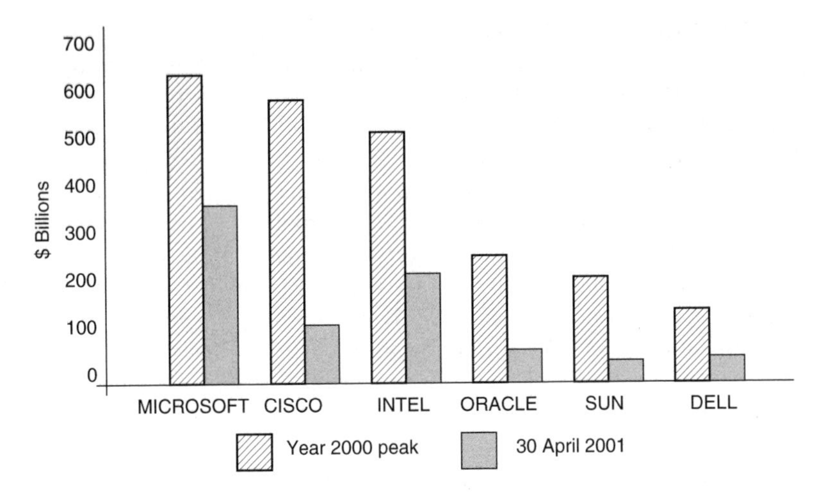

Figure 4.1 The shrinking market capitalisation of technology leaders in the United States.

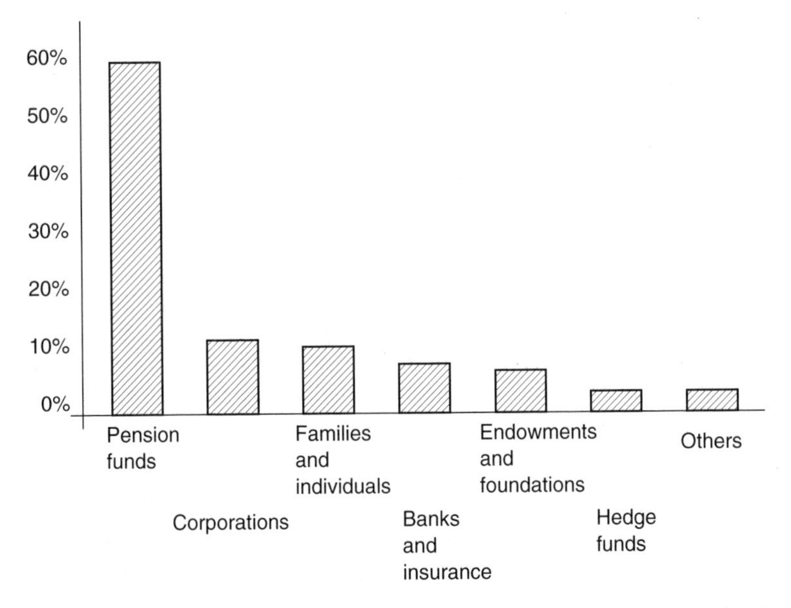

Figure 4.2 American sources of capital commitments for private equity in the heydays of 1998.

The amount of capital being invested by private equity entities varies from case to case and is frequently determined by the size of the company in which they invest. Often the target is medium-sized businesses with values in the range of US$50 million to US$90 million. In many cases, private equity bets endeavour to differentiate themselves from their competitors by increasing the level of money being invested, or by lending management skill to the financed company to improve its performance.

The biggest players in private equity investments pride themselves as being able to establish both local presence and expertise. They develop international connections and use analytics to help themselves in early identification of investment opportunities. One of their targets is firms whose owners face management succession problems. Private equity outfits also feature incentive schemes to encourage referrals of potential business leads from other companies.

When it comes to financial profits, returns from private equity are by no means a certainty. As the *Financial Times* noted on 27 July 2001, the United Bank of Switzerland expected to lose nearly Swfr700 million (US$406 million) on its private equity business in 2001, or more than twice as much as it earned in the previous two years (1999–2000) while it was trying to become a significant influence in the European private equity market.

In Zurich, analysts said that UBS Capital appears to have had relatively little exposure to the TMT sector, but it was suffering from a broader decline in its industrial portfolio. The financial press suggested that only 15 per cent of its portfolio was computer-related, compared with 18 per cent in consumer industries and 25 per cent in industrial products and services. There must however be a cause for heavy losses because:

- UBS, lost Swfr282 million (US$166 million) on its private equity business in the first quarter of 2001; and
- It issued a warning to expect further losses of Swfr350 million (US$206 million) to Swfr400 million (US$235 million) during the rest of the year, following a review of its portfolio.

UBS is not alone in this private equity investment misfortune. Its losses are more than matched by JP Morgan Chase, which took a US$1 billion write-off in early July 2001. The scale of those losses surprised analysts, since JP Morgan Chase had suggested that it expected its private equity arm to be profitable.

The reasons why banks usually invest in these and other uncertain ventures are fairly similar to the reasons why other people and companies are attracted to alternative investments at large. Usually, they revolve around:

- prevailing depressed market conditions;
- postponed planned investments or divestments by other firms;
- lower-than-expected gains in their classical business lines;
- deteriorating valuations across a range of industries, perceived as 'anomalies'; and
- the expectation that a windfall will cover other write-downs in their portfolio.

The stated rationale that investors are 'exploring new business domains', is a frequently given reason, and a ready excuse. Warren Buffett was right when he suggested that sometimes investors make more money by doing nothing rather than by rushing into deals they have poorly researched and risks they hardly understand.

Equities are not the only domain where private investment firms have been actively involved. Because the downturn in capital markets has put the crunch on stock offerings, the private equity business has espoused derivatives traded OTC as another way to make (or lose) money. Also, European private equity firms are increasingly turning to selling their investments to each other.

- These inter-industry sector deals are known as *secondary buyouts*, and they have been mounting in 2001.
- This is, in a way, *as if* Daimler-Chrysler sells cars to General Motors and GM reciprocates by selling its motor vehicles to Daimler-Chrysler.

Many private equity firms suggest that they have little choice in a market with a weak appetite for IPOs. At the same time, some finance companies are curiously in search of such acquisitions even if they have had problems raising money through their own share offers in a depressed market. Some venture capitalists who still have cash come to the rescue, particularly when they have investments in compatible industry sectors and hope to combine and create a larger, more cost-efficient, and therefore more valuable, entity.

The bet is that buy-and-build is giving private equity firms important critical mass, but in a depressed market private equity capitalists and the bankers promoting them get themselves into trouble. Even the investment banks that started up private equity operations in recent years have had second thoughts. In July 2001, UBS and Deutsche Bank said they were cancelling plans to spin off their private equity units, due to:

- weak stock markets; and
- the dim outlook for IPOs.

'The IPO route is no doubt already causing a lot of pain for those who structure deals based on an IPO exit,' said Jonathan Diggines, managing director of the private equity division of Aberdeen Asset Managers. 'For those in the bigger banks, an IPO exit is the key to getting your money back.'[8] Alternative investment professionals must consider the *exit strategy* both for themselves and their investors before following the private equity route, not only after.

6. Structured approaches offered to investors

When it comes to investments, the term 'structured' is used in the most liberal way. The concept behind a structured deal is that of overcoming some of the difficulties encountered in determining requirements related to the issuer, the issue, and the investor – hence the need to structure the deal in some way that may sound appealing.

In principle, *structural analysis* seeks to identify repeatable price patterns, using both quantitative studies and charting, for instance, price movements that occur consistently. In theory, *structured instruments* capitalise on patterns which can be identified and validated, and at the same time respond to the investment requirements of their intended market. In practice:

- It is not that easy to identify and validate patterns;
- Nor is it self-evident that structured instruments provide investors with capital protection.

A question that arises with the broad scope of the different structured issues is whether there is a distinction between functional and non-functional requirements. (The term *requirements* is indeed vague.) The pros say there is an underlying assumption in the development process of a structured investment deal, that requirements exist and can be captured. However, end-investor requirements are far from homogeneous. There should be a distinction made between:

- Functional requirements, which can be defined as *what* the investment does; and
- Non-functional requirements, which regard *how* the investment works in relation to the organisation supporting it.

With regard to the issuer, it is essential to focus attention on organisational factors. More generally, non-functional requirements concern all stakeholders, because they identify and mediate any conflicts before going on to model the new financial instrument. The practical examples in this and the following section concern functional requirements. One of the non-functional requirements, that of protecting directors and traders from court action, has been discussed in Chapter 3.

In mid-2001, Barclays Bank brought to the market a new instrument targeting individuals and institutional investors. High Interest Index Linked Deposit Account Issue Three (HI-ILDA3) advertised a return of 8 per cent gross annual equivalent rate (AER) fixed on the investor's cash, as well as something presented as a risk-free return linked to stock market performance. How exactly this was, or could be, 'risk free' was not explained.

HI-ILDA3 has been available in sterling or dollars to individual investors, aged 18 or over at the date of application, in sole or joint names, and to trustees of funds. A basic clause is that no more than 40 per cent of total deposit can be made into the high interest cash deposit account, which offers 8 per cent. The other 60 per cent (or 100 per cent if the investor so chooses) was going to an index-linked account. In effect, this structured deal is two accounts in one:

- an interest-based deposit account, and
- an index-linked account.

Given the contractual clauses, the 8 per cent offered to the 40 per cent of total investment was reduced to 3.2 per cent when spread to the total money at stake.

The investor has been offered the possibility to choose which stock market index he or she wishes to 'track' (although the average individual investor is unlikely to know how to track an index). The alternatives are the FTSE 100, for sterling investors, and the Dow Jones Global Titans index, for dollar investors. The return will reflect 50 per cent of the growth achieved over three years of the respective index, whose final level is calculated through averaging during the last year of the term of the index-linked account. The bank's sales literature further stated that:

- 'Your original deposit is safe, whatever happens to the index during the term of the account', and
- 'Your investment can be for any sum from £10,000 to £1 million or US$15,000 to US$1.5 million.'

This is supposed to be free of charges or fees, a clause becoming standard in many alternative investments. Fees are integrated into the gains of the issuer, becoming non-transparent to the end-investor. The investor will receive half the gains associated with 60 per cent of the investor's capital; the other half goes to the issuer. On the other hand, in a downturn, 100 per cent of the risk is on the investor's side.

Correctly, the issuer took care to underline that HI-ILDA3 is not sponsored, endorsed, sold or promoted by the London Stock Exchange, the *Financial Times*, or FTSE International. Also, there is no warranty or representation whatsoever, expressly or implied, either as to the results to be obtained from the use of the FTSE-100 index, or the figure at which the FTSE-100 index stands on any particular day or otherwise.

It has also been stated that Dow Jones is not related to the issuer bank, nor does it make any guarantee or representation whatsoever expressly or implied, either as to the results to be obtained from the use of the DJ Global Titans index and/or the figure at which the DJ Global Titans index stands on any particular day or otherwise. Specifically Dow Jones does *not*:

- Recommend that any person invests in HI-ILDA3 or any other securities;
- Assume any responsibility or liability for the administration, management, or marketing of HI-ILDA3; or
- Consider the needs of HI-ILDA3 or the bank in determining, composing or calculating the DJ Global Titans index or has any obligation to do so.

Therefore, the Barclays alternative investments offer explicitly stated that the Dow Jones does not have any liability in connection with HI-ILDA3, whether in negligence or otherwise, to any person for any error in the DJ Global Titans index and is not under any obligation to advise any person of any error therein. Along the same lines, the *Financial Times* and FTSE International are not to be liable, whether in negligence or otherwise, to any person in the FTSE-100 Index, nor be under any obligation to advise any person of any error therein.

The bank has been right to specify all these waivers of responsibility, yet they are written in small print and many people do not read the small print to understand what underpins their investment's future. By contrast, the anticipated performance of '8% Gross/AER on Your Cash and a Risk-Free Return Linked to Stock Market Performance' is written across the front page of the promotional literature, as the enticement to investors.

On the positive side, this particular alternative investments offer by Barclays has better non-functional characteristics for the stakeholders than most of its competitors' deals – and it guarantees, at least some part of the investor's money. Therefore, to my book, it constitutes one of the better examples in alternative investment offers. There are others where I could find only negatives.

Let me add that guaranteed capital is by no means a universal practice with structured deals. Sometimes hedge funds join forces with a credit institution to offer a principal-protected note. An example is Permal, which proposes its clients a note with three-year maturity, 100 per cent principal protection by Société Générale (credit rating Aa3 and AA-) and, on the upside, 75 per cent of the performance of the hedge fund structure. This has the advantage of less risk than unprotected alternative investments, and an extra feature of weekly liquidity. The minimum investment: US$100,000.

7. Ginnie Mae and other debt instruments

If the current push to sell alternative investments to the consumer succeeds, eventually individual investors might hold not only the risks of hedge funds but also many other risks in their portfolios, including those from banks and insurance companies. The ability of financial institutions to facilitate risk-sharing should not be underestimated. As personal wealth increases, an individual person's, or family's balance sheet might contain a mortgage on a condominium as a liability and an investment in a Ginnie Mae fund as an asset.

The Government National Mortgage Association, known as Ginnie Mae, is a US government agency. It was created in 1968 to promote home ownership by fostering a public market for home mortgages. Since the early 1980s these same home mortgages, which constituted the bread and butter of savings loans, became securitised and found their way first into institutional investors holdings and, subsequently, into personal balance sheets.

What the investor is essentially offered is to buy part of a pool including dozens of mortgages, each of which has a cash flow. The other aspect of this development in personal investments is that risk management, once the exclusive province of insurers and bankers, now emerges as a topic of wider interest at an individual level. But have end-investors the knowledge and technology necessary to become risk controllers?

Short of incorporating training on risk and risk control into the educational programme, general public sensitivity to risk associated with all investments, and particularly non-traditional ones, will remain low or non-existent. The general public is unlikely to understand, let alone refute, arguments used to promote alternative investments.

- *If* consumers are expected to actively enter into alternative investments, including reinsurance deals through capital market offerings,
- *then* they must be trained to understand that there are both serious offers and less serious ones in the market. The challenge is to screen them.

Those investment offers retained after a first screening should be thoroughly analysed. This requires skill and expertise. Take a new bond offer by another well known bank as an example. Bond B proposes to retail investors something which it calls 'extraordinary yield chances with an overseeable risk'. This statement invites the query: 'Who is the overseer?'

- Is the average bank depositor expected to appreciate the risks embedded in a complex instrument?
- Is he being provided by all the insight, including confidential information, necessary to an overseer?

In a manner resembling that of HI-ILDA3, the promotional material by the issuer of Bond B says that the level of interest is dependent on the development of the European stock market index Euro STOXX 50. It then advises that with an increase of the index of just 3 per cent a year, starting from basic worth, the investor would receive 8 per cent interest annually. Should the performance be below 3 per cent a year, there is a minimum annual interest of 1 per cent. In other words, very little. Then the investor is given a list of the 'evident' benefits. The promotional literature points out that:

- 8 per cent, in comparison with the market, is a very high interest rate;
- the minimum interest is dependent on the development of the stock market;
- the capital is at any time available at the daily course[9] (no mention is made as to who establishes it); and
- 100 per cent of the capital is paid back at the *end* of the term (which is evidently a constraint).

As in the case of HI-ILDA3, the investor should be happy to get back his or her capital at the end of the term, provided there is no credit risk. If the bank guaranteeing the return of the investor's capital goes bust, the investor can kiss his money goodbye.

None of the literature promoting these alternative investments speaks of the credit risk assumed by the investor. Yet, this can be critical. What the merchandisers of alternative investments usually say is that their offers are not correlated with that of equities and/or fixed income instruments. However, what they do not explain are the market risks and credit risks involved.

Not only in the case of HI-ILDA3 and the Bond B scheme, but in practically all alternative investments offers, no mention is made of the type of embedded risks. End-investors not trained to appreciate the meaning of capital exposure, and the amount of it they are assuming are at a disadvantage in protecting their assets.

In late October 2001 people who invested in short-term guaranteed investment bonds were set to become the latest victims of plunging stock markets. The lesson to be learned was that there are a lot of pitfalls with these different 'guaranteed' debt instruments, and even more so with the 'structured' deals.

Today, training investors and potential investors in risk management at an individual level is considerably more important than in the past. This is true not only in connection with the current crop of alternative investments, but also because the capital markets are increasingly asked to underwrite catastrophic events in insurance. This is a limited liabilities version of famous 'names' of London's Lloyds Insurance.

8. Investing in CATs and superCATs

There are some fundamental notions behind understanding investments in insurance policies. Classically, the insurance industry manages major hazards through a network of professionals. Its risks are spread horizontally, or pooled, among several direct insurers. The risks are then spread vertically to international reinsurance companies, which are capable of covering higher damage claims.

All of the insurers involved in this business are liable and they cover the risks with adequate premium reserves. This traditional system, however, can only insure against losses to the degree that they can be covered by the premium reserves earmarked for a specific purpose, or by capital and reserves.

The problem is megarisks. Many HI-ILDA3 analysts consider catastrophe derivatives part of the insurance industry consolidation that has been taking place for several years. As the market advances and innovates, there have been developments such as catastrophe, or CAT and superCAT bonds, which are not really bonds.

To begin with, investors in CAT derivatives operate at a disadvantage to insurance companies because they do not benefit from float – that is, the premiums people and companies insuring themselves pay at the front end to receive insurance protection. Warren Buffett says that float comes to an insurance firm at a negative cost; that is, a cost of less than zero. This is a major 'plus' to the insurance company, but not to the investors buying CAT bonds.

Basic characteristics of CAT bonds

CAT bonds are corporate bonds with a clause requiring bondholders to forgive or defer some or all payments of interest or principal if actual catastrophe losses surpass a predefined amount, or trigger. If that happens, the insurance or reinsurance company that is the bond issuer company can pay damage claims with the funds that would otherwise have gone to the bondholders. Notice that in addition to corporate bonds, the range of risk-finance instruments currently traded in the market also encompasses:

- Contingent surplus notes;
- Exchange-traded catastrophe options; and
- Catastrophe equity puts.

These are part of major structural changes, current and expected, which reshape the competitive landscape of insurance markets. They are the result of capital markets financing and of more intensive competition, driven not only by the globalisation of insurance but also by recapitalisation requirements. Another motor is the move towards consolidation which is gaining momentum against the backdrop of:

- Fiercer foreign competition;
- Continuing weakness of many local insurers' balance sheets;
- Mounting government pressure; and
- The fragmented character of some markets.

Another vital element in bringing the resources of capital markets into CAT bonds and superCAT reinsurance, is the fact that an increasing number of countries seem to adopt a solvency-oriented approach towards regulation. They are also gradually dismantling tariffs and product-related restrictions. Furthermore, insurers now put emphasis on cost-effective and innovative forms of distribution to hold their own in an increasingly competitive but less regulated environment.

Table 4.3 shows the statistics for catastrophe-linked securities from 1997 to 2000. The experts say that investing in insurance-linked securities reduces the overall riskiness of an investment portfolio, by reducing its

Table 4.3 A comparison between insurance industry and the capital market

	Insurance industry	Capital market
History	300+ years	6 years
Contracts	Trillions	$50–$60 billion
Rating	30+ AAA Insurers in Europe alone	No rating by independent agencies
Loss payments	Billions	?
Market continuity	Known	Unknown
Limits to exposure	$1 billion	About $300 million

volatility. In a small way, and up to a certain point, this might be true. The problem however remains that the average investor understands very little of catastrophe insurance, let alone superCAT instruments, and of derivatives in general.

- *If* the investor does not understand that both man-made catastrophes and natural catastrophes, tend to significantly increase,
- *then*, he or she is essentially buying something blind, pouring money into instruments which include many unknowns and definitely escape his control.

More straightforward is the argument that catastrophe bonds usually pay interest rates close to those for similarly rated esoteric structured paper, which may be even more risky. Sigma[10] published a statistic that a representative sample of 17 catastrophe bonds issued from 1997 to 2000 were priced at an average spread of 420 basis points above the risk-free London Interbank Offered Rate (Libor), even though their expected losses averaged just 0.6 per cent.

Instruments for alternative risk transfer

In an effort to provide insurance for risks that reinsurers are incapable of covering, as well as for risks that were previously uninsurable, alternative risk transfers (ARTs) offer a way of funding risk insurance via the capital market. With ARTs, risk is securitised and sold on the capital market, primarily to institutional investors such as pension funds, as well as to hedge funds.

- The reinsurance CAT risk is quantified using appropriate time-adjusted mathematical models, and
- It is usually endowed with an appealing rate of return to make it appealing.

Normally, alternative risk transfer policies are being followed when it is possible to quantify risk. This is very important given that they aim to transfer catastrophic risk exposure. Not every practice is, however, 'normal' and quite often the risks being taken are not properly identified and quantified, with unpleasant surprises as a result.

There are several similarities between ARTs and alternative investments. One of them is that ART policies have been developed during the last few years but they still lag behind the classical insurance business by a wide margin, as shown in Table 4.3. No doubt, in future, the capital markets will mature as an alternative risk transfer mechanism, but this is not the case today.

The insured company and the insured person (as opposed to the investor) should notice that the classical insurers' channels do not give 100 per cent risk protection. This is unachievable. But they do provide a range of choices for risk transfer, including the use of derivatives such as ARTs, which insurance companies currently employ for their own account.

Alternative investments and ARTs have in common the concern shown by regulators towards them. With regard to ARTs, these concerns are provoked by complex voidance clauses and narrowly defined events. Currently, different working groups address these issues, including a Basle Committee subgroup and the Property & Casualty Insurance Industry Working Group. Two fundamental principles of insurance which need to be re-evaluated are:

- the transfer of risk; and
- the process of sharing losses.

The work currently in process may redraw the rules of the game as well as reinforce the change that has taken place in the past few years, including greater retention, wider coverage, and higher limits. It may also lead to a better definition and taxonomy of risk exposures, including Pillar 1 charges, as well as a clarification of possible implications of Pillar 2 (insurance supervision) and Pillar 3 (disclosure and market discipline).

In conclusion, each of the investments (emerging markets, securitised products, private equity, structured approaches, other debt instruments, insurance derivatives – CATs and superCATs) involve individual credit and market risks to investors. When traded through hedge funds, however, leverage and lack of transparency see to it that their amalgam of risk exponentially increases, even if, as it is hoped, diversification might provide some degree of risk mitigation. Much of this risk mitigation is dependent upon the particular hedge fund investing, and therefore on the strategies and skills of its managers.

5
Hedge Funds, Multimanagers, and the Macromarkets

1. Introduction

A brief history of hedge funds will provide a perspective to the issues discussed in this chapter. The first hedge fund was formed in 1949, by Alfred Winslow Jones who invested his own money and other assets in his dealings. Jones employed several of the current hedge fund features, such as:

- leverage;
- performance fees; and
- long/short strategies.

By 1966, Jones's fund had outperformed the then highest mutual fund's five-year return by 85 per cent. This attracted a diverse lot of investors as well as imitators. By the late 1960s, some 200 hedge funds had been formed, some of which still survive among the 4,000–6,000 hedge funds that exist today.

It took almost four decades, from the late 1940s to the mid-1980s, for hedge funds to become an important financial industry sector and partner to major entities, from credit institutions to pension funds. But while they are part of the bloodstream of banking, hedge funds have not necessarily gained the bankers' and clearers' confidence in terms of investment policies or of performance. 'We watch hedge funds as counterparties very carefully, but we cannot leave out of our business their business,' said a senior banker in London.

The failure of high-flier hedge funds, such as LTCM in September 1998, the closure of Tiger Management in March 2000, and the muddy business of the Manhattan Investment Fund (see Section 7) are part of the story of asset managers who need to:

- boost leverage; and
- take inordinate risks

to achieve greater levels of return of investment. Both inordinate exposure and the absence of regulation have given hedge funds a bad name. Not all hedge funds, of course, fall into the bottom class. Some of them are well managed and contribute liquidity to the market.

Three years after the LTCM affair threatened the world's financial system, money was flowing into hedge funds at a remarkable US$4–$5 billion every month. Analysts suggest that around US$500 billion is invested in the thousands of hedge funds operating worldwide; with 80 per cent of that amount held in the largest 400 hedge funds. All of it is unregulated and unsupervised. We have spoken of this fact.

To date, the large backers of hedge funds have been banks and institutional investors, but, as we have seen, the trend is now attracting private investors, particularly those who are financially naive. The recent volatility of global markets is a gift to funds whose investment strategy magnifies the market price fluctuations from which they feed. With traditional equity markets showing few signs of stabilising and bond markets depressed, investors who played safe in the past are joining the high rollers of hedge funding.

Big names make the difference because there is always a tendency to imitate what the better-known entities are doing. In late 2001, CALPERS, the large Californian pension fund, stated that it planned to place about US$5.5 billion in hedge funds. AstraZeneca, the pharmaceutical company, and Abbey National are following the same path with part of their pension schemes. What are the strategies on which they bet? This is the theme of the present chapter.

2. Hedge funds' investment policies and leveraged strategies

One of the reasons given by the hedge funds for their better performance than other investors is their skill in handling nervous markets, and most particularly downtrends. They claim to exploit anomalies better than other entities and do it quickly. The argument often used is that company re-ratings, mergers, and acquisitions and other activities have offered opportunities for hedge fund managers in recent years.

This may be true. At the same time, however, in the 2000–2 timeframe a lot of hedge funds are holding cash, a move that appeared curious to many investors. When this subject was raised, hedge fund managers responded by saying that investors pay them to help them meet their targets, and given the market's uncertainties the best returns to be had at that time were from holding cash. That is something the average investor also knows, fairly well, how to do.

Hedge funds are better known for more aggressive policies. Their culture and the strategies they follow are often interpreted to mean they are better equipped than other entities in dealing with uncertainty in business. The majority of economic agents tend to be risk-averse when presented with a choice: they prefer lower but safer returns over uncertain higher returns. In a way, this means that entrepreneurial risk is generally perceived as a negative. Hedge funds operate on the opposite principle.

- They aggressively follow risk policies in search of double-digit returns.
- They also work on the assumption that their management is better informed than the external providers of capital, be they lenders or shareholders.

Asset selection and risk management

Hedge fund managers claim that they make the asset selection challenge less daunting and add value by screening the universe of opportunities. They say that they employ rigorous due diligence processes, developing a thorough understanding of the inherent risks and identifying superior investment opportunities. In short, their objective is to provide individual investors and companies with access to 'unparalleled' opportunities based on their specific investment needs.

Always according to hedge fund managers, this is achieved by following ingenious, innovative strategies. In practice, however, the comparison of investment strategies between samples of eight different hedge funds, in Table 5.1, illustrates that these ingenious strategies have significant divergence. It is simply not possible that all of them are ingenious at the same time. There is no copyright in banking.

But there is a need for rigorous risk control, and risk control is not a characteristic of hedge funds. On one occasion I found one of the hedge fund partners who took the risks, also looked after exposure. The risks which he took, he took them steadily, while he controlled the exposure 'from time to time'.

On another occasion, when asked which way he controls risk, the manager of a very complex fund of funds answered: 'I do the calculation myself every morning'. To my question *if* he is using supercomputers

Table 5.1 Strategies on asset allocation followed by eight different hedge funds

	Hedge funds								
	1	2	3	4	5	6	7	8	Average
US long/short	24%	38%	40%	46%	47%	–	50%	–	30.5
Macroinvestments	18	26	–	20	15	–	6	24	13.5
US emerging growth	11	20	–	–	–	–	–	–	3.8
US equity long	10	10	52	20	27	–	10	–	16.1
Japan	9	–	–	–	–	–	–	–	1.1
Event-driven	9	–	–	10	11	–	10	–	4.8
Europe	8	–	–	–	–	–	–	–	1.0
Emerging markets	5	–	–	–	–	–	–	–	0.6
Fixed income long	–	–	–	–	–	–	–	55	6.8
Fixed income hedge	–	–	–	–	–	–	–	16	2.0
Private placement A[a]	–	–	–	–	–	25	–	–	3.1
Private placement B	–	–	–	–	–	22	–	–	2.6
Private placement C	–	–	–	–	–	18	–	–	2.2
Private placement D	–	–	–	–	–	14	–	–	1.6
Cash	–	6	5	4	–	–	–	3	2.2
Other	6	–	3	–	–	21	24	2	7.0
Sum	100%	100%	100%	100%	100%	100%	100%	100%	

[a] Different types of private placements.

and powerful mathematical models he answered: 'No. I don't need them. I can do it by hand.' Those sorts of lies bring business confidence to the abyss.

Rigorous risk management is an absolute necessity because no matter what the specific risk category, and along with it the industry sector, the investments made by hedge funds include leverage. Their analysts and portfolio managers seek to identify shifting opportunities in constantly changing financial and economic environments usually through a bottom-up, research-driven approach.

The most popular strategy among this sample of hedge funds shown in Table 5.1 is the US long/short strategy with 30.5 per cent of assets on average. Three out of the eight hedge funds in the sample allocate nearly 50 per cent of their money to long/short. Next in popularity is US equity long, with 16.1 per cent on average, and just above 50 per cent of assets for one of the hedge funds. This is followed by macroinvesting with 13.5 per cent on average, with three funds allocating 20 per cent of their assets or more.

What is interesting is the position hedge funds take with regard to cash. In late 2001, when these statistics were compiled, one-quarter of them kept a little more than one-fifth of their capital in cash. Among the eight, three were fully invested, and another three kept between 2 per cent and 6 per cent, which is a relatively small amount intended to provide some flexibility.

These statistics do not provide a pattern that could lead to the definition of a more general strategy characterising all hedge funds. Each one has its own, and it is most likely convinced that it is the right one. Differences also exist on the choice of US equity long investments – buy and hold. During my research, some hedge funds were focusing on healthcare, and tended to include companies involved in:

- drug discovery and sales;
- instrumentation for medical and laboratory use;
- medical services centred on information technology;
- drug development in pharmaceutical, biotechnology, and generic drug companies;
- medical services such as owning hospitals or other healthcare facilities; and
- providing skilled nursing services and healthcare information companies.

The difficulty of obtaining performance metrics

It is usually very difficult, if not outright impossible, to verify the results of a hedge fund's real performance, because what the investor is usually given is a chart such as the one in Figure 5.1, which compares past deliverables of a given hedge fund with the index on the basis of, say, US$1,000 invested at a given point in time. In this exhibit, the timeframe is 1 January 2000 to 31 July 2001. The point to remember with this chart and others like it is that they never include the longer term exposure in:

- credit risk;
- market risk; and
- operational risk.

The graphical presentation resembles in many respects the earnings before interest, taxes, depreciation, and amortisation (EBITDA). In common with other proforma reporting, which is not regulatory, it misleads

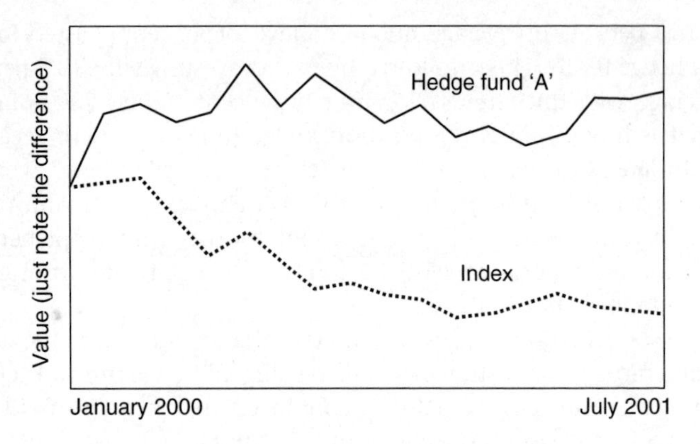

Figure 5.1 A comparative chart on investment performance.

rather than truly informs the investor. Neither is there any evidence given that the aim of capital preservation and steady performance is being achieved with any consistency.

Warren Buffett, the best investor alive today, says that EBITDA figures are useless in making investment decisions. Buffet is right, at best they are useless, and at worst they can be outright misleading. The unreliability of a cooked-up EBITDA has been demonstrated in many occasions. A case in point is KPNQuest.

In 2001, Jack McMaster, KPNQuest's chief executive, proudly told *Communications Week International* (CWI) that his company was EBITDA positive.[1] If so, KPNQuest would have been one of the first of the pan-European new carriers to be able to show that it was starting to generate enough cash to fund its operations. A year later, in May 2002, the crash of KPNQuest raised serious doubts over whether EBITDA is of any use at all in measuring the financial performance of businesses – and their staying power.

Yet, in spite of its unreliability, the earnings before interest depreciation and amortisation has become the key indicator for new entrant companies, particularly in the telecoms and in technology at large. Among those firms, as well as many financial analysts, EBITDA has been seen as proxy for operational cash flow, which is wrong.

- By relying on EBITDA firms are effectively reducing their own chances of survival.
- The sheer weight costs of setting up and supporting large corporates outruns the company's ability to turn up the volume of cash.

Also proforma reporting masks the basic facts that have classically characterised financial solvency. All too often, investors have to wait until companies go into administration to find out the right information about the extent of liabilities and their excess over assets. This is an outright result of lack of transparency, and leverage magnifies its impact.

To further appreciate this argument it is wise to keep in mind that EBITDA reporting, which preceded proforma reporting, was originally designed to window-dress financial reports of industries with high debt loads, such as cable television. Popularised in the 1990s by the dotcoms, proforma earnings exclude fundamental costs such as interest and marketing (and why not R&D, manufacturing, and general management overhead?).

To make matters worse, almost every company has its own type of proforma reporting. What these schemes have in common is that financial transparency disappears. Transparency and proforma, such as EBITDA, contradict one another.

- The CEO and board members who believe their company's proforma may dig their own grave.
- Investors, who trust a company solely on the basis of proforma, can easily wake up with a nightmare.

One of the key reasons, for example, for Vodafone's long decline in 2001 and 2002, was the loss of market confidence in EBITDA. Vodafone had a terrific EBITDA of £7 billion (US$5 billion) but its cash flow was low. In November 2001, an article in *Business Week* made the point that the different proforma and EBITDA earnings reports confused rather than illuminated investors.[2]

A different metric, with cash flow acting as proxy, may be more interesting as a benchmark, though it is by no means fail-proof. This is the average revenue per user (ARPU), which often acts as a good prognosticator. In the case of Vodafone, ARPU had been declining for some time, a very bad sign for a cash-hungry industry where a healthy stream of cash is essential. Hedge funds are not known to use ARPU, but they are famous for their leverage.

ARPU could be a very useful metric for investors looking at companies invested in by hedge funds, indeed, a much better metric than EBITDA and proforma, which are a means of creative accounting. But ARPU, too, can be manipulated. No unit of measurement remains reliable where there is no quality assurance provided by supervisors, to guarantee that standards are observed.

- Both the metrics and the quality of financial reporting should be controlled by regulators, or designed by professional associations and then supervised by regulators.
- Neither of these suggestions is imminent: in an era of globalisation, we do not even have global accounting standards.[3]

Lack of sound, rigorous tools and metrics for financial analysis, and of thoroughly documented investment choices, is a worry. Many hedge funds are run by people with little track record. Large amounts of money are flowing into the hands of recent graduates with an irrepressible urge to prove themselves and make personal fortunes. Finally, as far as the stability and viability of the world's financial system goes, the combination is potentially explosive. In other words, very few hedge fund managers are old enough to have a sense of financial history, or are able to look back at the fallout from other market bubbles.

3. Funds of funds: the multimanagers of hedging

The use of the word *hedging* in connection with derivative products, alternative investments and hedge funds is misleading. What hedge funds do is to take long and short positions in the market, in theory, in an effort to reduce market risk, but in practice to attain a high return on investment. This earns potentially rewarding commissions and attracts new depositors.

What happens in practice is frequent disappointment by end-investors. Illiquidity and other risks left aside, there is no guarantee that promises about returns will be fulfilled. As a recent article put it:

> Many investors were disappointed by their alternative investments in 2001.
>
> The emotional disappointment cannot be analysed…the expected returns should be revised downwards accordingly.[4]

Notice that this publication is pro-alternative investments, not against. Yet, facts are facts and it is better to call a spade a spade.

The myriad of hedge funds that sprang up around the world (particularly in the United States and the United Kingdom) believe that they 'know the market'. The truth is nobody truly knows the market. The stocks on which a hedge fund goes short might rise because of unexpected market turnarounds, because the company it shorted announces good financial results, or because some other big market player bets in the opposite direction.

Many young hedge fund managers have a good theoretical background, but in practical terms they still have to make their mark, and they do so by using other people's money. One of the mistakes often made by aggregators of risk, SAIVs and funds of funds is inadequate *backgrounding* of hedge fund managers and their ability to deliver. Although it is true that even the best players can fail in investment decisions, the lack of background information compounded with leverage can spell disaster.

It is simply not enough to *be* a hedge fund manager in order to *perform*. In February 2000, the highly experienced stockpicker Julian Robertson shut Tiger Management after losing US$11 billion, or half his company's assets. In 2001, Robertson's alumni known as Tiger 'cubs' had posted returns of as much as 47 per cent, but still had a long way to go to match their old boss, who from 1980 to 1999 posted an average return of 26 per cent a year.

The points made above about backgrounding, and the fact that the past is no predictor of the future, are valid with respect to a single portfolio manager or *multimanager* funds. The speciality of funds of funds is to invest in several hedge funds at the same time, by allocating part of their available capital to each of them.

- This capital often comes out of separate accounts, and
- the aim is to offer investors a way to gain exposure to a mix of strategies and investment styles.

As we saw in preceding chapters these different styles may be macromarkets, long/short, plain shorting, event-driven, market neutral, and so on. The underlying principles are that a fund of funds follows a multistyle in investments, and that each fund in the pool applies its principles to the market it deals with. But the aggregator of risk can also have its individual style.

What then are the risks? First and foremost, going short is a leveraged business, which means that there is no limit to the losses the hedge fund and its investors could suffer. However, some hedge funds put up to 50 per cent of their money in long/short strategies. Something similar is true about investing in the macromarkets. Some hedge funds put up to one-quarter of the assets they have been entrusted with in macroinvesting. Others, who 'know the market better' bet as much as three-quarters of their geared assets in the macromarkets.

Hedge funds' managers also seek out what they believe to be *inefficiencies* or *anomalies* in the market. This is precisely what the managers of LTCM had done on a large scale. The Nobel Prize winners and other high-flying LTCM partners forgot about the principle that the market is unpredictable. Also, the banks and institutional investors who financed them paid no attention to the fact that as counterparties hedge funds must be analysed for credit risk. All things being equal:

- lots of leverage means a great deal of credit risk to the fund's counterparties; and
- gearing increases the loss threshold and can make spell disaster not only for the fund of funds itself but also for all counterparties.

Loss thresholds, practised by hedge funds and some commercial and investment banks, consist of offering the customers loan facilities to absorb their losses and to face urgent requirements for trading connected with payments and settlements. In principle, the bigger the circle of *multimanagers*, the greater the loss threshold. With these practices, hedge funds and the credit institutions financing them significantly increase their exposure.

It needs no explaining that funds of funds, multimanager policies boost the likelihood of any one counterparty in the group going under. That is why leverage and loss threshold practices must be watched very carefully. Apart from business intelligence, which is now part of banking, watchful practices require the development of new algorithms and heuristics to enhance *interactive computational finance* for better risk management.[5]

Is it possible to create a model to represent the fund of funds exposure? A 'fast and dirty' approach would be to use the square root algorithm. It serves in computing the complexity present in multimanager environments involving leveraged financial instruments compounded with multimanagers and with uncertainty in the markets. For example:

- *If* the risk management complexity with one hedge fund is X;
- *then* with a pool of two hedge funds it is $1.41X$, with 10 it is $3.16X$, and with 20 it is $4.47X$.

The square root algorithm is valid, other things being equal, but this is not always the case. Say, for instance, that the complexity of managing exposure associated with hedge fund A is low, because this entity is only moderately leveraged (for instance, by a factor of 5–10), is fairly transparent, and its strategy is judged mainstream. But the complexity of a second hedge fund is high because it is leveraged by a factor of 30, is not at all transparent, and specialises in shorting. *Then* the reference for X should be the higher complexity of this second hedge fund B, not of A.

A different way of looking into this issue is that one has to account for the fact that, in these portfolios of leveraged liabilities, practically everything can be found: risk arbitrage, equity long/short, equity market-neutral, macromarkets, fixed income arbitrage, and so on.

- The idea is to benefit from the specialist expertise of the different portfolio managers within the hedge funds and the assets over an investment cycle.
- But good sense requires that the investor should never forget the need to control risk – and that he is directly responsible for it.

This is a duty, which cannot be relegated by the investor to the hedge fund, SAIV, or aggregator or risk. Admittedly risk control with funds of funds investments can be a very involved task.

Since the multiples of '*X*' represent the risk management complexity, 4.47*X* is a lot if we account for the fact that *X* is already big and the task of managing it is most demanding. Since no single market or asset class consistently outperforms, it follows that no single strategy is the best in all markets. Hedge funds tend to use a variety of strategies, as was seen in Table 5.1, in Section 2.

To summarise:

- The aggregators of risk say that combining many hedge funds into one portfolio can produce more stable and enhanced long-term results.
- In real life, however, there is absolutely no assurance that a multi-manager asset allocation provides protection; all that is certain is that it increases the portfolio's complexity.

SAIVs and investment management divisions of banks and brokers who sponsor a number of hedge funds should bear this fact in mind. Those selling alternative investments should, first and foremost, and in a fully documented manner, present to their investors the risks – including the risks of illiquidity and the potential total loss of capital.

Furthermore, every bank designing an alternative investment, whether with one hedge fund or with a group of 10 or 20, must see to it that the specifications comply with the toughest regulation in the Group of Ten countries, not with the most lenient ones. Even if hedge funds are not supervised, commercial banks have to care about compliance. Failure to do so can be very costly.

4. Some of the better hedge fund managers and their macrostrategies

There is not one, but many different *macrostrategies* used by hedge funds, SAIVs and other entities inclined towards taking large risks. One of the characteristics that these macrostrategies have in common is that they are established and followed by global asset managers who employ an opportunistic, top-down approach. Usually macroplayers are looking for major changes in global economies, and they are hoping to realise profits from:

- significant shifts in interest rates and/or exchange rates;
- important twists in a country's economic policies;
- anomalies in securities, whether they result from a country's economic policies or other reasons.

What is known as *global macro* is a style of hedge fund management that looks to make either *directional* or *convergence/divergence* trades based on macroeconomic factors. In theory, the securities being traded and in which hedge funds invest are global, rather liquid, commoditised products such as stock index futures, bond futures, and currencies. In practice, however, all these deals are illiquid and highly risky.

In *directional trading*, macroplayers make a bet that an event will occur due to a change in macroeconomics. This change does not need to be only financial. It may be the enactment of a new law, a change of political party which promises switches in policy, a new international agreement which will lead to a directional move by certain types of securities, or a manifested lack of support for the economic status quo.

A now classic example is the bet George Soros made against sterling in 1992. He saw, correctly, that the German Bundesbank and the British government would allow sterling to break the EMS bands that were established at the time. In his book *Soros on Soros*,[6] George Soros says he made this directional trading bet after he asked a question to the chairman of the Bundesbank at a public conference and Dr Schlesinger was undecided in his reply.

It should be noted that macromarkets are difficult to manage and even more difficult to redress after a fall. Soros himself said so in a letter to shareholders of Quantum after the interest rates debacle of 1994, which wiped out some of the hedge funds – among others, Steinberg's, one of the original hedge funds that till its fall, was one of the star performers.

In *convergence/divergence trades*, macroplayers make a bet that some events will go in one way and other events will take a different course.

An example of this is utilising index futures to short the European equity market(s) while going long in the US equity market. Another example is going short and going long, at a certain ratio, in the same stock market. Today, this is one of the two most popular strategies followed by hedge funds, and demands a lot of research if it is to be successful.

Almost independently of tactics used in tracking macromarkets for profits, it must be clear that convergence/divergence is a very complex strategy requiring both deep skill and high technology. The same is true about playing on the correlation of important economic factors. Currency exchange and interest rates, for instance, correlate. As a Merrill Lynch report was to comment: 'The 3 percent trade weighted euro appreciation since February (2002) is equivalent to 50 basis points rate hike'.[7]

Both industrial demand and consumer demand enter the macromarkets equation. Quoting from Merrill Lynch report on the Japanese economy: 'Salient points are: The current up-cycle is sub-par to previous ones, with the output acceleration lagging about 2 percent points behind the 1994 and 1999 cycles.... So far, (industrial) demand has been sub-par, with overall shipments lagging previous cycles...(but there is) a surprisingly strong consumer demand....'[8]

- Theoretically, a macroeconomic analysis is able to guide the hand of traders, investors, and hedge fund managers in taking currency positions.
- Practically, this is questionable because government statistics are often biased, and currency exchange trends are influenced by a lot of factors.

There are foreign currency crashes as well, such as the Turkish lira in 2001 and 2002, because of political reasons, along with the issues underpinning the law of supply and demand that are still a much weightier determinant of a currency's price than wishful thinking and other rhetoric. For this reason, it is very important to track international flows of capital and unearth the correlation between:

- investment inflows to and outflows from a given country; and
- this country's financial stability, which impacts on currency strength.

Once the players in the financial markets realise that their assets are not matched by sufficient guarantees and they do not benefit from large returns on investment or significant productivity gains, they begin to rapidly withdraw their funds. This puts massive pressure on domestic currencies and ultimately causes a currency crisis to break out.

Most evidently, money centre banks, hedge funds, and institutional investors who lead the crossborder stampede are not free from blame. Little or no account is often taken of political and structural defects when deciding on whether and how much to lend to emerging countries. Most often, the big investors take no proverbial long, hard look at the varying risk situations in individual emerging markets. One of the solutions that they find, port-mortem, is to:

- repackage their macroeconomic blunders; and
- sell them as alternative investments.

Both expert advice and a factual and documented financial analysis should support the macromanager's trading principles. The way these principles are put into effect varies from one macroplayer to the next, as documented by the case studies in the following section. But there is always an underlying strategy, at least among the best-managed hedge funds.

> 'I like the sections on macro strategies,' said one reviewer, '(but I) thought it is a pity that there was not more detail on specialist performance, head hunters specialising in hedge funds etc which would have been interesting.'

Head hunting is indeed one of the weaknesses of hedge funds. Personally, I see it as a way of avoiding the need to develop its own human resources, which indeed is a pity. The hired hand, by a headhunter, may be another Nick Leeson of Barings fame; John Rusnak, charged with fraud in the Allfirst Bank (Allied Irish Banks) scandal;[9] or Michael Berger whose case is discussed in Section 7.

5. Examples of strategies followed by macromanagers[10]

Mr ALPHA aims at taking advantage of speculative trading and investment opportunities on a global scale. He trades and invests both long and short in a broad range of stocks, corporate bonds, government bonds, currencies, commodities, commodity futures, options, forwards, swaps, and other derivatives.

ALPHA's gambling style is to be involved in highly leveraged, speculative dealing in investments where prices can be volatile. He likes to keep the aggregate value of all direct investments to less than 15 per cent of his company's net assets, at the time of acquisition of each such investment. If the value of these investments exceeds 15 per cent of the company's net assets because of losses on other portfolio positions, growth in the value of such investments or redemptions, he takes action to lessen the potential illiquidity that could result if a special situation becomes a large part of his portfolio.

Dr BETA is also a macroplayer, but he works differently. He uses computer-trading models in 20–25 markets, and normally has positions in about two out of three of these markets at any one time. Another of his characteristics is to simultaneously employ two systematic trend-following trading programs. With one of these programs he manages one-third of his assets and follows an intermediate-term approach, which seeks to mathematically quantify the:

- intermediate price trends; and
- volatility of both financial and non-financial markets.

His other program with two-thirds of assets, uses a long-term approach and trades less actively than the first. This one is designed to participate primarily in very substantial market trends, and will frequently have no position in approximately 50 per cent or more of the markets it trades. Figure 5.2 presents a graphical overview of BETA's dealing strategies. Currently this second program:

- trades approximately 30 markets; and
- features broad participation in both traditional commodities and financial futures.

	Intermediate term 1/3 of assets	Longer term 2/3 of assets
Positions	Positions in 66 per cent of 25 markets	Positions in less than 50 per cent of 30 markets
Criteria and trends	• Active trading • Price trend • Volatility	• Less active trading in commodities and financial futures • Substantial market trend only
Models	• Computer trading models	• Macroeconomic models

Figure 5.2 Dealing strategies by one of the hedge fund macroplayers (identified as Dr BETA in this text).

Ms GAMMA is a global macro hedge fund manager inclining towards emerging markets. Her investments include public and private equities, debt securities, convertible securities, commercial paper, lease-related instruments, money market instruments, put and call options, forward currency contracts, derivative securities, synthetic instruments, repurchase agreements and sovereign debt, including Brady bonds. The choice is dynamic and, typically, her turnover is very high. GAMMA:

- uses fundamental analysis for company selection; and
- employs macroeconomic factors, such as political events, for determining the geographic territory of her choice.

The recognition of statistical patterns is the strong point of Mr DELTA, who is both a systematic and a discretionary trader, the second option being his forte. DELTA uses computers to identify patterns and receive an input on recommended trades, but he himself makes the final decision on how many contracts to buy or sell, and on when to buy or sell.

- Due to the size of his operations, DELTA tends towards financial futures with one- to five-day holding periods.
- He usually trades with roughly six to one leverage and has few draw-downs, the goal being to make a 30-per cent return each year with no peak-to-valley draw-down greater than 10 per cent.

Ms EPSILON bases her investment decisions on a combination of economic, financial, and political factors that affect market prices, her analysis of market dynamics, and her evaluation of potential risk and reward of a market position. She uses price and market analysis only to determine optimal entry and exit time, as well as target price. EPSILON pays particular attention to the risk and reward potential of each trade, by:

- examining how this potential fits into the risk profile of her entire portfolio; and
- scrutinising whether it adheres to the overall goal of gradual and steady capital appreciation.

The company with which EPSILON works has a staff of traders, economists, researchers, and market analysts who monitor and evaluate worldwide events, which could affect various markets. These analysts also develop investment strategies. The macromanager minimises exposure by examining the efficiency of instruments she wishes to use to express a market view, determining the optimal size of a position, and studying the correlation of a position or market sector to other positions and sectors in her portfolio.

Dr ZETA invests in international currency, financials, commodities, and securities markets, employing discretionary trading and utilising a combination of technical and fundamental analysis to select the proper instruments and markets. His trading decisions are based upon political and economic factors, the output of valuation models, market trends and expectations, interest rate arbitrage, inventoried positions in the portfolio and risk management objectives. Through computer-based technical trading models, ZETA monitors markets on a 24-hour basis and tracks loss metrics to maintain a predetermined level of risk.

These are some of the best case studies that I have found. Many others were not so neat. Practically, all of the macromarket strategies we just saw contribute to significant capital flows and, to understand the risks associated with them, it is essential to put them in the context of their impact on the global financial order. It is to this issue and these risks that the remainder of this chapter is devoted.

6. Capital flows, macroeconomy, and 'Tidal Wave XXI'

Large capital flows have been the *alter ego* of macrostrategies and macromarkets. Their size and frequency has been steadily eroding the world's economic and financial fabric, leading some conservative economists to suggest that we are confronted by a *Tidal Wave XXI,* where XXI denotes the new century. These economists also suggest that in order to try to rein in the tidal wave and carry out damage control, it is necessary to analyse:

- Where this money comes from?
- Who is transferring the money?
- Who is taking away the money and why?
- How fast this vast amount of money changes from one investment site to another?
- What triggers traders to make the changes?
- What is the effect of the changes being made?

Capital flows represent money lent and invested mainly in a trans-border sense. A direct result of huge crosscountry capital flows is that the total accumulation of indebtedness in the world today vastly exceeds the amount, which could ever be paid under existing terms and conditions of repayment. This makes it even more urgent to provide answers to the six queries outlined in the above bullets, and proceed with solutions that will protect the fabric of the world's financial system by avoiding systemic risk.

The whole issue of damage control to transborder capital flows comes down to the problem of which authority is best equipped to play the regulator's role within the framework of macroeconomic surveillance, and which other regulatory authorities should offer policy advice. Linked to this query is the existence of a comprehensive mandate to guarantee orderly supervision of capital accounts and crossborder money transfers. There are two candidates for this central function: the IMF and the BIS.

In 1944, at the Bretton Woods Conference, the IMF was assigned the task of promoting and monitoring an open, stable international monetary system. However, as they currently stand, the IMF's Articles of Agreement do not contain any authority to supervise capital transactions and transborder money flows.

Basically, it is left to the discretion of member countries to either maintain capital flow restrictions they consider necessary, or to introduce new capital controls. This division of responsibilities between the major central banks and IMF is an impediment to global supervision. A key element of a well-run global monetary system should be the obligation of member countries to:

- subject crossborder money flows to prudential supervision;[11]
- while liberalising current account transactions and eliminating foreign exchange restrictions.

One of the origins of the inadequate treatment of current account and capital transactions, as well as the absence of their steady supervision in a global transborder sense, has been the post-Second World War monetary system based on fixed exchange rates and tight controls over capital flows. This was abandoned in the early 1970s, but no mechanism was provided to:

- promote the need for monetary policy stability;
- guarantee a system of checks for the expanding world trade; and
- supervise the practice and effects of highly increased transborder money flows, largely unrelated to the trade of commodities.

It became evident only gradually that something consistent had to be done to satisfy the requirement for establishing institutional rules able to regulate transborder capital. This is most important at a time when international capital flows have become a vital feature of the world economy, and innovative financial instruments see to it that existing controls are circumvented.

Technology played a dual role in connection with the macroeconomy and the 'tidal wave'. The rapid growth of crossborder capital transactions was aided by advances in information and communications technology, and reached virtually explosive proportions in the 1990s. With this, it became increasingly clear that capital movements cannot be excluded from the process of deregulation and the increasing interrelationships in the world economy. However,

- country-by-country government regulation cannot effectively control the mechanism behind capital flows; and
- the lack of a massive common database and of intelligent artefacts to mine that database hampers damage control efforts.

To appreciate the need for a whole set of conditions, ranging from prudential regulations to appropriate identification procedures, the establishment of dynamic limits, and sophisticated technology to bring all this together in real time, it is wise to remember that the growth of crossborder capital movements has moved much faster than regulations themselves. As a result, money flows of around US$1.1 trillion a day are passing unimpeded through the old structures.

Originally, global money flows were connected to international commerce and they were concentrated in the developed countries. Money travelling transborder for commercial purposes was met by capital imports for direct investment purposes. These rose nearly thirty-fold between the mid-1970s and the end of the 1990s. By contrast, in the main industrial countries, inflows for portfolio investments increased nearly fifty times over that same time period.

In the 1990s, private capital flows to developing countries also soared. The expectation of high earnings unleashed a strong ripple effect, while government privatisation programmes offered opportunities for international investors to enter emerging markets. Today, capital flows connected with international commerce represent a mere 3–5 per cent of transborder capital movements.

Much of this money is *speculative*, connected with the macropolicies of different hedge funds and other institutions. Some of it, though, finds its way to the real economy. According to the IMF, new direct investment in developing countries increased more than five-fold, from just under US$40 billion as an annual average in 1989–92 to just over US$200 billion in 1997–99. In these same timeframes, inflows of portfolio investment picked up from just over US$27 billion to US$104 billion.

This explosion in money flows made private capital the dominant source of funding for an increasing number of emerging economies – which is positive. The bad news is that it also led to overleveraging of countries and companies resulting in Mexico's crises in 1982 and 1994, the East Asia crisis of 1997, Russia's meltdown in 1998, and Argentina's bankruptcy in 2001–2.

Two other significant changes from the past should be recorded. One has to do with the investment horizon; the other with instruments being used. Institutional investors who are behind the boom of cross-border money flows of the 1990s have a much shorter time horizon than banks. This makes their investment less permanent and therefore more volatile.

The nature of finance products used in capital flows, other than cash, has also changed. They became more diverse and much more leveraged, adding to the volatility of the market, and providing ways and means to bypass capital controls by the different countries. The positive aspect of all this is that it generated a trend towards integration of national financial systems into an international financial market that includes developing countries, even if various barriers to crossborder transactions are still in place. The negative is the resulting fragility of the global financial system and the fear that major failures may tear the financial fabric apart. This is the Tidal Wave XXI syndrome.

7. The effects of speculative capital movements

The current international monetary system has evolved over nearly six decades from the Bretton Woods agreements. Though many things have changed since then, among them the advent of speculative waves of transborder monetary flows, one of the two pillars on which the original concept rested remains a de facto freedom of transborder capital movements.

What has changed in this connection is that while initially very few countries, such as the United States, the United Kingdom, Switzerland, and Germany, benefited from it, today the countries taking advantage are many and some of them are finally fragile. In addition, increasingly more governments would like to liberalise the movement of money in and out of their jurisdiction if and when they can afford to do so. Hedge funds, commercial banks, investment banks, and other entities are taking advantage of open frontiers in a financial sense.

By contrast, the other pillar of Bretton Woods, that of a par-value system of exchange rates, has disappeared. It has been replaced by a system of diverse exchange-rate arrangements, or by regional common currency like the euro. The former sees to it that each country looks after its exchange rate regime, until a wave of speculation sweeps away existing guidelines.

As a consequence of the Mexican debt crisis of 1994–95, and subsequent similar events in other countries, there has been much debate about how the financial architecture of the global system could be improved.[12] The idea is to pave the way for the financial and commercial markets to function better, while helping developing countries, which are dependent on a steady inflow of private capital, to develop. However, there are flaws in this process:

- as transborder capital flows towards emerging markets intensify, there is evidence that too much money is worse than too little; and
- short time horizons characterising these capital flows, the synergy of leveraging and derivatives, the search for a quick profit by hedge funds, and mismanagement at a local level combine to create financial nuclear bombs.

The major crises of the late 1990s: in East Asia (1997), Russia (1998), after that in Brazil, and in 2001 in Argentina dampened the high expectations of liberalised capital markets. It also revealed the weaknesses of a system that falls foul of credit risk and market risk, leading to suspicions that there are substantial risks inherent in opening up of domestic capital markets too quickly. To these political problems and other issues add the undependability of corporate governance as well as creative accounting, and you get: *geopolitical* and *geofinancial* risks.

The fact that economies with seemingly sound macropolicies but mostly fixed exchange rates encounter severe crises has been seen as a sign that the regulation of international financial markets had failed. The highly volatile nature of short-term capital flows bears the brunt of criticism, as well as the fact that it is now possible for crises to be transmitted from country to country – an example being the contagion from Argentina to Uruguay in May/June 2002.

Active traders typically investing globally, and seeking changes in the economic backdrop, rapidly exploit these changes. When they happen, highly speculative capital movements destabilised more than one national economy. As a result, weak and undersupervised financial systems in developing countries, as well as political interference (i.e. mismanagement) in these countries' economies, have come under scrutiny. In many cases, large amounts of imported capital were channelled into projects that had no chance of meeting profit expectations.

Expert advice counts. In mid-2002, Hicks, Muse, Tate & Furst, a private equity company, signed up Henry Kissinger to advise on politics and the world economy. Advice by cognisant people with proven intellect is important as providers of capital must accept the consequences of investments that instead of producing extraordinary profits range anywhere from lower returns to the total loss of invested capital.

There are few possibilities to hedge against such losses, which may be more a result of mismanagement than anything else. For this reason, providers of capital must be careful with commitments, which should not remain uncontrolled even over small lapses of time.

What I just mentioned is another reason for transparency by hedge funds, and it is true of all cases – especially if the profitability of a project is difficult to assess from outside the fund itself and the place where the investment is made. A good principle to follow is that the higher the level of uncertainty, the greater attention should be paid to limits in the amount of money:

- invested; and
- lent by banks, institutional investors, and high net worth individuals.

Essentially, hedge fund investing has much to do with the risk propensity of providers of capital, hence the need for risk control limits. There is no universal model that will allow the investor to estimate in advance the exposure assumed with one or other macroeconomic investment. Even bread-and-butter type investing may have bitter surprises, as was demonstrated when Ford paid out US$3.5 billion for the Firestone tyre recall.

As far as investments abroad are concerned, the effects of nepotism have been another pitfall. Owing to close links in the majority of the developing countries between domestic financial intermediaries and their governments, a surprisingly high number of foreign lenders assumed that their loans were de facto officially guaranteed. This proved to be a costly illusion, with the financial catastrophe being partly repaired by the fire brigade of the IMF.

Strong official support for a policy of stable exchange rates also contributed to underestimating foreign exchange risks of the international lending business. Argentina is an example. Given the undersupervised nature of global financial markets, and the lack of effective regulation in many countries, different sorts of government guarantees led to the creation of a sizeable volume of foreign debt denominated in foreign currency – which cannot be repaid. Contrary to claims by hedge funds and SAIVs:

- there are few if any experts who know how to perform in volatile markets in developing countries;
- nor are there local counterparties with experience, proven track record, and commitment of own funds in the bets that hedge funds make abroad.

> 'Sloane Robinson might disagree with the (first bullet point),' said a reviewer. 'Their emerging markets fund is up 448.1 percent from inception to 31/03/02 (= 32.3 percent compound annual return).'

LTCM, too, was producing in the first years of its existence 40 per cent and 30 per cent returns. Then came the crash. Many other hedge funds also have been bleeding. For instance, in January 1999, James Allwin, head of Institutional Investment resigned after a Morgan Stanley Dean Witter hedge fund lost $300 million.[13]

> 'We need some figures on actual losses of hedge funds, derivatives and other alternative investments. It is all very well speaking of risks in general, but (figures help) to put these into context,' said a reviewer.

Good advice. This is precisely why I just mentioned the $300 million loss by the Morgan Stanley hedge fund. The reader should, however, be aware that if a regulated institution publishes its losses, the huge unregulated hedge fund industry does not. They become known either after a bankruptcy or near-bankruptcy, as in the LTCM case; or, as a result of court action. This is the Bear Stearns/Michael Berger story.

Mid-April 2002, as clearing broker for the Manhattan Investment Fund, Bear Stearns, which was involved in one of the high-profile hedge fund frauds, was cleared from paying almost all of the $1.94 billion in damages claimed by the bankruptcy trustees. The origin of the claim was debited to Michael Berger who ran the British Virgin Island-domiciled hedge fund, convicted of hiding $400 million in losses from clients.

- Despite originally pleading guilty, Berger withdrew the plea in late 2001 on the grounds of mental incompetency.
- 'Mental incompetency' is a curious claim by a hedge fund manager to whom people and companies had entrusted their assets.

Investors represented by the bankruptcy trustees had hoped to recover some of their losses by implicating Bear Stearns in the fraud. But when the firm was cleared of liability, the trustees sued it for damages instead. This is a fairly common move in cases where a collapsed fund has little or no assets on which to put a hold.

In a litigation release in January 2000, the Securities and Exchange Commission said the Manhattan Investment Fund began to sustain losses from September 1996 that totalled more than $300 million.

Berger was reporting to investors that the fund had returns of between 12–27 per cent annually. By late August 1999, Berger told investors the fund had a net asset value (NAV) of $429 million when in fact its NAV was less than $28 million.[14]

It is both instructive and interesting to take note that Michael Berger hid the fund's losses from investors by creating false account statements that materially overstated the performance and value of the hedge fund. In an unregulated industry what one person of lesser ethics can do, another person can do too. As a hedge fund manager, Berger had been short-selling technology and internet-related stocks between 1996 and 1999, when the prices of these securities were skyrocketing.

Investors were evidently disappointed when a US district court dismissed $1.8 billion of the $1.94 billion lawsuit against Bear Stearns, while the judge said she could not rule on the remaining $140 million that was outside her jurisdiction. That should be a lesson to investors who put their money and their faith into dubious leveraged deals (run through 'mental incompetency') hoping to do a killing and ending by killing their own assets.

6
Risk and Return with Derivatives

1. Introduction

This chapter addresses itself to derivatives. We consider what they are, what they do, how and where they are traded. Also, what are the risks to financial institutions, hedge funds, and other investors and what is the exposure associated with the growing use of derivatives. Finally, the chapter brings under perspective the need for regulation of derivatives trading – a subject further analysed in Chapter 9.

Regulation of OTC derivatives trades has become very important because too many banks and other institutions take king-size risks with derivatives. When big banks come to the brink usually it is taxpayer's money that bails them out. Credit Lyonnais is an example. In the 2000–2 timeframe, this happened twice with Berliner Bankgesellschaft. Mid-July 2002, the going joke in Berlin was:

> Profits will be privatised,
> But losses will be nationalised.

The classical definition of a derivative financial instrument is that this is a future, forward, swap or option contract. However, the Statement of Financial Accounting Standards 133 (SFAS 133), by the FASB re-defines derivatives as financial instruments with the following characteristics:

- having one or more underlying, and one or more notional amounts, payment provisions or both;
- usually, requiring no initial net investment and, if needed, this is rather small; and
- requiring or permitting net settlements, or providing for delivery of an asset that puts the buyer in a net settlement position.

Derivatives are also known as off-balance sheet (OBS) instruments, due to the fact that, in the early 1980s, the Federal Reserve had allowed banks to write them off-balance sheet (this practice has changed because with SFAS 133, of June 1998, derivatives must be recognised in the balance sheet. The same is true in the United Kingdom, according to Accounting Standard Board directives).

Derivatives have a role to play in the modern economy, when used to fulfil real business needs and not for speculative reasons. For instance, at a cost and for an assumed amount of risk, they make possible to plan export trade at a virtually fixed exchange rate, or swamp a floating interest rate with a fixed one.

2. A sweet and sour taste of derivatives

Derivatives can be classical or exotic. In the United States, the FASB has defined a long list of OBS transactions as *typical*. These include: commitments to extend credit, standby letters of credit, financial guarantees written (sold), options written, interest rate caps and floors, interest rate swaps, forward contracts, futures contracts, resource obligations under foreign currency exchange contracts, interest rate foreign currency swaps, obligations to repurchase securities sold (repo), outstanding commitments to purchase or sell at predetermined prices, and obligations arising from financial instruments sold short. A different way to look into what has become by now classical derivative typology is to distinguish between (in alphabetic order):

- collateralised debt obligation (CDO);
- collateralised mortgage obligation (CMO);
- credit derivatives;
- currency, commodity, and equity swaps;
- futures and options on futures;
- floating rate for fixed-rate payments;
- forward interest rate agreements (FRA);
- equity and currency options;
- interest rate swaps (IRS);
- securitised mortgages;
- stripped treasuries or STRIPs.[1]

Usually some 78 per cent of these deals take place over the counter. The balance is transacted through exchanges. Derivative financial instruments are dynamic and their innovation is steady. All told, the number and variation of derivatives is wide and is growing quickly. This is particularly the case of new and complex financial instruments, which are designed in response to requests by industrial clients, other banks, institutional investors, and risk aggregators.

There is another list of so-called, *exotic* derivatives mostly done OTC. Among financial products included in this list are: all-or-nothing, barrier, binary, butterfly, complex chooser, compound (nested), down and out (or in), discount swaps, embedded options (embedos), inverse floaters, knock-in and knock-out, lookback, one touch, outperformance, path dependent, quanto, step-lock, up and in (or out), and many others.

With both classes, complexity and life cycle impact on risk. Ordinary options, futures, and swaps typically have a long life cycle. By contrast custom-made instruments, like exotics, have a time horizon that depends on client needs. The more custom-made and unusual the instrument is, the shorter its market appeal will tend to be, but the life cycle of inventoried positions can be quite long. Therefore, averages regarding a derivative instrument's time horizon are largely meaningless.

The same is true in regard to a kind of 'average exposure' assumed by the counterparties who trade in derivative financial instruments. Since the differences between derivatives products are so many and profound, nearly every OBS vehicle has to be considered on its own merits and demerits. The same is true of its: risk characteristics, market liquidity, and possible reward for risk.

Cognizant people in the financial industry regret that derivative instruments have drifted into speculation. The greater risk comes from the fact that many firms do not have the skills necessary to control assumed exposure. As V. Fitt, of the UK Securities and Futures Authority stated back in the mid-1990s: 'Behind the big guns is a growing number of smaller outfits anxious not to miss the boat, who cobble together OTC derivatives capabilities in an attempt to keep up with the play and get their share of the market – with limited regard to the dangers'.

All repetitively successful people know how to appreciate the dangers, and how to be in control. It is the drifters who fail in this account. Yet, everybody is informed by clear-eyed regulators about the dangers with derivatives, the instruments, and the derivatives market at large.

- 'I cannot believe that all these derivatives people are competent,' suggested W. Heyman, of the Securities and Exchange Commission.
- M. Shapiro, another SEC Commissioner said: 'The downside of a customized derivative package is the complete or near complete absence of a secondary or an interdealer market.'

Behind these and similar comments lies the fact that risk management with derivatives is wanting: 'In many cases, senior management does not have a good handle on what risks are being taken,' says Dr Henry Kaufman, probably the best economist in life today. 'Bad risk management of derivatives could sink a firm in 24 hours', M. Carpenter, a former CEO of Kidder Peabody once suggested. Indeed it did. Kidder Peabody was dismembered and sold by General Electric, its parent, to stop the accumulation of toxic waste.

There are reasons why knowledgeable people are so concerned about the derivatives aftermath. Take interest-rate derivatives as an example. An estimated 75 per cent of all outstanding derivatives contracts tend to be interest-rate derivatives, which to a significant extent means bets on bonds and interest rate-sensitive securitised instruments – with the result the disastrous aftermath of 1994, when the Fed increased the interest rate in six consecutive moves.

The 1994 losses by hedge funds through overexposure with leveraged fixed interest rate instruments are legendary. George Soros' Quantum Fund lost $600 million (big money at that time); Steinhardt's fund lost $1 billion, out of $4 billion in equity; David J. Askin's $600 million pool of exotic mortgage securities, lost nearly all its net worth in a flood of margin calls.

Julian Robertson's Tiger Management suffered a similar fate and found it difficult to recover, though eventually it did so and lived six more years. Leon Cooperman's Omega Advisors took a first-quarter 1994 beating of about $600 million. Granite Capital and Granite Partners, which gambled in mortgage-backed financing (MBF), are other hedge funds which got very badly burned. These are real-life examples on hedge fund failures, often forgotten by alternative investments fans.

Bets through currency exchange swaps are another example on Murphy's Law: 'If something can go wrong, it will'. The experience of Japan Airlines (JAL) at the end of 1995 shows how misjudging the future when using derivative financial instruments can affect the treasury and P&L of companies.

Since the mid-1980s JAL took out forward currency contrasts to buy dollars for yen to hedge the future purchase of aircraft. But the dollar weakened against the yen, resulting in a loss towards the end of 1994 of Yen 176.3 billion ($1.7 billion). Through creative accounting these losses were being ignored until the aircrafts were purchased. Then, the derivatives losses were spread over the life of the assets through higher depreciation.

- Nobody at JAL was ready to admit that so much money went down the drain as a result of speculation thought to be a sort of hedging.
- But an accounting change brought red ink to light, not only at JAL, but also at Showa Shell. Other examples are Sumitomo Corporation, Procter & Gamble, Olivetti, and Metallgesellschaft.

Showa Shell lost over $1 billion, in 1993, as a result of massive foreign exchange deals done through derivatives. Other entities reported to have lost several billion dollars in currency exchange during the early to mid-1990s, were the Japanese Postal Savings Bureau (KAMPO) and a major Indonesian bank.

Procter & Gamble lost $102 million in 1993 by taking ill-judged bets on future interest rate movements. A year later, Olivetti reported a loss of $223.4 million of which only $3.4 million were from computers (its product line). The origin of the 98.5 per cent of the losses was officially stated to be bonds – or, more precisely, derivatives based on bonds.

Metallgesellschaft speculated on oil futures and lost a cool DM 5 billion ($3.3 billion) which grew to DM 8 billion counting other losses. This makes an excellent answer to the argument by funds of funds that themselves and their alternative investments is 'hedge'. Metallgesellschaft also was 'hedged', but the losses at one leg of its deals were huge while the gains at the other leg of its derivatives deals were minimal.

3. Demodulating the notional principal amount exposure

For starters, derivatives carry market risk and credit risk. Both are embedded into the contracted amount known as notional principal (more on this later). Counterparty exposure with swaps is an example. Even if all swaps are executed under ISDA swap agreements, containing mutual credit downgrade provisions, and even more credit latitude is only permitted for transactions having original maturities shorter than one year, there is a significant amount of counterparty risk.

- Counterparties may be financially unable to make payments according to the terms of the agreements, whether these are swaps, purchased options or forwards.
- Gross market value of probable future receipts is one way to measure this risk, but this is meaningful only in the context of net credit exposure to individual counterparties.

Since counterparty risk is omnipresent, all swaps, purchased options, and forwards, should be carried out within credit policy constraints established by the board. If a counterparty exceeds credit exposure limits, no additional transactions should be permitted until the exposure with that counterparty is reduced to an amount that is within the established limit.

Another example is an asset sale and repurchase agreement (repo), an important derivatives tool. Repo deals are made both for trading and for treasury management purposes. They are becoming more common as *lending* is nowadays increasingly securitised. Repos are also a bridge to speculative deals. For instance, short selling of equities.

When the asset in a repo is certain to come back to the selling financial institution, at some predetermined date, the risk on that asset sold remains essentially with the selling bank, as full market risk. But an additional credit risk arises from the possibility of failure of the counterparty to the repo. The potential size of such counterparty exposure depends on the:

- type of security involved;
- arrangements for margin and interest payments;
- maturity of the repo, movements in market prices, and other reasons.

The exposure is the net cost of replacing that particular asset should the counterparty default.[2] Outright forwards purchases are less common than repos, but the full credit risk remains. Therefore, it is not considered prudent to offset forward sales against forward purchases in assessing credit risk unless the transactions are with the same party, and even then there may be legal issues to be considered.

Yet, in spite of these reservations, multiple risks and possible torrents of red ink, derivative financial instruments can play a useful role in the economy *if* and when they are used for true hedging purposes, rather than for speculation. Even if the law of the land does not explicitly require doing so, a well-managed entity would be keen to:

- establish for off-balance sheet instruments adequate capital reserves;
- follow solid accounting principles;
- put in place rigorous risk management techniques; and
- practice daily disclosure of exposure to top management.

How should this exposure be computed? The usual answer is through *value at risk* (VAR), but this is a half-baked response. VAR only covers from one-third to two-thirds the instruments in the portfolio, depending on their type, complexity, and other criteria.[3] What about the balance?

A far better answer than VAR is *credit equivalence*. A number of institutions have moved or are currently moving away from the percentage rule of exposure, which dominated in the early to mid-1990s, into an analytical basis of *replacement value* of transactions with counterparties. This accounts for notional principal amount.

A *notional principal amount*, also called face amount, is a concept, which comes from swaps. It is specified by the contract, but it is rarely exchanged. It may be a number of shares, currency units, kilos, bushels or other metrics identified in the derivatives deal, which establishes the counterparties obligations based on this notional principal.

Notice that the notional principal is the only legal obligation expressed. We should capitalise on it for risk control reasons:

- using valuation and pricing formulas already employed in trading; and
- doing stress tests of the computed replacement value till maturity of the transaction.[4]

One of the better ways to proceed is that credit equivalent is calculated on the basis of a maximum of an envelope of possible replacement values during the lifetime of the product under consideration. Financial products availing themselves to this procedure are IRS, interest rate options (caps, floors), swaptions, and other fixed income options.

Here is, in a nutshell, the math of demodulation. Say that for an IRS, the notional principal of a contract is $100 million. We mine our IRS database and find that in the distribution of *absolute values* of gains and losses in connection to fixed/floating rates:

- The mean is 2.4
- The standard deviation is 1.

Then, at 99 per cent level confidence (two tailed distribution) the risk being taken is: $x + 2.6s = 2.4 + 2.6 \times 1 = 5$, and the resulting demodulator is: $100/5 = 20$.

This exercise can be repeated at portfolio level, demodulating the different derivatives contracts to establish credit equivalence, therefore *capital at risk*. Say that the total notional principal amount with derivative products we hold stands at $1 trillion. The market value as of today, the corresponding exposure in real money is $60 billion. Taking the total derivatives exposure as a frame of reference, the demodulation from notional principal to real capital at risk is:

$$1{,}000/60 = 16.6$$

I do not advise a global approach because it is bound to be inaccurate. It is better to demodulate derivatives instrument-by-instrument or by homogeneous family of transactions. Once we have calculated the right ratio of risk for redimensioning the notional principal amount, credit equivalent becomes a most valuable tool for OTC trades. Exchange-traded derivative financial instruments can be marked to market, which is not true of those OTC. Two possibilities are therefore open:

- Developing an eigenmodel per instrument (as contrasted to the value of the denominator), which may be expensive, time-consuming, and not always accurate.
- Establishing an algorithm according to the principles by Dr Enrico Fermi, which permits to demodulate homogeneous families of instruments at an acceptable level of accuracy.

Demodulation, credit equivalence or whatever you like to call it, is a flexible and fairly accurate method, which permits to estimate exposure at real-time basis bringing management's attention precisely where it belongs. The best solution for sound risk management is to ask what can go wrong, and to quantify the answer. As the mathematician Carl Jacobi advised: 'Invert, always invert'. Demodulation is an inversion.

4. The changing pattern of derivatives trades

There is no question that the use of derivatives reflects a broader trend towards financial innovation, and that there has been an explosive growth in the trading of derivative securities. The question is at what cost to the individual investor and to the economy. A short historical review helps in providing perspective, making the answer easier to understand.

One of the reasons derivatives are attractive to hedge funds, funds of funds, and other institutions is that they allow their originators to unbundle and repackage risks, allocating them to investors willing to assume them. Theoretically, from an investor's perspective, they can profit from new instruments, particularly as (sometimes) these can help bypass regulation and other constraints, such as taxation.

- Other investors might find them attractive, because of the rewards they expect.
- Risk and reward, however, is a double-edged sword, the shape of which is depicted in Figure 6.1.

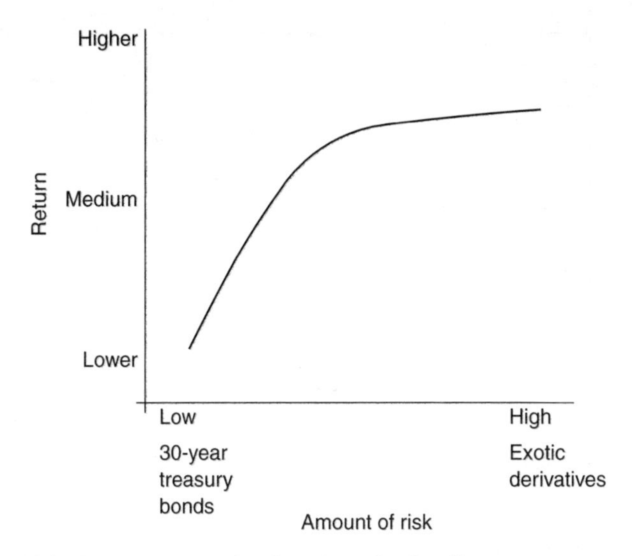

Figure 6.1 Risk and return are correlated nonlinearly: the effect is not proportional to the cause.

Practically, the risk continues to rise but reward tapers off. The concept of absolute returns with low levels of volatility proves particularly elusive, no matter what the alternative investments evangelists are saying. Major losses require a very long time to return to the starting position. There is a bifurcation of objectives targeted by: investors and the merchandisers of risk.

It is not surprising that a growing number of financial and non-financial companies have embraced derivatives, and with them alternative investments, as an integral part of their strategy. When real-life events confirm the assumption made by traders about the direction of market moves, derivative products can become a factor of significant gains. As the examples in Section 2 documented, the opposite is true when the bets go wrong. They can destroy the company or the investor.

- Contrary to what many investors believe, or people think, this is not a win–win situation.
- Investors should remember that *the doors of risk and return are adjacent,* and they are usually indistinguishable.

Since 1986, when derivatives became a financial playground, the notional principal amount has grown enormously. Those traded on organised exchanges throughout the world reached about US$24.5 trillion in 2001;

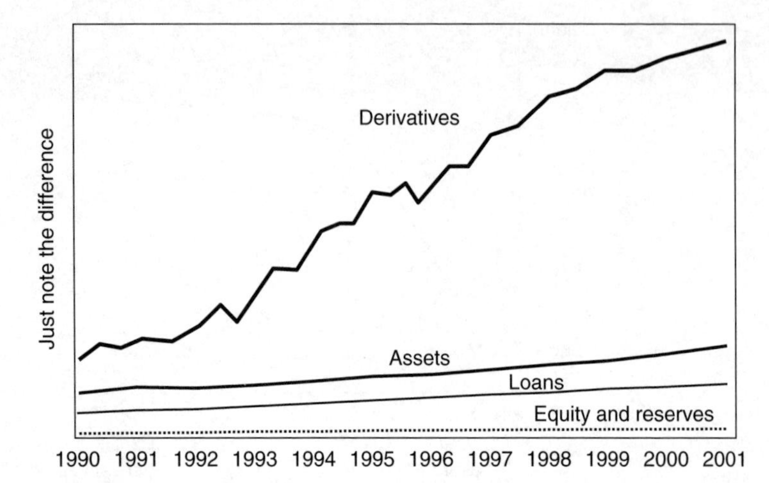

Figure 6.2 The rapid growth in derivatives versus the slow growth in assets, loans, equity, and reserves.

OTC trades grew much more. Figure 6.2 illustrates their growth compared with assets, loans, equity, and reserves. The trading activity, which has spread throughout the world is characterised by a changing geographic pattern, in terms of the weights of each market:

- In 1996, North America represented 83 per cent of the global derivatives market.
- By 2002, apart the fact derivatives trades increased tremendously, market share also changed with North America representing about 50 per cent of the global market.

Many foreign banks present in the United States are more active in derivatives through their New York office than in their home base. In a meeting on Wall Street in the late 1990s, I was told about Australian banks, which had a greater derivatives exposure in New York than in their home offices in Australia.

In 1996, Europe had a tiny 3 per cent share of the derivatives market, while the balance (more than 14 per cent) was to be found in Asia. Since then, the fastest growth of all has been in Europe, which in 2001 shot to about 30 per cent of the total, a ten-fold increase in five short years. Given that another 2 per cent or so, in derivatives trades today, takes place outside North America, Europe, or Asia, this leaves Asia with some 18 per cent of the global market, at the time of writing. This may look as a small increase in percentage terms, but it is a large one in traded volume of derivatives.

There are reasons why a boom in derivatives trading has taken place in the last three decades. Some are technical: the existence of floating exchange rates since 1972, and the increase in interest rate volatility. At least one reason is mathematical: the development of algorithms for pricing new financial products has helped in the promotion of derivatives trades.

A good example is the Black–Scholes formula,[5] which made the pricing of options feasible. A new financial product, however, does not necessarily have an assured future because it is being priced; neither is it guaranteed that its sales only have one way to go: up. Much depends on the state of the economy, and the risk appetite of traders and investors.

All things being equal, the better the state of the economy, the better received are new products, in general, and derivatives, in particular. In a healthy economy people and companies tend to assume more risk. This explains the exponential growth of derivatives between 1996 and 2000.

It is interesting to notice that the man, who invented options in about 600 BC, was Thales of Militos, a mathematician and philosopher. He cornered olive oil production through options, and became a millionaire in the process.

- The fact that a philosopher became a high net worth person suggests that the story with derivatives has not been all bad.
- Yet for others, the way to a small fortune with derivatives was to begin with a large one.

Figure 6.3 shows an example of market growth, based on options contracts traded daily on the Chicago Board Options Exchange (CBOE). Trading started in 1973 and a year later there was already about 30,000 contracts a day. This number grew rapidly during the following years until the crash of 1987–88 when it fell dramatically. By 1992, the exponential growth began again, surpassing the 1987 peak and continues to grow.

Many people have offered advice on the risks embedded in derivatives. 'The growth and complexity of off-balance sheet activities and the nature of credit, price and settlement risk they entail, should give us all cause of concern', Gerald Corrigan, former president of the New York Federal Reserve has said. 'Sophisticated trading strategies and complex instruments, by their nature, require robust risk management and controls', added C. Feldberg, also of the New York Federal Reserve. The amount of assumed risk left aside, often times trading in derivatives violates Shakespeare's dictum: "Think of many things but only do one

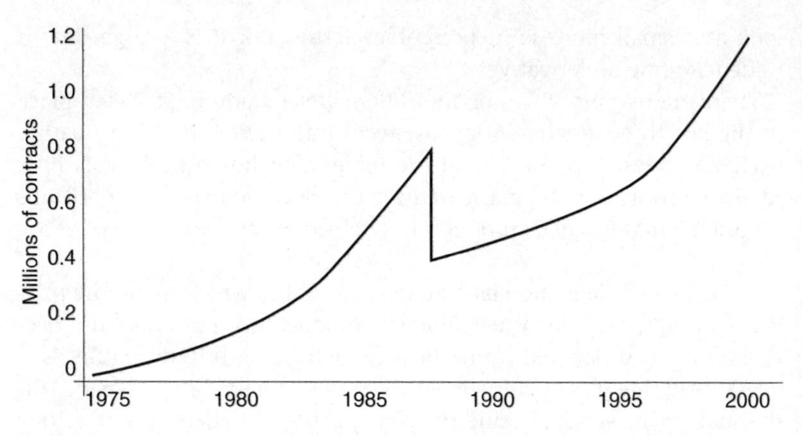

Figure 6.3 The volume of options contracts traded per day on the CBOE.

thing at a time." Incompetence in derivatives and other alternative investments raises attendant risk.

Some bankers have been more direct in describing the risks with derivatives. '26-year olds with computers are creating financial hydrogen bombs,' said Felix Rohatyn, formerly of Lazard Brothers.[6] 'We do not know the web of interconnections between banks established through derivatives,' suggested Alexander Lamfalussy, a former general manager of the Bank for International Settlements and of the European Monetary Institute, the predecessor of the European Central Bank.

As the risks are great, there is no substitute to steady, real-time vigilance. Stress tests and worst case scenarios are an integral part of it. 'The worst case scenario of derivatives valuation and the nightmare scenario are not the same thing,' said John Howland-Jackson, former chairman of Nomura International. A 1993 joint report by the US regulators was to add: 'The complexities and interdependencies inherently associated with multi-legged positions are such, that a sudden failure of a major market participant might disrupt the financial system'.[7]

In terms of historical precedence, futures trades (and derivatives losses) were known to have occurred in the early eighteenth century. In one instance, investors agreed a share price in the Mississippi Company and made a downpayment for delivery at some future date. During the autumn of 1719, shares officially traded for 10,000 livres or so (up from 50 livres, their issuing price), but they were sold in futures contracts for 15,000 livres.[8] In December 1719, the market tanked and many investors went bankrupt.

In the boom market of 1719 in France, the equivalent of call options were also available. Called *primes*, they permitted investors to pay a deposit of 1,000 livres for the right to buy a Mississippi Company share at 10,000 livres if its price shot past this target value. As these examples demonstrate, over the centuries plenty of means have been available to investors to increase their gearing and beefing up of their hope for profits along with their risks. But the day of reckoning never failed to show up.

5. The current huge derivatives exposure

Derivatives exposure can be enormous. Figures released in March 2001 by the Office of the Comptroller of the Currency (OCC) show derivatives concentrations at unprecedented levels due to megamergers among credit institutions. In the United States, three commercial bank holding companies account for 91 per cent of the admitted derivatives positions held by all US financial institutions and other parties. The three largest US credit institutions hold the following amounts:

- JP Morgan Chase, US$24.5 trillion;
- Citigroup, US$7.9 trillion; and
- Bank of America, US$7.7 trillion.

At the time, a European bank held the number two position in derivatives exposure worldwide, just between, JP Morgan and Citigroup. This was Deutsche Bank with euro 10 trillion (US$9.2 trillion). Since derivatives grow at about 25–30 per cent per year with inventoried positions increasing more than 15 per cent, these figures are by now much larger.

Such huge derivatives risks serve as a reminder of the convergent credit risk, market risk, and operational risk, and indicate that the global economy is entering a critical phase. Authorities must be ready to take firm action in implementing emergency economic measures, as the situation demands, and the banks themselves must be aware that their reputation is at stake.

Not only is a large derivatives exposure weakening a credit institution, it also makes it vulnerable to other shocks. In the timeframe after Enron's bankruptcy on 2 December 2001 to 11 February 2002, when I completed this part of the research, JP Morgan Chase's stock fell 15.6 per cent, because new risks were revealed from Enron's off-balance sheet vehicles.[9] *If* a large bank fails, the aftermath is much more than a disaster to its stakeholders as it can take with it the world's financial system. This is the *first order* systemic risk.

Reputational risk and systemic risk correlate. As I have explained in Chapter 3, reputational risk is one of the key reasons behind the establishment and observance of prudential limits in exposure with derivatives and all other financial instruments. Once a company's reputation is ruined, its ability to generate income evaporates. Yet, limits are resented by traders and bankers because they conflict with the independence of:

- loans offers;
- derivatives traders; and
- desk managers.

In many credit institutions, limits also pose cultural problems. Without limits, every business opportunity looks like the chance to make a small fortune; a chance one may not have encountered for a long time. Nick Leeson must have surely thought so when he brought Barings to bankruptcy through his exposure. The same is true of John Rusnak, the Allfirst trader who in February 2002 allegedly lost $750 million and with this threatened the independence of Allied Irish Banks (AIB).

Institutions, their cultures, and their employees must be challenged to accept the setting and observance of limits. The high stakes of modern finance is in a situation where every asset should be subject to constant and rigorous critical review. To do so, senior managers should be able to:

- understand the information relating to transactions;
- compare it with all sorts of limits;
- make sense out of these tests; and
- take immediate corrective action when necessary.

The surest way to ruin a business is to drain it of capital and reserves. The constant risks a bank is taking can be divided into two larger classes: those taken in the dealing room and those in credits and loans. Those taken in the dealing room, which are largely in derivatives, represent roughly two-thirds of a credit institution's total exposure, and also involve the counterparty's creditworthiness – not just market risk. A different way of looking at this statistic is that:

- Treasury operations today represent a much greater exposure for the bank than its classical business; and they involve both market risk and credit risk.
- Credits and loans typically fall under the commercial division, and make up the other third of global risk the institution is taking.
- But credits and loan risks also find their way into derivatives because of the huge loans banks make to hedge funds and other counterparties who use the money to trade in derivative instruments.

Conscious that this bubble is unsupportable in the longer term, banks try to unload part of it to institutional investors and their retail clients. They do so through alternative investment vehicle. Notice that in this game the managers of alternative investments are more responsible to each other than to their clients.

While banks are faced with a compound risk from their dealing room and their loan activities, in the case of hedge funds, practically, all the risk being assumed is in the dealing room; a great deal of derivatives exposure. The following section, about financial institutions, explains how this risk is assumed and the implications for the banks, and for end-investors.

6. Financial institutions and their derivatives risk

The core capital of the majority of banks is so little compared with its derivatives exposure that it would last a very small amount of time in a crisis. What sort of strategy is in the mind of financial institutions when they are assuming inordinate risks? One of my professors of business strategy at UCLA taught his students that a company's true strategy is never written in big pronouncements – it can only be observed over the years. The same is true of the status of financial reserves.

In the early 1980s, when Mexico almost went bankrupt, while Brazil and Argentina were not very far behind, Bank of America, Citibank and Chase Manhattan had locked all of their capital into these three countries in non-performing loans. Publicly, there has been no evidence that that money was returned, although as Walter Wriston used to say, 'Countries never go bankrupt'. This is only half way true. Argentina did go bankrupt in 2001, while the IMF kept its money under lock and key.

Organisations are made of people, and people find it hard to learn from past mistakes. Many large banks and many medium-sized ones from the First World have been in a similar situation in the late 1990s with Russia, Indonesia, South Korea, and other countries. What is more, their core capital grows slowly if at all, while, as mentioned, the derivatives exposure increases by leaps and bounds every year – with the exact percentage depending on the institution and its risk appetite.

What of the relevant returns from derivatives to these banks? Sure enough there are also profits with derivative financial instruments. Yet, losses from derivatives, curiously, tend to grow faster than profits as is evidenced from the annual statements in which the regulators in the United States, United Kingdom, Switzerland, Germany, and other countries require that banks must report their *recognised* but not realised gains and losses.

In other words, hedge funds are not the only entities to be overexposed in derivatives trades, even if the lack of regulation sees to it they can keep their losses secret. In fact, a large part of the risks with derivatives is that all sorts of financial institutions trade the bulk of them among themselves. Moreover, as it has already been stated, commercial banks provide loans to hedge funds and then trade with these same hedge funds in derivatives products, compounding credit risk and market risk.

Of course, the size of the derivatives portfolio is not at imminent risk at 100 per cent its notional value, but what is known as the *toxic waste* (that part of the money at greatest peril) is part of it. The extent of this capital at risk depends, to a large extent, on the type of inventoried positions and general economic climate. Under current conditions, a demodulator (see Section 3) of 20 might do,[10] but in a crisis this demodulator shrinks to six or five. This is the experience from the meltdown in East Asia in 1997 and from the bankruptcy of the Bank of New England in the early 1990s.

- Under current conditions, Deutsche Bank's toxic waste due to derivatives would be around 18,500 per cent its capital.
- Should a global economic crisis hit, the exposure due to derivatives becomes, almost overnight 74,000 per cent the bank's core capital.

This picture of a bank's exposure looks distinctly unfetching. Like all other credit institutions, Deutsche Bank has assets. When these statistics were published the bank's assets stood at euro 996 billion (US$906 billion), but a credit institution's assets do not belong to the bank – they belong to its clients. The large potential discrepancy between core capital, assets, and derivatives exposure of this bank is illustrated in Figure 6.4.

The assets held by credit institutions are also invested in loans, securities, and other instruments, whose value fluctuates. Recent collapses in indices have been seen worldwide: alongside the 75 per cent collapse of Nasdaq from March 2000 to July 2002, for example, the German Nemax Index fell from 9,400 to 1,300, or more than 85 per cent over the same period. The implications of such fluctuations for telecommunications, Internet, high tech and other growth sectors, where the large banks are key investors, are obvious.

Moreover, large derivatives contracts mean extreme exposure in just one of a bank's many business channels. The 1992 European Union Directive on capital accuracy defines *large exposure* as being assumed with a client or group of clients, equalling 10 per cent of the bank's funds. On these calculations, we see derivatives exposures that are very large; practically erasing from the picture all of the bank's funds.

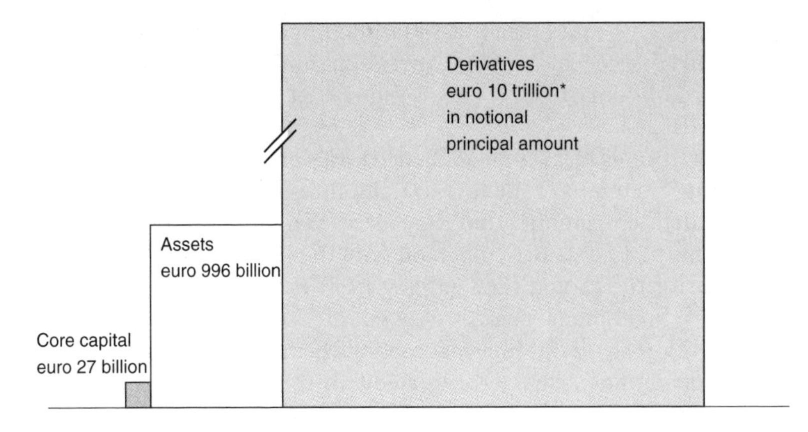

Figure 6.4 Deutsche Bank joins the club of superleveraged financial institutions.
* Statistics as of 31 March 2001, published by BIS.

Some other statistics are also pertinent. When analysts talk of *large commitments*, they tend to take US$1 billion in notional principal as the cut-off for a larger derivatives contract. This would represent about US$50 million in *loans equivalent risk*. A US$10 trillion notional principal in the portfolio would tend to include 4,000–6,500 large derivatives contracts, many of these, if not the majority would be beyond the $1 billion benchmark, therefore representing large commitments.

It is important to underline that this US$1 billion level is nothing out of the ordinary. Each of the top ten money centre banks has a derivatives exposure in notional principal of more than US$3 trillion, and therefore an enormous amount of large derivatives commitments. The US$3 trillion corresponds, on average, to about US$150 billion in real money risk and it may represent up to 2,000 important contracts. Therefore, the scenario of a three-digit number of large derivatives contracts held with the same major counterparty is within the realms of possibilities.

7. Risks for hedge funds dealing in derivatives

It has been estimated that as of August 2001 the volume of derivatives contracts worldwide hit US$300 trillion. Demodulated by 20, which would be a reasonable ratio under current conditions, this means US$15 trillion in real money that can, overnight, turn into toxic waste and be lost. This could reach US$60 trillion in case of panic because, as we saw, the demodulator of derivatives exposure shrinks from 20 (under normal conditions) to 5.[11] This is equivalent to 200 per cent of the world's GDP.

The situation is bleaker where hedge funds enter the derivatives market, as they do not have the financial resources of large banks, and their low cost depositors money, but they carry even more exposure to derivatives. This highlights the vulnerability of the hedge funds own capital; as well as of the capital they employ from end-investors through the alternative investment schemes they sell.

Furthermore, with only a few exceptions hedge funds do not have the orderly operations characterising credit institutions, which set limits and monitor derivatives risk. It is self-evident that they need to do this. At least the well-managed banks monitor their exposure with different types of limit structures by:

- counterparty;
- type of instrument;
- volatility-based market risk;
- currency- and volume-based market risk;
- liquidity prevailing in the market.

Tier-one institutions also set triggers for corrective management action once a market threshold or counterparty threshold has been reached. By contrast, poorly managed banks have substituted the system of limits system through VAR (see Section 3),[12] which is somewhat irrational because VAR is computed *a posteriori* while limits are set *a priori*.

Well-managed banks also have the policy of distinguishing between first-order risks and second-order risks. In setting limits, *first-order risks* are: interest rates, currency rates, equities, other commodities, and credit spread. *Second-order risks* are: option delta, gamma, theta, kappa, rho,[13] yield curve, swap spread, cross-currency basis risk, and interest rate basis risk. A close watch on both first-order risks and second-order risks is necessary to closely monitor derivatives exposure.

The changing pattern of derivatives trades, and with it of investments, requires greater attention to be paid to risk control, not less. Prior to the 1997 meltdown, the derivatives market in East Asia revolved predominantly around vanilla products, which were unlikely to pull down the market in the near future. However, this is changing. The market's development is dependent upon the liquidity of the underlying security, which is characterised by thin trading in a post-crisis market.

What about the old continent? As we have seen, in the years that followed the 1997/98 meltdown in East Asia and Russia, a large development in leveraging through derivatives took place in Europe. The foundations for more complex trades developed as people and companies look to swap out of their principal risk into another class of exposure. Due to this, market activity centres on:

- yield enhancement by any means;
- equity transactions carried out as protection for mergers and acquisitions; and
- cross-product hedging, leading to caps, floors and swaptions in different currencies.

The move towards greater complexity in derivatives trades, which began in the United States and Europe, is now migrating to Asia. An example is the South Korean derivatives market, with its OTC equity and equity index options, overnight index swaps, IRS, and increased secondary trading. Korean bankers look at these instruments as areas promising growth, while foreign investors are hedging against the weakening won, and exporters are hedging their dollar receipts into won.

The good news is that, today, Asian banks are more aware of contagion between individual economies, and are beginning to protect themselves on a larger scale than in the pre-1997 crisis environment. Collateral agreements are widely signed in some Asian countries, particularly in Northern Asia, and introduced in South-East Asia. According to some experts, collateral agreements have made for a healthier all-round financial system, with institutions starting to unwind cross-holdings. Others disagree.

One of the risky sectors of the off-balance sheet instruments landscape is that of *credit derivatives*[14] (see also Chapter 4 on insurance derivatives). Credit derivatives have a growing popularity among credit institutions, as banks use them to protect themselves against loan defaults. Today, these securities are mainly bought by institutional investors, including insurance companies, which assume the banks' counterparty risks. However, there are indications that they start infiltrating into alternative investments offered to consumers.

It has been suggested that the speed of growth of the market in credit derivatives is due to the finite amount of AAA and AA paper forcing everyone down the quality curve. Banks today try to securitise many of their corporate loans through credit derivatives, because the instrument seems to have finally found a market, but it takes a lot of skill to develop sophisticated solutions for new instruments, as well as rigorous ways for real-time risk control.

My impressions from meetings, which I held on design, marketing, and risk control connected to alternative investments has been that high-grade skill is in short supply in the banking industry, because too many institutions spread themselves too thinly. From hedge funds to credit institutions, available skill is allocated towards innovation: designing more complex instruments than those offered by competitors. Risk control has taken a backseat and this creates major dangers for investors.

8. Can regulators control the risks of derivatives?

As opposed to conventional financial products where problems are generally better understood and the rules are codified, much of the modern regulatory environment for geared instruments is guided by fuzzy industry standards of which, until the mid-1990s, the regulators have silently approved as being acceptable – for lack of better solutions. Typically, a bank could select one of several scenarios, which it followed in terms of off-balance sheet exposure.[15]

During the late 1980s and early 1990s, central banks were not very active with regard to the control of off-balance sheet instruments. The clearest analogy is with the regulatory approach taken towards the airline industry, with its new generation of aircraft and its high technology reservation system, including auctions on the Internet. Here, too, regulatory authorities had been closely watching the developments but were providing few direct standards because rapid product innovation and technological breakthroughs overtook them.

The paradox in both industries, financial markets, and civil aviation, has been that the state of affairs was suggestive of the disarray in management control and technological standards of the 1920s, rather than what one would expect in the 1980s and 1990s. There were many instances of emerging problems that nobody really dared to tackle until the mid-1997 emerging markets meltdown, followed in 1998 by the bankruptcy of Russia and of LTCM.

In civil aviation, for instance, Boeing and Airbus used (and continue using) different display colour-coding schemes, as well as completely different lexicons to describe systems with similar goals. Even among mission-critical components that act similarly, there can be significant discrepancies. Yet, the details dearly affect the safety equation.

An analogous problem is apparent in aspects of banking with regards to novel instruments such as exotic derivatives and alternative investments. With VAR models, each bank follows its own standards in internal reporting, with the result that management decisions on risk control are heterogeneous and comparisons become difficult if not outright meaningless. Table 6.1 shows an example of VAR 'standards' used by major institutions for internal management accounting reasons and for internal control purposes.

On the one hand, banks have to comply (and do comply) with the VAR reporting standards established by the Basle Committee, such as the 99-per cent confidence interval. On the other hand, for internal decision purposes they use the 95-, 97.5-, and 98-per cent confidence levels – probably because lower confidence levels help to minimise the capital at risk being reported to the credit institution's senior management. This is regrettable. The ten credit institutions identified A–J in Table 6.1 are from the same country, but the VAR languages they use are quite different, and the results not at all comparable from one bank to another.

The setting of standards applicable throughout the financial industry, including the results of stress tests, which we discuss in Chapter 8, is the more urgent, as not only have pension funds, mutual funds, and other institutional investors branched out into highly geared products in an attempt to improve their performance, but also with alternative investments the consumer is brought into the high-risk arena where he or she can lose all their capital. Regulations limit the proportion of a pension fund's assets that can be allocated to derivative instruments, but:

- not all pension fund managers remember to inform their shareholders and their investors that they are active in alternative investments; and
- there is currently no regulator or legislation protecting the consumer from risks taken with hedge funds, with the exception of those mentioned in Chapter 2.

This suggests the need for further legislation and regulation. However, in the United States, where the pressure for legislation is greatest, banks and brokers are mounting a vigorous anti-legislation action, claiming it would be counterproductive – including an argument of 'irrational constraints and ultimately more risk for investors'. Despite this, the Controller of the Currency now requires banks to:

- disclose the dollar value of all their derivative contracts on the sick list;
- account for the compound effect of bad loans and derivatives losses; and
- guarantee that exposure is aggregated for sound risk management reasons.

Here is the loophole. As a very large part of what enters a leveraged derivatives trade is a *book entry* – and therefore a virtual asset – at times

Table 6.1 Major assumptions and associated differences underlying VAR estimates presented in annual reports to one of the European regulatory authorities

	Bank A	Bank B	Bank C	Bank D	Bank E	Bank F	Bank G	Bank H	Bank I	Bank J
Confidence interval (%)	99	99	99	99	99	98	97.7	97.5	95	95
Holding period (days)	10	10	10	10	30	1	1	30	1	1
Aggregation method	Correlation	Simulation	No correlation	NA	Correlation	Simulation	Correlation	Correlation	Correlation	No correlation
Maximum daily VAR	471	121	80	NA	118	47	30	1090	21	6.9
Minimum daily VAR	389	64	20	NA	63	19	10	366	4	3.2
Average daily VAR	415	81	NA	280	100	34	23	NA	10	4.4

NA = not available.

everybody might win. This however forgets that at other times, with other book entries, everybody loses. Red ink can be hidden up to a point, but not when it becomes a torrent.

Governments have also been swept along by the possibility of financial engineering: the debacle of Italy's alleged derivative manipulation to meet the Maastricht Treaty's budget deficit targets is a case in point. The lesson to be learnt is that, as has been the case with business, industry, and financial institutions, rigorous regulatory disclosure and accounting rules are necessary also for governments' derivatives deals.

The European Union's stability pact sets stringent budget limits, and these require accounts free of financial window-dressing. *If* this cannot be done, *then* it is useless to set tough benchmarks in the first place.

As far as market discipline on behalf of sovereigns is concerned, it should be noted that the IMF imposes stringent financial rules in its aid package to emerging countries. It is also trying to ensure that major risks of hidden liabilities and obscured counterparty twists are not overlooked in financial reporting by governments.

Two contradictory sets of rules – one for governments, the other for business and industry – are not acceptable. There should be worldwide consistency in rules and regulations, in particular among the countries of the Group of Ten, which should be setting the example. Governments should not put aside prudent accounting rules and use twists in financial reporting as it suits them.

The need for forward-looking risk control is well exemplified by the dollar weakness of 1994 and the severe stock market corrections of mid-1997, August–October 1998 and April 2000–July 2002. These events affected many mutual funds and pension funds, while some of the hedge funds were devastated during all three of them. This has sparked a debate in the industry about:

- the extensive use of hedging strategies;
- the truth surrounding the issue of derivatives used mainly as hedges; and
- the time to maturity which should be targeted by leveraged instruments, less than AA-rated counterparties, and novel types of transactions.

The task of prudential legislation and regulation is not an easy one. Many believe that the OTC market is almost impossible to regulate. Only after the huge losses by many big banks and other, medium-sized credit institutions, and the hedge funds themselves, in the August–October 1998 period, did people begin to change their 'wait-and-see' attitude. However, it took the market meltdown of 2001, for people to realise that:

- US long/short, and most particularly shorting, strategies (see Chapter 5) can be self-destructive; and
- if left to their own devices, speculators can bring corporate, national and even the global economy to its knees, taking end-investors along with them.

Despite these perils, the pressures towards non-regulation of alternative investments remains strong. Current risk control models are limited, and difficulties with them have found resonance with bankers eager to fend off tighter legislation. In all likelihood, alternative investments cannot be regulated as a single product because their transactions encompass several areas of the financial market, as well as different instruments. Supervisors, however, should try hard to find a good regulatory solution targeting exposure both by type of alternative investment and in a compound manner.

7

Scrutinising Alternative Investment Strategies Intended to Give Higher Returns

1. Introduction

Whether we talk of alternative investments or any other business, investment strategies are made by people and, other things equal, the higher are their skills and the experience of these people the more effective the strategies will be. In 2001, a study at MIT concluded that the difference between hiring the best person and hiring an average person can be as high as 50 : 1. The best person will:

- have a polyvalent background;
- be innovative and imaginative;
- challenge the obvious;
- be flexible and adjustable; and
- have a deep sense of planning and control.

These are managerial and professional skills. Management is responsible for a company's success or failure, and the same is true about an investment plan's performance. Effective plans require perspective. In regard to planning, Harry Truman once said, 'You can always amend a big plan, you can never expand a little one'. Dwight Eisenhower was to add, 'The plan is nothing. *Planning* is everything'.

A plan must be documented, and a sound documentation is typically qualitative and quantitative. Decisions must be taken in function of the qualities and the quantities characterising an investment plan's existence, the way in which it works and the deliverables it will provide.

'Your main contention is that the risks taken with alternative investments simply do not justify the risks,' said one of the reviewers, 'but it is also your job as author to provide the statistics to back this up'. He further added 'The performance of funds, and not just the particularly bad ones, needs to be presented to give credibility to your argument'.

Just for the record, as the careful reader will appreciate, the first sentence in the reviewer's statement simply does not make sense. Probably, he wanted to say *risk* and *return*. Instead, what he is writing is *risk* and *risk*. Risk is all what seems to be in his mind, and for good reason.

While risk and return are indivisible, *risk-and-risk* turns assets into ashes. This chapter shows *how*, by bringing to the reader's attention the failures of hedge funds in the relentless pursuit of double-digit profits and high commissions. 'Gambling is when you bet something you cannot afford to lose', says a proverb. Hedge funds gamble with the investor's assets.

Quoting Alfred Nobel: '.... The exaggerated chase after money is a pedantry which spoils much of the pleasure of meeting people and destroys a sense of honour in favour of imagined needs'.[1] (Or 'solutions.') The bones of the old man must have turned in his grave when two Nobel Prize winners and their pals run to the ground LTCM wiping out the assets investors entrusted to them. Neither is this a one-tantum example.

Finally, with regard to 'hedge fund statistics', the author has other, more important responsibilities to his readers than to answer the same and same question about unreliable information provided by hedge funds. This reviewer's query has been repeated time and again as if it came from a broken gramophone record. (In any way, in Section 2 will return to this issue of statistics in conjunction to a very similar point by the same reviewer.) This chapter addresses investor strategies, which can mitigate some of the risks.

The first quarter of 2002 saw a wave of selling of fund management outfits by their parent companies to the tune of about 20 disinvestments. Among others, Zurich Financial sold troubled Zurich Scudder Investment to Deutsche Bank Services. HypoVereinsbank sold Foreign & Colonial to Dutch insurer Eureko. Commerzbank was selling Jupiter Asset Management, a money loser, and Royal Sun Alliance was selling its money-management unit to Friends Ivory & Sime.

2. Assessing the claims made on behalf of alternative investments

Banks and insurers that have not been selling their fund management outfits were repositioning them or cutting them back. Caisse des Dépôts et Consignations of France pushed its CDC Ixis into the high-fee business of alternative investments involving private-equity and hedge fund deals.

The Caisse de Dépôts and similar moves are betting that investors will not understand the risks they are taking with alternative investments (see Section 4). Or, at least, they would not appreciate that planning an investment strategy is a steady business. Most crucial is the ability as well as the will to:

- develop alternatives without myths and hype;
- receive a fair amount of dissent about every investment plan;
- examine the possible pitfalls and their likely origin(s); and
- receive feedback and be ready to amend the plan as market forces change.

This requires not only know-how and dedication, but also technology for intraday *investment tracking*, down to the detail of single positions. It also needs courage to decide on *disinvestments* even if this means licking one's wounds. Cornerstone to proper investment tracking is the ability to avoid *conflicts of interest*, which invariably lead to major troubles.

Secretive deals like Raptor 1 and the other non-transparent partnerships in Enron's constellation are the exact opposite of what I just stated. An example of hedge funds which had the courage to change course in early 2000 are Quantum and Tiger Management (see Section 6); the latter chose to go out of business.

Steady investment tracking and the avoidance of conflicts of interest are pillars of good management. They should characterise all offers made by hedge funds, funds of funds, commercial banks, investment banks, SAIVs and other entities. This is not the typical case. Yet, what I just said applies to all notes linked to hedge fund performance, whether or not they provide a guarantee that at maturity investors will receive back, at least, the capital they put in.

> 'The compelling question again with this chapter is the issue of higher returns', said the reviewer. 'There is nothing which actually provides cold hard statistics as to the returns with different classes of alternative investments, comparing them with traditional investments'.

The reference made in Chapter 6 to a Crédit Suisse comment on (deceptive) hedge funds performance pre-empts this argument. Let me, however, add that this is an argument I have heard many times when talking to hedge funds pros – but in reverse. Typically, I get two sorts of answers when I am saying that the claims being advertised about 'much higher returns' with hedge funds are undocumented.

- The more polite one is: 'Sorry, we cannot release internal data'.
- The more brutal one reads: 'This is the information on returns and you better believe it. We don't plan to explain how we do our business'.

Usually, this second response is followed by the question: 'Are you convinced now?' Without the minimal doubt, I am not. Fifty-seven years of professional experience taught me not to believe in magic and never to go by word of mouth. I want hard facts and documented data. Typically, these two things are *not* forthcoming with hedge funds.

It is, therefore, preposterous for a hedge funds manager to insist 'give me data', when he knows first hand that his industry is largely on Cloud 9 rich in 'soft numbers' but thrifty on hard data. The funny side of this argument is that creative accounting treacheries can be sometimes ingenious, not unlike a sequence of events shown by the Israeli TV in connection with the April 2002 police action in Jenin.

What was supposedly a Palestinian fellow, who died in the fighting, was carried covered in a blanket by his pals through the field of operations, so that foreign reporters could take a good shot at the make-up funeral. One of the pals, however, lost his foot and the blanket fell down. The 'dead' rose and ran away, but he returned to the blanket and the procession started once more so that the media did not miss the show. Next false step, the little crowd broke up, and this time the 'dead' definitely disappeared through his own motor power – like alternative investments claims.

Is this funeral procession for the media really relevant to a discussion on alternative investments? It is, for two reasons. It serves as a proxy to the answer the reviewer asked through his question on hedge fund 'statistics'; and it helps to bring into perspective another characteristic of alternative investments and hedge funds. The 'high liquidity/less liquidity' case.

In early 2001, I was told by the director of alternative investments of one of the best-known banks that the fund of funds he wanted to sell me was highly liquid. He also said this was true of alternative investments at large. To be more convincing, he gave me a monthly research report by his institution, which wrote so black-on-white: 'Alternative investments are *always* liquid'.

Subsequent to this meeting, I protested to the bank's senior management that this is a false statement. I also pointed out that with this sort of printed literature and of claims, the bank was taking inordinate legal risks. There were as well some other complaints, but the most important remained that high liquidity was carried around like the dead in the blanket, but in an environment where the legal system functions very well.

The warning that I gave to this big bank seems to have had a result, because the new edition of its alternative investments literature included some interesting bullets; which described the alternative investments it offered in a more exact manner:

- Leverage
- Performance fees
- *Less liquidity*
- No benchmarking.

The merchandisers of risk, however, stood fast on another claim: 'Positive returns in *every* market environment'. The knowledgeable reader will appreciate that this is patently unheard of. In no financial market and for no financial instrument, this can be the case – whether classical or alternative.

In fact, because many investors are cautious about alternative investments, *principal-protected* notes have become popular. While each month several billion dollars are poured into the different risky products by hedge funds, aggregators and merchandisers of risks, some institutional clients will not buy unless at least their capital is protected. Analysts suggest that just one institution, Société Générale, has issued more than US$3 billion of principal-protected notes in private or public form.

- The idea of protecting at least the capital, even if its owner is willing to put at risk the interest this capital would earn, is a good compromise between risk tolerance and risk aversion.
- But it is wise to remember that this scheme has embedded in it considerable *credit risk*, and there may be liquidity problems for banks that offer money-back guarantees.

Given the risks being assumed, how can these credit institutions afford to offer such guarantees, which could become a huge drain to their treasury?

- One approach is to reinsure the capital at risk with an insurance company, if one is found to be able and willing to assume this exposure.
- Another solution is to invest a proportion of the capital in zero-coupon US Treasury bonds, or similar credit risk-free instruments, and to leverage another portion through derivatives.

The plan behind the transactions suggested by the second bullet typically assumes that, at target date, the zero coupons yield most of the principal sum. The balance of the capital is then invested in hedge funds on a highly leveraged basis. This strategy has plenty of potential to disappoint. Not only are such 'solutions' not fail-proof, but they also require high technology to make them work.

The bank must continue tracking the hedge funds performance and adjust its delta and gamma hedges quickly in order to avoid spectacular losses.[2] Investors should do the same.

- Every investor should account for downturns. Hedge funds are no exception to this statement.
- Downturns in the capital market are in no way exceptional in a historical context.

Aware of loans risks and capital markets risks facing every commercial bank, regulators developed what they call a CAMEL rating, according to Gary Hector.[3] This is granted on a five-point scale with '1' being the highest and '5' the lowest. The letters of the acronym stand for:

- *C*apital adequacy;
- *A*sset quality;
- *M*anagement;
- *E*arnings; and
- *L*iquidity.

Hedge funds, SAIV's and many other institutions offering alternative investments are not subject to CAMEL rating. For them capital adequacy is unrequired; this permits overleveraging and shorting games. Shorting the capital markets through loaned equity makes asset quality questionable and liquidity dangerously low.

Many hedge funds and most special alternative investment vehicles are not registered as an *investment company* under the US Investment Company Act of 1940, nor are they registered as an *investment advisor* under the US Investment Advisers Act of 1940. Although they trade in securities, they are not registered or regulated under any comparable non-US jurisdiction. Accordingly, their stakeholders, including shareholders and end-investors, do not have the benefit of the investor protections provided by the aforementioned legislation.

3. The merchandising of risk: basic facts which are important to pension funds

One of the factors leading to booms and busts in the capital markets is the fact that analysts tend to replicate one another in their behaviour. Recent evidence is found in the promotion of a host of technology stocks whose share prices have first shot to the stars and imploded on re-entry. Computers, communications, and media are a case in point.

- When traditional valuations made stocks look expensive, the analysts did not react by saying, 'sell'.
- Instead, they cast about for explanations that would justify existing price levels and beyond.

Alternative investments demonstrate much of the same behaviour. However, the risks being taken through investing by means of hedge funds are significant, and the quality of leveraged assets is in no way guaranteed. Wall Street firms, such as Morgan Stanley, Goldman Sachs and J.P. Morgan Chase, say they are alive to the danger and tend to comment negatively about German, French, and Swiss banks, as well as subsidiaries of insurance companies, for their multimanager hedge fund business (see Chapter 5). Precisely, they criticise:

- taking on greater risk through leveraged financing; and
- involving their own clients in alternative investments.

Both private pension funds and regulators should be most attentive to the message conveyed through these two bullets. A recent publication on special risks in securities trading outlines the rules prevailing in Switzerland and makes the distinction that there are basically two types of investments. Those with limited risk, and those with unlimited risk.

The purchase of equities and options involves limited risk; at worst, the entire amount of money is lost. But 'there are certain types of derivatives that can require additional outlay of capital over and above the original investment'. Unlimited risk is typically associated with forwards, futures, writing put and call options, and the obligation to make margin payments, which 'can amount to many times the original level of the investment'.[4]

Pension funds must appreciate that the amount of risks involved with derivatives and alternative investments, has its consequences. In some countries, like France, private pension funds are not permitted. In others like the United Kingdom and the Netherlands, pension funds are big business – but they should become a big risk business. For this reason, the European Union plans to restrict pension funds' investment in private equity, real estate, and derivatives. Its member countries are considering limiting company pension funds' exposure to high-risk investments.

A motion introduced by the Spanish government has proposed specific limits on pension fund's freedom to put money into unlisted investments, in a way going beyond the 'prudent person' principle. This principle says that pension funds can invest in a diversified range of asset classes that ensures that they meet their pension promise to their members. The Spanish 'plus' to it puts restrictions on:

- investment in the pension fund's own company;
- investment in unlisted vehicles (such as private equity), derivatives and exposure taken with hedge funds.

Beyond Spain several other EU member states have argued that quantitative limits should be imposed to increase the protection of investors and pensioners. For his part, with the same objective to make pension funds safer investment vehicles, after the debacle of Enron, George W. Bush has proposed limits on how long companies can require employees to hold company stock in 401(k) plans.

The US 401(k) are pension plans. The plight of Enron's workers and retirees is behind this proposal. Investors and retirees of this 'hedge fund with a gas pipeline' lost more than $1 billion on Enron stock held in their 401(k)s, which should induce every pension fund manager to think twice before committing the retirees' assets.

Neither is acceptable the excuse that intermediaries will absorb the risk in case of a catastrophe. With intermediaries taking care not to expose themselves to the losses, end-investors are assuming major risks often without paying due attention to the fact that the instruments they buy are highly geared and their risk and return curve is far from attractive.

Profits and losses always condition the investors' behaviour as Figure 7.1 suggests, but with the lack of precedence on how capital invested in alternative investments will fare, the end-investors find themselves in the narrow band of hope right in the middle of this graph. Institutional investors, and most particularly pension fund managers, who patronise the hedge funds, must be cautious and they should understand that many hedge funds have low credit standing.

Precisely because the risk of loss is major, both to the lenders and to the investors, since the LTCM debacle, the financing of hedge funds has become a much tighter affair than it used to be.[5] Regulators see to it that banks do not lend them more than three to seven times their capital,

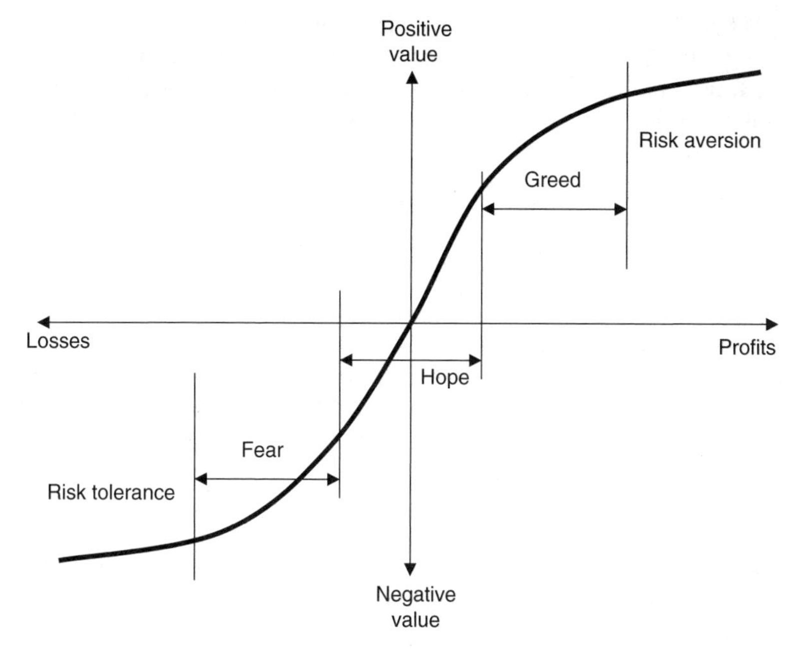

Figure 7.1 Profits and losses condition investors' risk appetite and risk tolerance.

while the same commercial banks borrow as much as 12 times their capital, leveraging themselves through bought money.

- The banks have been reducing their own credit exposures to hedge funds by bringing in outside end-investors.
- At the same time, institutional investors have picked up the slack in financing hedge funds.

Many insurance companies and credit institutions say that the capital of hedge funds is contributed mainly by wealthy individual speculators and they do not take part in it. Such statements do not pass a careful scrutiny. Not only banks and insurers, but also mutual funds, pension funds, even charities, lend capital to hedge funds and invest their money in the instruments they are selling.

Another statement, which is only half-true is that hedge funds are assets and liabilities managers. They are asset managers of their depositors' money: what they have invested in the fund is really *risk capital*. But many hedge funds are poor managers of their liabilities, which come with leverage, the amount of money they borrow, and the repurchase agreements they make.

What about the returns? If everything goes right with the gambles being taken, then the different end-investors will receive between 70 and 80 per cent of resulting profits, given the various management and other fees the hedge funds and banks would deduct at the source. Therefore,

- the end-investors take 100 per cent of the risk including the capital they invest;
- but can only hope to receive 70 per cent or less of the profit.

Some hedge funds allow the possibility of investors withdrawing the investment from the fund when there is severe underperformance. This can be, however, largely theoretical as hedge funds are not liquid and recovering the money invested can itself send them to the wall. For this reason, most agreements are longer term, a year or more, though some do allow disinvestments once a month.

Under most prevailing conditions, a decision to disinvest is at best guesswork. If, and only if, the bank can see all the positions in a hedge fund's portfolio, and comprehend what is in them, it can guard against a downturn rather quickly. This is difficult to achieve in any effective way through the low technology today featured by many credit institutions.

What is needed to capitalise on a disinvestment clause, if there is one, is a real-time passthrough solution, like that which has been engineered by top-tier computer and communications companies. These companies are using enterprise resource planning (ERP) software enabling them to achieve on-line passthrough to databases of their business partners. Cisco provides a good example.[6]

Figure 7.2 helps to explain the sense of the *passthrough* in the alternative investments supply chain. Both real-time watch *and* appropriate legal clauses for rapid disinvestment are necessary because, like any other entity, hedge funds can go bust, and their high gearing can wreak havoc in the financial market.

Few of the people and companies who go for alternative investments really appreciate that to deliver the lower two-digit return on investment, which they promise, hedge funds must take enormous risks and sometimes these risks backfire.

Precisely for this reason, serious investors ring the alarm bell. In 2001, Warren Buffett, who heads Berkshire Hathaway and is considered to be one of the best investment specialists alive today, warned his shareholders that American investors are living in a 'dream world', if they are still counting on returns of 15 per cent or more on their investments. But is anybody listening?

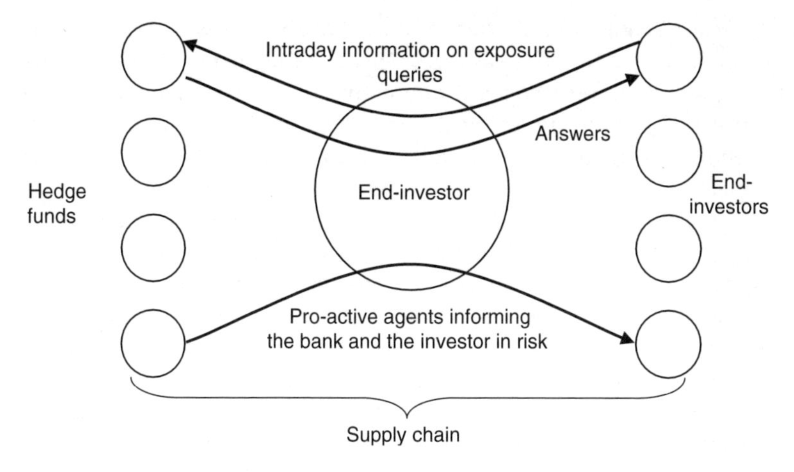

Figure 7.2 Real-time passthrough to the hedge funds exposure is a 'MUST', both for the bank acting as intermediary and the end-investors.

4. Appreciating the risks of going retail

A fairly prevalent opinion among investors, based more or less on historical evidence, is that in the longer run stocks deliver higher average annual returns than bonds. Another widely held view, particularly among financial analysts, is that stocks should be purchased for the purpose of achieving capital gains, and bonds should be bought for obtaining a fixed income through coupon redemption.

Still another oft heard view is that derivatives are for hedging, but they can at the same time deliver double-digit profits fuelled by a unique confluence of circumstances in financial markets, and a massive outperformance of stocks, as we knew until March 2000. Indeed, this dual incarnation of derivatives as hedgers and profit makers, is the background argument for alternative investments:

- Managers, analysts, and investors, who have such expectations regarding earnings, growth, continuing performance *and* safety of capital, can be mistaken.
- The sharp correction of technology stocks in 2000–2 is a reminder of what happens when the upside is the focus of attention, with only lip service paid to the downside.

The exposure assumed with derivative instruments and many other alternative instruments cannot be compared with credit risk free products like

US Treasury bills and Treasury bonds, British Guilts, German Bunds, French OAT, or Dutch Treasuries. On the other hand, if the investor appreciates that the proposed alternative investment assumes a large market risk *and* it is not credit risk free, then he should more than double the profit figure he is demanding – just as American investors do in connection to investments in Indonesia versus investments at home.

This is the best advice I can give to retail investors contemplating alternative investments. Understanding the risks at retail level is most urgent because, as we have seen, alternative investments are becoming increasingly offered to the retail customers of credit institutions, through a sort of long-term 'savings plans'. The usual advice is that in order for investors to protect their wealth, 20 per cent of their money should be in alternative investments. This is patently false. It is a mousetrap by unscrupulous people to catch those who are uninformed of the risks and unaware of the dangers.

Many who know how to evaluate risk and return suggest that their main worry comes from the fact that hedge funds and credit institutions with their fund of funds have shifted strategy towards leveraging the private sector using alternative investments as their tool. Investment advisors advocating leveraging and non-transparent alternatives as investment opportunities for their clients need to be very clear about to whom these investments are being targeted – not just for reasons of ethics but also to avoid the legal implications.

- Selling leveraged, highly risky instruments to consumers is not vastly different from predatory lending.
- In years past, predatory lending has been castigated as an unlawful practice. This, however, is not yet the case with alternative investments.

The merchandising of alternative investments at the retail level is predatory lending in reverse. In 2000, a study by the US Treasury said the practice of predatory lending 'involves engaging in deception or fraud, manipulating the borrower through aggressive sales tactics, or taking unfair advantage of a borrower's lack of understanding about loan terms'. This definition fits well the retail sale of alternative investments because they exploit 'an investor's lack of understanding about the risks of leveraging'.

Predatory lending is a term used, among other cases, in connection with mortgages extended under terms that are more onerous to borrowers than prevailing market prices, a predatory investment is one which is likely leveraged, complex and obscure in its fundamentals, has no fair market value, and its liquidity is low or nil. End-investors or borrowers fall under the spell of predatory practices either because, in the case of investments, they are not well informed about the risks; or, in the case of borrowers, they do not know the sources of finance that may be open to them and/or their credit standing is low.

Different forms of past *alternative investments* have led to the tulip mania, the South Seas scam, the Mississippi bubble, and other financial catastrophes. There is an analogy with alternative investments, where they are addressed to people who cannot understand the exposure they are assuming. In both cases, those falling into the trap are either misinformed about the risks they involve or they do not want to be informed because they are too insecure about their own decision power.

The best way to stop the bubble-in-the-making through predatory investments is that regulators and the banking industry focus on the need for investor education, as the best means to stop the next financial storm from gaining force. Some types of investments lack *soundness*, a notion, which since coming into use in 1966 has never had an official description but is generally considered meaning navigating in uncharted waters in an investment sense.

Credit risk, market risk, and operational risk must be brought into perspective through an investor education programme. As personal investment portfolios become popular because of growing affluence, investors must learn to appreciate the risks embedded in securities. They must also understand not only what is credit risk but also the reasons for *credit deterioration*, as well as how to calculate *capital at risk* putting together credit and market exposure information.

Education and guidance needs to be positively oriented, illustrating the steps that banks, brokers, and other institutions must take to protect their clients. Investor education must include several steps to avoid inadvertently purchasing abusive financial instruments. This requires:

- learning about originators;
- finding out about their marketing tactics; and
- being informed about what kinds of complaints have been outstanding so far.

There should as well be a warning about legal or litigation risks. Investor education is critical not only for retail investors, but for banks who may unknowingly buy and market high-risk instruments. For instance, guidance must be provided to help avoid investing in securities backed by unsecured loans or in products peddled as being liquid which in reality are highly illiquid. Investors should be trained on how to review the prospectus and its supplements, and understand the risks the investment instrument involves.

Part and parcel of investors' education is to learn how to recognise one of the main mistakes many investment managers made when the Nasdaq turned south at the end of March 2000 that was to think that the change in the market's mood would not affect profits. Part of the reason for this illusion is that in the S&P Industrial Index the average company saw its profit margins jump from 4.2 per cent in 1992 to 6.6 per cent in 1999, a level last matched in 1966.

Many analysts expected those margins to hit an all-time high of 7.7 per cent in 2001 in spite of the early 2000 slump. In October 2000 many analysts and investment advisers incorrectly prompted investors to stay in technology stock, because 'that kind of margin expansion would lift corporate earnings'. Some people even say corporate earnings would grow by 13–14 per cent in each of the next two years. As a result, investment managers saw the S&P 500 reach 1675 by early 2001, a 10-per cent rise from April 2000 level, before it took a prolonged turn for the worst.

The lesson to retain from this example is that when it comes to investments, even the pros can make big blunder. As a *Business Week* article had it right after the Nasdaq rout, Lehman Brothers chief US investment strategist Jeffrey M. Applegate, whose Virtual Economy portfolio had surged 66.6 per cent in a matter of four months believed that growth stocks will again trounce value issues (read Old Economy stocks) for the seventh year in a row.[7]

Based on this belief Applegate made big bets on premier names such as America Online, Cisco Systems, IBM, Microsoft, Oracle and Sun Microsystems, and up-and-comers like 'fiber-optics powerhouse' JDS Uniphase. Technology stocks, plus AT&T, Qwest Communications, and Sprint, made up a hefty 75 per cent of the portfolio, versus a 41 per cent weighting in those two sectors in the S&P 500 – and we know what has happened since then to AT&T, Qwest, AOL, Cisco, Oracle, Sun Microsystems and the other high techs.

5. Leveraged trades and conflicts of interest

From one case to the next, conflicts of interest with respect to alternative investments follow a fairly similar pattern. A common scenario is that Hedge Fund A is a trading advisor as well as the manager to investment company B, which may be a bank. An inherent conflict of interest exists between A's fiduciary duty to assist B's board of directors in the selection of a trading advisor for B, and A's interest in acting as its trading advisor. Furthermore, there is a high likelihood that:

- A's trading advisory and management agreements with B have not been negotiated at arm's length; and
- A's trading decisions are not subject to review by any independent third party, which works to the detriment of investors.

If B is an alternative investment vehicle set up by Bank C, then *most likely* B was formed and is operated for the sole purpose of permitting investors to place assets under the management of A, or of say ten different hedge funds: $A_1 \dots A_{10}$. Multimanagement agreements (see Chapter 5) often hide the fact that the different managers may have financial and other incentives to favour certain accounts in terms of risk and return.

There is as well another complication if B owns a start-up investment management company formed for the purpose of managing assets and from time to time directly places funds under management with this company. Decisions regarding whether and how much of B's funds are to be placed under management with the start-up investment management company will be made in the sole discretion of A. B, however, will have an interest in the profits and fees earned by the investment management company, which leads to further conflicts of interest.

The ability of B and its affiliates to co-invest with A in so-called strategic investments also creates potential conflicts of interest. Although the right to co-invest will generally be exercised by investing in a different entity, there is typically no limitation on holding the entity's interests in a manner, which may put the investors in the fund at a disadvantage.

Some regulators are actively hunting these cases of conflict of interest in the domain under their authority – but many hedge funds escape regulatory supervision, particularly those based offshore (the majority of them). In other cases, they have little to do by way of compliance because the regulatory guidelines are wanting. A case in point is the risks associated to cross-investments.

In an interview he gave in July 2002, Dr John Kenneth Galbraith brought attention to the similarities between United Kingdom's split capital investment trusts and the US trusts which crashed in 1929. He also brought attention to the high leverage of hedge funds and other institutions, including their dual lending and trading relation to banks, particularly in connection with the downfall of some mighty investment trusts in the great depression of 1929.

Galbraith described the risk from cross-investments as the *classic* and *erroneous* development that comes when one company invests for speculation in another company, which in cases may be its own daughter. This reference fits well with the SAIV as well as the shell companies which closely link a credit institution with its clients, so that the downfall of one of them can have dramatic results on the other(s). The case of the *prepays* and the offshores involving J.P. Morgan Chase, Citigroup, and Enron – investigated in July 2002 by a US Senate Committee – is an example.

We should never disregard the lessons learned in the past. In the big bull market of the 1920s, for example, Goldman Sachs set up a series of huge investment companies, starting with Goldman Sachs Trading Corporation (created in late 1928). After issuing stocks to gullible people, this company set up Shenandoah Corporation, another investment trust. A short time later, Shenandoah launched the even bigger Blue Ridge Corporation, investing heavily in the new creation and benefiting from the rise in the value of its stock:

- This has been a pyramiding structure, waiting for an opportunity to crash.
- It has also been an exhibition of conflict of interest, not unlike that of today's alternative investments.

Conflicts of interest also arise even among the best pension funds. In mid-July 2002, it was revealed that directors of CALPERS, America's largest employees pension fund with assets of $150 billion and responsible for minding the retirement of 1.3 million people, were involved in potential conflicts of interest. These threatened to erode the pension fund's sterling image.

Three of CALPERS board members received political contributions from companies the bank invested in, raising questions of influence. Five members of the pension fund's board owned stocks also held by CALPERS.[8] Business ethics experts say this should never happen because it puts board members in a position to profit from advance knowledge about the entity's investment decisions.

To make matters worse, rather than being the leader in putting corporate accounting right, in July 2002, the board of CALPERS shelved a staff recommendation calling on companies to expense options.[9] Warren Buffett, who is upright, did expense options at Berkshire, Washington Post, Coca-Cola, Gillette, and other companies where he is involved as chief executive or board member. Many other companies including General Electric and Amazon.com did the same.

6. Be careful what you wish for

One of the major contributions of Arthur Levitt, as chairman of the Securities and Exchange Commission (SEC) in the 1990s, is that he did his best to stop a practice involving conflict of interest concerning certified public accountants (CPAs, chartered accountants) and their consulting arm. CPAs typically make more money from consulting than from auditing. The problem is that their consulting activities may influence their auditing findings and reporting. The risk Levitt had seen is that:

- Large consulting fees paid by the audited firm, are incompatible with the auditor's neutral opinion.
- Therefore, Levitt's message to the Big Five CPAs has been: 'Be careful what you wish for'.

The SEC rule, approved on 15 November 2000, placed the burden on corporate audit committees which must now tell shareholders how they decided that hiring the same firm to do auditing and consulting did not, and would not, compromise the auditors' objectivity in certifying the accounts. Enron's, WorldCom's, and a long list of other debacles have demonstrated that this SEC rule, the product of a compromise, was not strong enough.

Similar conflicts of interest exist with commercial banks, specifically between their managing of retail accounts and their merchandising of highly risky alternative investments to consumers. Retail clients do not have the necessary experience to question whether what they are offered makes sense. The bank's conflict of interest behind the promotional literature potential investors receive is not transparent.

In the long term, this is bad. Repeated conflicts of interest erode business confidence. Other conflicts of interest result from the fact that the hedge fund and/or SAIV not only co-manage, with commercial banks, accounts corresponding to alternative investments, but also administer other client accounts as well as trade for the proprietary accounts under their wing.

A conflict of interest, which emulates insider trading is evident in the fact that hedge funds and SAIV may use the same information and trading strategies for all of their client and proprietary accounts. This necessarily obliges them making choices favouring or penalising specific accounts, and therefore investors who have put their money in them. One of the ironies of this particular case is the practice of hedge funds managers investing their own money in their funds.

- On the one hand, this helps to give confidence to investors that the fund will be managed prudently even if it undertakes leveraged trades, and will not be diluted.
- At the same time, it creates a potential conflict of interest, as when the bets turn for the worse, managers may pull out in time, leaving the vehicle to crash.

Investors therefore need to demand ironclad guarantees that traders and hedge fund managers will not step over this line. In the United States, some funds have begun using a random allocation procedure, in order that their traders and managers are not redeeming their investments first – when worst comes to worst. But is this a guarantee?

- Who says that this has become a policy?
- Who polices the random numbers?
- How much dependability can be placed on the results?

Experts say there may be a significant amount of other information to make insider preferences feasible. What surprises the author is that in spite of all these perils, many people think of alternative investments as the new messiah. It looks as if good sense has taken a leave.

At a poll taken at a Bond Investors' conference in London in February 2002, despite the fact that only 18 per cent of the audience had invested in hedge funds, 65 per cent answered positively to the query: 'Do you believe that hedge funds can help *reduce* your portfolio risk?'[10] The author of this book does not. Numerous differences among various accounts need to be balanced, such as:

- their size;
- investment objectives;
- redemption policies;
- trading practices; and
- regulatory considerations.

Nobody, really nobody, knows how to do such balancing. The hedge fund or SAIV may not enter into the same trades at the same time, nor take positions of the same proportionate size, for all the accounts managed by it. Consequently, the performance of various accounts managed by the entity may vary. Yet, the investor has been offered a simple view regarding performance by the entity. In this sense:

- The simplicity of a classical investment contrasts with the complexity of risky dealing by fund managers.

- The investor may not understand what it means taking a position in bonds of a country, which is or may be in trouble; and this is further compromised by the activities of the hedge funds themselves.

Neither are hedge funds, funds of funds, SAIVs, and other merchandisers of risk known for the accuracy and continuity of their risk control system. Some of their clients suffer from exactly the same deficiency, and this sees to it that exposure can run wild. Figure 7.3 shows what would have been a sound approach to tracking risk through a statistical quality control (SQC) chart by variables.[11]

- 90 per cent of the bankers and hedge fund managers I asked if they use control charts by variables responded: 'What is SQC?'
- The other 10 per cent responded they used risk adjusted return on capital (RAROC), a credit control by attributes for loans to hedge funds).

This 10 per cent were bankers, not hedge fund managers. The fact they use RAROC is commendable, but it is not the same thing with the steady update of statistical quality control charts. Steady vigilance is mandatory for both: risk control purposes, and rate of return.

For instance, it is not unusual for investment managers' rates of return to decline as assets under management increase. Assets under management fluctuate in accordance with addition and redemption activity. In their sole discretion these entities determine the level of capital they

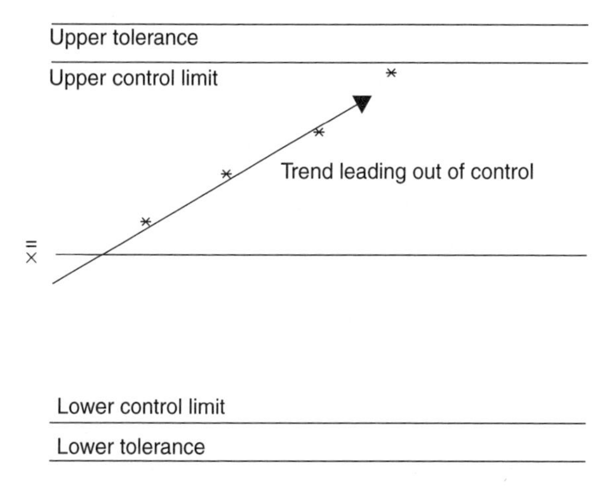

Figure 7.3 A trend line helps to identify a situation getting out of control.

manage, again one of the reasons given for prudence on the part of hedge fund managers.

The list of potential conflicts of interest can be a long one, fed by the stated practice that different trading advisors currently manage several client accounts, and at the same time their own proprietary accounts, eventually acting – even if by accident – in an unfair or unequitable fashion with respect to some of the accounts. Few institutional investors take into account this risk.

The performance of the different accounts can vary quite significantly creating potential conflicts, frictions, and legal action. The degree of satisfaction or dissatisfaction with deliverables often reflects the huge reliance on the trading advisor, as the profitability of an alternative investment depends upon his or her:

- ability to trade in various markets;
- ingenuity in selecting strategic investments; and
- persistence in monitoring the activities of other advisors to which the hedge fund delegates a portion of its activities.

Trading advisor's strategies and methods can change over time, with instruments and markets added or deleted. This shifts the relative emphasis in the alternative investments' portfolio. The intermingling of different portfolios and accounts does not result in an improved performance for all: some suffer, while others benefit. As we have seen in Chapter 3, these are the seeds of future legal action.

These preoccupations about conflict of interest and insider trading are most pertinent today, when laws and regulations designed to protect investors from zealot merchandisers securities and of the risks associated to them, are being bypassed through derivatives and other gimmicks. Since new financial instruments are, by definition, 'new', legislators and regulators are sometimes at a loss in terms of controlling the abuse of investors. 'Confidence is a difficult thing to put your finger on. You don't reverse investor confidence overnight', said Dr Alan Greenspan, the Fed chairman, in his Congressional Testimony of mid-July 2002.

6. The experience of Quantum and Tiger

Companies and private individuals tempted by alternative investments should appreciate that hedge funds are not the infallible entities their promoters say that they are. The members of their investment policy committee, which sets the overall strategy, including capital concentration, can fail like anybody else. On the other hand, every analyst other than the fund's own can make the in-depth fundamental and technical analysis necessary to seek a dominant market position.

Precisely because nobody really knows which way the market will go, and everybody can make wrong guesses: Julian Robertson closed down Tiger Management, his hedge fund in late March 2000. A few weeks later, George Soros revealed that he no longer intended to invest in alternative strategies and would be pulling out of his two funds, Quantum and Quota.

> 'Quantum and Tiger are not representative of the industry,' said one of the reviewers, 'and to suggest that Robertson and Soros are role models for the investment community is a dangerous generalisation. Perhaps we could take some funds which are still operating'.

Soros and Robertson are not representative of the hedge funds industry only in the sense that when they were going strong they were the tops – and they left a legend behind them. Others have not. Besides this, Soros, Robertson, and Steinhart had the courage (and the decency) to close down their funds when they saw that risks were in excess of returns. Others have not; instead they continue losing the investors money which is not their's anyway, and some are lying to their investors for long years as the case of Berger, in Chapter 5, documents.

Therefore, rather than getting nervous about Soros and Robertson being taken as the better examples of hedge fund managers, the pro-hedge funds reader should ask himself the question: 'Has the wisdom of the ages convinced two of the most successful investors (or speculators) of our time to quit their usual business?' Or have two billionaires merely decided to park their assets in safer investments in times of high volatility and a great uncertainty about what lies ahead in the financial markets?

- The 20 months which followed the phasing out of Robertson's and Soros' funds prove that the great masters were right in their decision.
- Since then, however, their shoes have been filled by many folks whose feet are at least two or three sizes smaller.

It needs no explaining that Quantum and Tiger have been the largest and most successful global macro funds, yet they were both hit by losses from 1998 onwards. For years, their initially high return investment strategies aimed at early recognition of macroeconomic trends, like movements in currencies and interest rates.

The good news to their investors has been that they were achieving a double-digit level of returns through leveraged positions. But times changed, gearing became in some ways counterproductive and the financial warlords lost their hand. As a result, Tiger and Quantum suffered considerably:

- Tiger lost an estimated US$2 billion in autumn 1998, as the yen market grew unexpectedly stronger;
- Quantum lost an estimated US$2 billion in March/April 2000 when Nasdaq's technology sector went into a tailspin.

In terms of currency exchange, the euro's sustained weakness worked to the detriment of the funds whose managers misread the general economic trend. Also, as the liquidity in the financial markets declined in a substantial way, it made the macroplayers much more exposed on account of their high leverage.

The irony is that past successes of Tiger and Quantum became a liability. Quantum's past gains led other hedge funds to study and emulate its investment strategies, which made it increasingly more difficult for them to find counterparties for transactions. Also, apart from providing a significant amount of new competition, past successes put in place standards on annual return hard to repeat, let alone exceed, year after year.

A combination of greater market volatility and an explosion in hedge funds, which increases competition saw to it that the monthly return of global macrofunds went below the index for alternative investments such as long/short equity or event-driven deals, while the assumed risk remained significantly higher. This turned past risk and return standards on their head; a fact of which few end-investors are aware.

There is another aspect to the losses Quantum and Tiger have suffered prior to voluntarily leaving the alternative investment. If a fund generates negative returns over a period, as has been the case with Tiger and Quantum, this red ink must be made good before the fund manager can charge investors a performance fee. The prospects of leaner returns are by all likelihood a further reason why Julian Robertson opted out and George Soros scaled back.

The other very important factor is that one cannot always be right in one's guesses. Failing is human. Let me take a very simple example. In May 2001, well before the tragic day of September 11, United Airlines (UAL) president Rono J. Dutta has been quoted as blaming the airline's US$305 million first-quarter loss in part on a 27 per cent increase in fuel prices from a year earlier. Could not he hedge through derivatives? Yes, ... but UAL stopped hedging fuel prices at the end of 2000, believing that they were bound to fall as the economy slowed. But the reverse occurred.

'It's unusual for fuel costs to go up like this into a recession', said Dutta.[12] It is unusual but it did take place. The same way hypotheses made by hedge fund managers turn sour, and because of high leverage, fortunes are lost.

Neither is it true that the crash of technology stocks is the one and only reason for misfortunes. 1998 was a bumper year for technology. Among hedge funds' managers' big losers in 1998 were Leon Cooperman, Marty Zweig, and Jo DiMenna. The biggest of all losers on record was John Meriwether, of the now famed LTCM. At the end of August 1998, Meriwether's hedge fund had lost US$2.1 billion, or 50 per cent of its assets. A month later it came to the brink of bankruptcy.

In 1998, Leon Cooperman's Omega Overseas Partners lost 21 per cent of its value. Even harder hit were the Infinity Investors fund, down 28 per cent; Latinvest fund and Apam High Performance Capital fund, each down 33 per cent; Everest Capital International fund, down 42 per cent. Appaloosa Investment I and Palomino funds each down 43 per cent; Oscar Investment fund, down 54 per cent; Everest Capital Frontier LP and Everest Capital Frontier funds which lost 61 per cent of their assets in the third quarter of 1998.

That is an impressive list of better-known hedge funds – which took with them investors' money down the financial precipice, in just one year. A worse landing, that same year 1998, was seen in three hedge funds run by McGinnis Advisors. They filed for bankruptcy protection because they could not meet margin calls from their brokers and bankers. Other funds were forced to liquidate significant portions of their holdings to meet margin calls – which is a splendid example of *the costs of leveraging*.

These hedge fund managers, like thousands of others, thought they not only know the market, but had also mastered it. They simply could do no wrong, and nobody could stand up to their expertise in making double-digit profits, or in repeating that feat, time and again, with impunity in regard to risk. But they were devastated twice within four years:

- in 1994 with the bond market meltdown, as the Fed kept on increasing the interest rate; and
- in 1998 with the credit market crash, and the beating administered by the stock market.

Nobody really knows the financial market in all its breadth, depth, and ramifications. Hedge funds are not the only ones to suffer large losses. With stocks taking a severe hit in the April 2000 to mid-2002 timeframe, some of the better-known companies bled. The stories of Lucent Technologies, Nortel, Cisco, Ciena, Juniper, JSD Uniphase, Xerox, even Sun Microsystems are too well known to be retold. For a time, after being beaten by the market on repeated occasions, hedge funds seemed to be losing some of their will to fight in all fronts. Yet, they found the end-investor as the ultimate risk taker. The consumer and his or her hard-won retained earning came to their rescue and high stakes by hedge funds began again at full velocity.

8. Promises made with alternative investments and the lack of market discipline

Alternative investments are sold on the hypothesis that:

- there is plenty of opportunity for outperforming the market while invested capital is not at risk (which is the first myth);
- both high returns and capital preservation are guaranteed (the second myth);
- they have low correlation to traditional stock and bond markets, a feat today offered by no other instrument (the third myth);
- they feature no currency risk for US$, sterling, euro, Swiss francs, or other main currency; because there is product for each currency (the fourth myth); and
- they have a nearby date of redemption (the fifth myth).

End-investors should understand and appreciate that nearly all of these arguments at best include their own embedded risk and at worst they are a cheap rhetoric. For example, two or three years to redemption is a long, not a short term and many adverse events can happen in between.

Investors could be confident about hedge funds, SAIVs, and other merchandisers of risk only when they abide with the requirements of Pillars 1, 2 and 3 of the New Capital Adequacy Framework of the Basle Committee – most particularly including the prerequisites for Pillar 3: transparency and market discipline. Typically, they do not.

- While the lack of market discipline among credit institutions seems in the way of being corrected, through Basle II.
- This does not apply to hedge funds as long as they continue to operate without prudential supervision.

The fact that the regulation of hedge funds is in some countries, like the United Kingdom, very weak and in others, like the United States, non-existent makes it possible to diffuse all sorts of false claims and get by with it. One of them is that, by miracle, investors need no more worry about currency risk.

It is true that the investor does not assume currency risk when buying an alternative investment in what he or she considers to be the base currency (dollars for Americans, pounds for British, francs for Swiss, and so on). However, he or she assumes all other risks embedded in alternative investments of which we have spoken in this and in the previous chapters.

Currency risk comes into the picture through two doors. First, not all different types of alternative investment strategies are available in hedge funds. The different flavours of alternative investments in pounds sterling and Swiss francs are rather limited. The largest selection is denominated in US dollars, and for other than American investors currency risk is ever present.

The second door is to be found in the fact that many hedge funds speculate on currencies, sometimes with big losses. Floating exchange ranges offer opportunities for making bets, but as all bets these involve surprises with end-investors left to foot the bill.

Regarding the myth of 'low correlation', being to a very substantial extent derivatives based, alternative investments rest on underliers which are real entities: an equity index, a bond, a currency, a short position, and so on. When the price of equities, interest rates, and currency exchange rates fluctuates, so does the worth of the alternative investment – only much more so, because it is leveraged.

As for the argument that non-transparent deals offer both high returns *and* guaranteed capital preservation, this resembles the state of mind of one who wants to have his pie and eat it too. Not only is this situation unattainable but also, where deals are at the edge of good investment sense:

- laws and regulations tend not to be properly observed;
- there is conflict between attaining high returns and preserving the capital; and
- a cultural clash eventually develops between prudent investors and those who manage their money by increasing the bets.

A fundamental business principle is that overexposure limits business strategy choices and handicaps changes in objectives. Added to these references is the fact that, at least for some investors, such as pension funds, loss of control of financial resources leads to ineffective management and therefore to a failure in fulfilling their fiduciary responsibilities.

Finally, the boldest myth is at top of the list: that there is 'plenty of opportunity for outperforming the market'. Nobody has managed to achieve this in the long run. It is not possible that over the longer term, everybody can always win. It is this mentality that leads to bubbles and panics.

Precisely because today the risks are so high and unpredictable, supervisory authorities have put restrictions on sales of alternative investments. Such restrictions, however, primarily concern residents of the United States, United Kingdom and Canada because these countries have better laws to protect nationals. In the final analysis, in a fast-moving financial world where new types of investments replace the old at a furious pace, the only true protection is the investor's mind itself.

The best, most recent advice has stemmed from unexpected quarters: former Enron CEO, Jeffrey Skilling, in his Congress testimony at the Congressional Committee investigating Enron's downfall. The Committee's Chairman asked him if he had learned anything from the crash of his company, and Skilling replied: '*Not to believe anything that does not make sense to my own professional experience*'. Investors must have the experience to manage risk and the resources to take the exposure of alternative investments; otherwise they should let them alone.

8
Assessing Strategic Risks through Stress Testing

1. Introduction

In the background of the attention being paid by governments, economists, and financial analysts to macroeconomics lies the fact that debt, consumption, and productive power correlate. Sometimes debt is used to increase the productive capacity of a company, of an industry, or of a nation, but in other cases, money connected to leverage filters mostly into consumption and from their inflation.

- Productive investments have a longer term return.
- But debt incurred to cover shortfalls in income has only a very short-term aftermath.

The results of leverage used in connection to financial instruments fall between these two bullets in their timing, and in the boom and bust cycle in terms of aftermath. Due to the bubbles greater detail on debt distribution and the leverage underlying it further substantiates worries over liabilities.

Within the financial sector of the economy, during the 1990s, the largest increase has been the 661 per cent rise in debt owed by issuers of asset-backed securities (ABS). With these derivatives instruments, securities are issued against the income stream generated from underlying assets. Next to this figure in liabilities growth, comes the debt owed by real estate investment trusts (REITs), which rose by 502 per cent in the decade of the 1990s.

These are US statistics, which should dearly interest the European reader because investors who fail to take global economic and geopolitical developments into account are leaving an important variable out of the risk and return equation. Since the markets continue being under

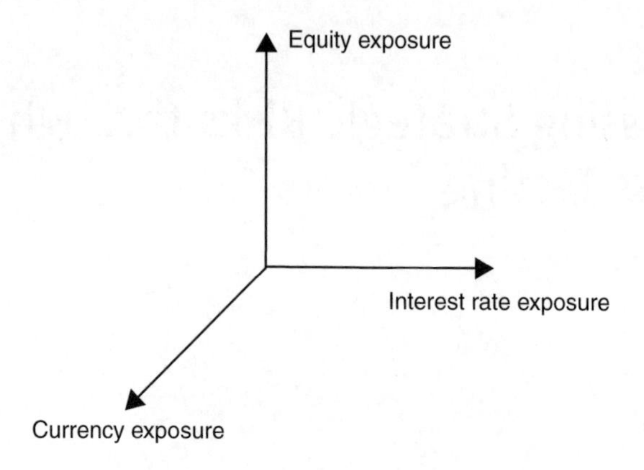

Figure 8.1 A 3-dimensional frame of reference which should be addressed through stress testing.

stress, and no one knows which sector or group might be the source of the next major investment theme, or upheaval, investors should look for opportunities in conservative, higher quality assets and be ready to act on them when their prospects become attractive.

'We are willing to invest our capital along three axes', says George Soros. 'We have a stock exposure, we have an interest exposure, and we have a currency exposure'.[1] This frame of reference is shown in Figure 8.1 and it has become the model of trading and investing of the majority of funds.

To get better insight on how the market develops and where are the hidden risks, stress testing must address all three dimensions at the same time, which is a compelling task. How do we know *if* 'this' or 'that' equity becomes attractive? Charting is one of the answers, particularly when we examine technical factors underpinning market trends. Past patterns and recent data might suggest a future downturn or breakthrough.

- Rigorous testing, however, requires more than a trend line.
- That is where *stress testing* may be able to help.

The reader is aware of the term stress testing since Chapter 4, where it was stated that what a serious investor who contemplates entering into alternative investments should keep in mind, is that *all* types of investments should be examined not only for risk and reward but also for *extra risk* and *extra reward*. Are the added basis points with junk bonds, or increased returns with leveraged equities, enough to compensate the investor for extra risks being taken?

The answer cannot be given through classical tests, because we are after something 'extra', an *outlier* in risk and return. Such outliers are often perceived as *anomalies*, which more often than not are the analyst's lack of a better, clearer conception. 'I have always found the word "anomaly" interesting,' says Warren Buffett. 'What it means is something the academicians can't explain, and rather than re-examine their theories, they simply discard any evidence of that sort'.

When it comes to the evaluation of strategic risk, all investors should appreciate that the doors of risk and return are side-by-side, and most often they are indistinguishable. To make sense of which door is which, we need tools much more powerful than normal testing. This is the role of stress testing, which is summarised in this chapter.[2]

2. Leverage, strategic risk, and VAR

Starting with the fundamentals, leverage exists everywhere in the economy. Whether the investor buys bonds, purchases stocks, or engages in some other transaction, the instrument he receives has embedded in it a certain amount of gearing, and therefore of risk. Practically every company runs on borrowed capital. Figures 8.2 and 8.3 consider the assets and liabilities side of balance sheets, and illustrate the extent to which credit institutions and other financial entities are geared.

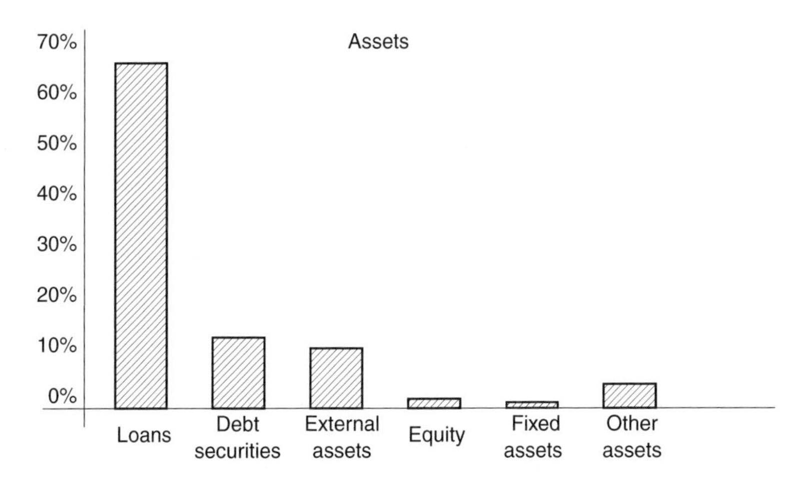

Figure 8.2 Percentage share in the consolidated balance sheet of Euroland financial entities at the end of 2000 (including the Eurosystem).*

* Statistics by the European Central Bank.

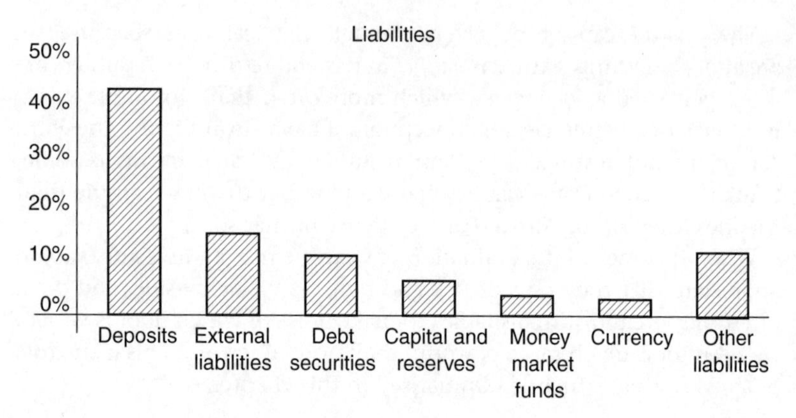

Figure 8.3 Percentage share in the consolidated balance sheet of Euroland financial entities at the end of 2000 (including the Eurosystem).*

* Statistics by the European Central Bank.

- Their assets are essentially leveraging the liabilities they have assumed.
- They are not supporting these liabilities in accordance with traditional investment strategies.[3]

In order to understand the significance of leverage, the reader must remember that banks generally operate with an equity cushion of only 8 per cent. This is the gearing approved by the regulators. The 8 per cent capital adequacy was established by the 1988 Capital Accord by the Basle Committee on Banking Supervision. The cushion, which characterises the New Capital Adequacy Framework (or Basle II), to be implemented in 2006, will use the 8 per cent as a standard approach and offer sophisticated banks the possibility of dynamic adjustments.

- An 8 per cent capital requirement corresponds to a leverage factor of 12.5, or 1250 per cent.
- This 8 per cent addressed loans exposure, and it was a practical compromise, not a theoretically established limit.

In the opinion of regulators, commercial banks can work with 8 per cent reserves because, as far as their banking book is concerned, they are relatively long-term investors. Accidents do happen, however, as with the 1929 depression in the United States and most other western countries, the Russian meltdown of 1998, and Argentina's bankruptcy in 2001, when there have been runs on commercial banks and a number of credit institutions ran out of cash. Also, collectively commercial banks may face a downgrading, as has been the case in the 1990s with 'Japan premium'.

Apart from credit risk that is addressed through capital adequacy for loans, something has to be reserved for market risk as well. The pre-requisite is a dependable measurement. With the 1996 Market Risk Amendment, the regulators require a daily measurement of exposure by banks, through the value at risk (VAR) model.[4] VAR numbers are supposed to give a snapshot of the bank's current market risk exposure through the computation of recognised, but not yet realised, gains and losses.

I have already explained why, as a measurement tool, VAR has many weaknesses. First and foremost, under no condition should VAR be interpreted as a predicator of future exposure in the bank's trading book, and therefore of the institution's longer term financial health. Neither is VAR God-given or all encompassing. It only answers one- to two-thirds of risk measurement requirements, depending on:

- the institution and its line of business;
- the composition of its portfolio; and
- the way it uses VAR and/or its derivatives.

Value at risk is also open to model risk, as are all other mathematical artefacts.[5] Therefore, a sound way of looking at VAR is as a fast and dirty approach to guestimating market risk. It works with relatively simple financial instruments, but not with the very complex deals such as those undertaken by hedge funds.

- Contrary to the leverage of banks, the leverage of hedge funds is a medium to high two-digit number. Fifty is not unheard of.
- As hedge funds are not required to report even the approximate figures of recognised gains and losses expressed by VAR, leverage can take a totally different dimension.

Before it crashed, LTCM had an exposure of US$1.4 trillion with a capital of US$4 billion: a leverage of 350 or 3,500 per cent. Admittedly, this is an extreme exposure. Yet, investors need to be wary of hedge funds, which claim that their leverage is 'only' 10 or 15. This may fail to account for the fact they are mostly running on bought money.

Money borrowed from banks and institutional investors, adds significantly to the leverage factor. Banks buy money at the going market price, and try to lend it at higher rate to consumers, companies, or hedge funds. This is, of course, trading in liabilities, which makes our economy function.

> 'You give us the leverage of LTCM and warn investors about hedge funds that claim leverage is "only" 10 or 15. You need to provide us with some statistics on what average leverage generally may be, and not assume that hedge funds are lying if leverage is low,' said a reviewer.

For the *n*th time, let me repeat that hard data about the leverage of hedge funds, and other 'statistics', are not available until the blow-up comes. In the general case, the performance of hedge funds is in no way supporting the reviewer's hopes. Here are some examples.

Most recently, *The Economist* aptly remarked that while hedge fund managers once talked about a *special skills-set* distinguishing them from mere fund managers, in other asset management categories, the facts talk otherwise. Today, most hedge funds are performing poorly,[6] and plenty are losing money, which hurts the bottomline of their investors.

Unable to see which direction the market goes, many hedge funds now speak of 'preservation of capital' rather than 'outperformance'. In doing so they forget that with huge credit risk and market risk the preservation of capital is a chimera – though it remains a label for suckers.

The real surprise is that while hedge funds struggle to preserve their capital, let alone to make money, there has been a market growth in hedge fund activity. In the second quarter of 2002 some $29 billion flowed into hedge funds worldwide. Yet, at the same time, an increasing number of hedge fund managers are giving up. Recent cases are: Bayard Partners in England, and Robertson Stevens in the United States.

The want for information about hedge funds performance until the bad surprises occur is precisely what is meant by the *lack of transparency* characterising hedge funds, funds of funds, SAIVs and other aggregators of risk. This reviewer, who is an institutional investor and at the same time a fan of hedge funds and of alternative investments, should have known the risk associated to this sort of business.

If the reviewer or anybody else has factual and documented statistics regarding the leverage of the above entities, I will be most obliged to get a copy. This is an open challenge. But I underline the words *factual* and *documented*. Any numbers on hedge fund gearing whose background is wanting would not do.

What *is* indeed available are educated guesses by market players: regulators of the banking industry, the bankers themselves, analysts and investors. The reason post-LTCM Group of Ten regulators require commercial and investment banks to report to them the money they lend to hedge funds, is precisely to be able to get a pick at hard data – at least at the liabilities side through loans being made to hedge funds and off-shores by banks.

Interestingly enough, the educated guesses on hedge funds leverage tend to be at the low side rather than at the high side. When LTCM went to the rocks, in September 1998, the guess among Wall Street experts was that its leverage stood at about 25 : 1. Almost overnight, as more information became available, the guestimate of LTCM's leverage jumped to 50 : 1 and stayed there for some time. Only after LTCM's salvage negotiations were completed under the aegis of the Federal Reserve Bank of New York, it was revealed that this hedge fund's leverage stood at an unprecedented and breathtaking 350-to-1.

This means a double high-level exposure: To market risk and to credit risk. To make up for the exposure that hedge funds are taking, the more serious firms specialising in alternative investments use the notion of *strategic risk* and of *value drivers* as applied to the different instruments, which they design and sell to end-investors. Some hedge funds managers point out issues leading to strategic risk, such as:

- the inability to perceive the aftermath of alternative business models;
- the failure to recognise opportunities and threats from emerging technologies;
- delays in defining and implementing innovative, compelling value propositions for customers and investors.

These are major strategic challenges in today's competitive environment, which can lead to loss of market position, failure to retain important clients, a haemorrhage of money, or a combination of these factors. What is done with the so-called 'value drivers' is less clear because their concept is confused, as it means different things to different people (see Section 3).

To meet the foregoing challenges, the better run hedge funds develop and implement systematic and rigorous methods, including processes and tools able to identify and manage strategic risk. But only a guestimated 5 per cent of hedge funds are able to do so. The value at risk algorithm is of absolutely no help in this connection. Only sophisticated tests can do, and that is the reason why stress tests are so important.

3. Stress tests are a culture: not a bunch of tools

Part and parcel of a risk reduction strategy adopted or to be adopted by an institution is the proposition that both value-based and growth-based analysis constitute a key input for assessing and addressing strategic risk. This concept makes sense, but prudent people should be concerned about the methodology, which they choose, the tools being used and their results. For instance for a value-oriented approach there are the so-called *value drivers* serving as operational means for:

- analysing alternative investment opportunities as they develop; and
- measuring the extent to which current and projected performance contributes to sustainable value creation.

This might make sense in theory but in practice the problem with a value-based analysis, is that this approach is highly subjective by the force of things; particularly when addressing strategic issues and strategic risks. Hard data (reliable statistics) do not exist on future events; even soft data (documented projections) are difficult to come by. Also, the methodology being used by the majority of analysts is heterogeneous and not necessarily reliable.

One way to overcome this adversity, indeed one that is instrumental in providing insight, is *stress testing*. We torture a system and its information elements until they confess their secrets. There are four different methods for stress tests:[7]

- scenario writing,
- sensitivity analysis,
- statistical inference under extreme conditions, and
- drills for a meltdown.

There exist some parallels between a stress testing approach and the search for anomalies in market pricing. 'Many of these events don't look like anomalies to me', Dr Fischer Black used to say. Black was right because by and large what other analysts called *anomalies* were extreme events, some of which eventually entered the mainstream of financial data.

In fact, there may be a good reason for an *anomaly*, for instance, a major correction. The October 1987 deep fall in the Dow Jones index was a 14-standard deviations event. Therefore, an analytical mind that finds information that contradicts existing beliefs, feels the obligation to look at it rigorously and use a magnifying glass. This is what stress testing is doing. The problem with the majority of people is that their mind is conditioned otherwise. Namely: to reject contradictory evidence, or, simply to express disbelief.

Stress testing has a great deal to do with alternative investments, because many hedge funds are active in non-investment grade debt securities and/or bet on stock indices, while all of them are highly geared, contributing to the liabilities which make up the market's leverage. Financial entities like hedge funds, banks, SAIVs, and other geared institutions, which believe that conservative investment strategies kill their value drivers, should be keen in stress testing and the analysis of results.

God is in the detail

The message the reader should retain from these references is how much personal skill counts in the gains and losses equation, and how great is the risk of bias. Despite advances with models at the time of writing, we simply do not have the means for modelling events like those described in some of the preceding examples, even in a coarse way.

This is not surprising because financial modelling is still a new science. All facets of it are not yet well known. The market turns around intraday and volatility is high. As Mies van der Rohe, the architect, used to say: 'God is in the detail', and *algorithmic insufficiency* sees to it that we cannot handle a great deal of detail through computers.

Some may dispute this argument, and I would be the first to agree that financial engineering has made great strides,[8] but the complexity of the instruments has also increased by leaps and bounds. There is no evidence that hedge funds, SAIVs, risk aggregators, and merchandisers of alternative investments are able to identify in a factual and documented manner the aftermath of all value drivers in regard to:

- revenue,
- cost, and
- risk.

This failure in approaching risk in full detail is by no means a critique of mathematical analysis. It is a result of the complexity of the instruments handled by hedge funds. It is much easier to do a value-based analysis with classical business lines, than with highly geared, novel and illiquid instruments.

For instance, we can estimate trend curves with net new money growth and average margins on assets, for products such as private banking and traditional asset management, but we are less able in computing the potential impact of complex alternative investment deals, let alone to do so in a factual and documented manner.

One way to provide evidence is to see to it that internal value driver projections and valuations are benchmarked against more classical business lines and assessments, and they are subjected to sensitivity analysis and *stress tests*. This will help to understand the fitness of our assumptions.

This is doable, but as I have already said the complexity of alternative investments makes it difficult to do a rigorous analysis. Also lack of transparency – therefore the poorness of databases – renders this job nearly impossible.

The good news is that stress testing can provide valuable results, because it has to do with extreme events. Mees Pierson said that the scenario it uses on extreme events is dependent on market movements on triggers associated to volatility and liquidity. The institution's executive committee also looks individually at high-risk clients – while it regularly datamines the entire client base.

High-risk clients require the greatest detail because they must not only be followed daily but also control can go on at an hourly pace if necessary. At Mees Pearson, typically, such control involves Monte Carlo simulation under stress conditions. Particularly targeted are:

- changes in volatility; and
- swings in derivatives prices whether these go up or down.

This strategy is followed in recognition of the fact that extreme events can hit hard any institution. Also known as bolt out of the blue (BOB), stress tests are usually associated with a large loss that leads the managers, traders, or investment specialists who are responsible to remark: 'I never thought of that!'

To my experience, the best way to learn about extreme events and their aftermath is to examine in the most critical manner: What has happened to others, how they restructured their risks, and how they altered their management practices under stress conditions. Every one of these steps requires detailed but also reliable information – as well as valid assumptions.

Cicero's key questions

Extreme events are uniquely informative about *how, where, when,* and *why* the assumptions, which underlie risk management practices become invalid. When, how, why, when, and where become known, they provide the basis for rejection of the implicit hypothesis that an institution understands the nature and significance of the risks it is taking and it is facing.

These are Cicero's[9] six evidentiary questions, and constitute the crucial queries to be made in the investigation of every risk and of the people behind it:

- *Who,* apart from the person who signed, contributed to or was witness to this decision?

- *How* did the persons involved, alone or by committee, come to this decision?
- *Where* has been the evidence, which led to the commitment being made?
- *When* was this decision originally made, and under *which* conditions?
- *What* exactly the decision involved? Was it subsequently changed or manipulated?
- *Why* was the decision made, which precise goal it targeted or intended to avoid? Was there a conflict of interest?

Of the four types of stress testing, scenario writing is the one best suitable for this investigation. By means of scenario writing, the management of financial institutions has a unique opportunity to extract value from past experience – its own and that of competitors. This requires a policy of investigating and reporting significant surprises and failures in meeting them, in order to establish a documented and factual basis for controlling ongoing risks, and improving future performance.

At a different level of sophistication the stress testing approach that I am suggesting uses the principle of experimental physics. This permits matter-of-fact sensitivity analysis. The principle was first presented by Dr Bernhard Rieman, in his 1854 habilitation dissertation. In the 150 years, which elapsed, it has become a foundation of modern science.

What Rieman essentially said is that once we have discovered and validated a needed new principle of scientific knowledge, we must integrate the best surviving features of our old experience and our new knowledge.

The two should merge into a new set of axiomatic assumptions, featuring the validated new principle. This is a challenge not only for the experimental physicist, but also for those who live and work in the world of finance and economics, because the principle of experimental physics includes design of experiments and test of hypothesis. Therefore, it permits to understand fundamental phenomena in a wide range of activities from physical science to technology, finance, the history of ideas, art, and statecraft.

The Fermi principle

One of the best examples on inference based on experimental spirit is how to approach an order of magnitude solution in connection to a problem with many unknowns. This has been illustrated by Enrico Fermi, who has to his credit one of the major breakthroughs in nuclear science. Dr Fermi asked his students: 'How many piano tuners are there in Chicago?' Part and parcel of this question are: the improbability that anyone knows the answer, and the number of unknowns that it involves.

Like the level of leveraging of hedge funds, and other 'statistics' obsessing the reviewer, this piano tuner problem has no standard solution and that is exactly the point Fermi wanted to make. But it is possible to make assumptions leading to an approximate answer.

- If Chicago's population is five million, an average family consists of four people, and one-tenth of all families own pianos.
- *Then*, there will be 125,000 pianos in the city, a guestimate.

If every piano is tuned once every five years, 25,000 pianos must be tuned each year. If a tuner can service four pianos a day, 250 days a year, this will make a total of 1,000 tunings a year. Therefore, there must be about 25 piano tuners in Chicago.

This answer is not exact. It could be as low as 15 or as high as 40. Enrico Fermi was a physicist and knew about the principle of experimental physics, proof being that he applied it in the most beautiful way. Hedge fund managers will be well advised to learn from this method and adapt it to *their* problem of risk control.

The metaphor of Fermi's piano tuners shows that if at the outset even an order of magnitude answer is unknown, we can proceed on the basis of different hypotheses and arrive at estimates that fall within an acceptable range. This is the secret in building a risk management system connected to a portfolio, which is in flux and contains instruments defying classical analysis methods.

- If our hypotheses and calculations are well done, errors tend to cancel out one another.
- As a whole, it is improbable that all of our deviations from the real value (which is unknown) will be underestimates or overestimates.

This is a basic principle of science. When the work that we do is truly professional, deviations from the correct but unknown values tend to compensate for one another. Therefore the final result will converge towards an order of magnitude, which stands a good chance to be right. The metaphor of Fermi's model fits hand-in-glove financial analysis of events under extreme conditions.

4. Stress testing outliers and nonlinearities

Stress testing is not just the better way to positioning ourselves against the risks of illiquidity and those resulting from globalisation; it is the only valid way. Let me start with a reference, which has the potential of being explosive. The first year of the new millennium became one of global financial crisis as analysts, bankers, and investors realised that, in the year 2000, the magnitude of financial assets reached US$400 trillion while the GDP of the world stood at US$30 trillion (one-third of this is the GDP of the United States)

- These US$400 trillion need servicing. To keep the economy running, reserve banks of the Group of Ten are obliged to continue pumping liquidity into the market.
- The criterion of 'how much' liquidity should be made available is that to avoid illiquidity at all cost. This is what the reserve banks of the Group of Ten did on the aftermath of September 11.

This was a step function in injecting liquidity, hence a nonlinear response (more on this later). Normally, liquidity in a market-wide sense is obtained by either flooding the market with new money, and/or reducing interest rates and capital reserve requirements which speed up the velocity of circulation of money. Both represent a change of policy affecting the macromarkets, and both can lead to inflation. Sometimes, however, there is no other way.

Since illiquidity followed by pumping liquidity in and out of the system has its risks, many reserve banks advise the financial institutions under their jurisdiction to drive hard in testing assets and liabilities under stress conditions, including that illiquidity. The supervisors themselves plan to conduct stress tests on a global scale. Behind much of these system tests lies the presumption that:

- we must always be alert to exceptional events which can upset all known balances; and
- we should appreciate that some of the events, which take place may have no precedence.

Rethink the cause and effect relationship

All banks and all hedge funds managers need to subject their assets and liabilities to tests of nonlinearities between *cause* and *effect*. This aids both themselves and their investors. The task is challenging and it is not easy, primarily because stress testing requires that we change mindset. Let me take two examples, of which the first is the simpler one: stress testing for outliers and stress testing for nonlinearities.

In stress testing, the risk manager selects a set of likely but rather extreme moves for key market parameters. He then subjects the trading book, banking book or a given portfolio to those moves – for instance events at 5, 10, or 15 standard deviations – measuring the simulated change in portfolio value.

In some institutions, the board or senior management endorses a table of market moves that is compiled by computing standard valuation changes. More or less, this is nonsense because the repetition of similar scenarios makes the stress testing exercise too bureaucratic. The board should establish the:

- Direction
- Guidelines
- Crucial variables it wishes to see tested; and
- some milestone values.

But the stress tests should be made with an open mind largely outside previous 'standards'. They should be conducted by the director of risk management together with rocket scientists. Such tests may use traders as part time advisors but they should be independent of trading desks to avoid different influences.

In principle, risk managers should be given the freedom to conduct their own analyses and experiments as well as introduce new critical facts to the study of exposure. The intraday control of risk is too dynamic to be run through preprogrammed tables even if the past can serve only as guidance. Among the guidelines for testing market risk through stress tests are:

- steepening and flattening of yield curves by XX basis points (10, 20, ... 50 or more);
- changes in interest rate spreads; changes in swaps spreads;
- increase and decrease in 1-, 2-, 3-month volatilities by XX per cent of prevailing levels;
- increase and decrease in one currency's exchange values against other major currencies by XX;
- increase and decrease in equity index values by 5, 10, 15, and 20 per cent;
- the synergy of increase and decrease in currency exchange and equity index volatilities; and
- the synergy of liquidity and volatility changes.[10]

The challenge of nonlinearities

The challenge of stress testing to the classical mindset is greater when it comes to nonlinearities. 'Anything linear is probably wrong', says Joel Moses, Dean of the School of Architecture and Planning, MIT. 'In complex systems you usually have feedback loops. In R&D, we've long had this notion of a linear chain from basic research to product development, and we know that that's wrong. Unfortunately, not enough people operate as if they know it's wrong'.[11]

What Moses says is valid in physics, in engineering, and in finance. Scientists studying nonlinear dynamics, that is, the equations that describe irregular motion, have found that predictions about the future are greatly dependent on initial conditions – and on the present status.

- Two situations identical in all but the smallest detail will develop to utterly different conclusions.
- This is the principle behind what is often called a deterministic chaos.[12]

Classical financial theory perceives a company as a black box, which has inputs and outputs, the latter being the result of production functions. The relations characterising inputs to outputs are taken to be mostly linear which in some cases is an approximation, and in others it is outright wrong. In reality, the large majority of input-to-output relations are nonlinear. Therefore, one of the major problems in modelling financial products and markets is the nonlinear and non-stationary phenomena of the economy. This should definitely be reflected in stress tests.

The mindset of people who become stress-testing specialists must change because today practically all of the existing models work on linear trajectories and use statistical estimates of hypothetical stationary processes. That is the region of changes, which can be fairly easily approximated, but often the approximation ends by being misleading.

For instance, the sort of events which have characterised the phenomena in the Far East booming economies in the 1997/98 timeframe happened just at some switching points of nonlinear trajectories reflecting sudden changes of continuity. At those points, typical chaotic, if not catastrophic, behaviour is to be expected with:

- bifurcations;
- big changes in direction; and
- avalanches due to seemingly minor effects.

Such phenomena are well known from nonlinear mechanics and from mathematical theory. The basic ideas behind them are about a century old, starting with Poincaré, Ljapunov, and others. Refinements have been made in the last two to three decades and these offer a wide spectrum of possibilities, which can be better exploited, and appreciated, in the context of stress tests.

5. The mindset required for historical and hypothetical stress tests

> 'Stress testing is a method of risk reduction/management for fund managers, not really something that an institutional investor would be doing,' said a reviewer, immediately thereafter implying that a pension fund manager – like himself – has no use for stress tests.

This is an awfully wrong hypothesis. An institutional investor who keeps bonds and equities – without leverage and without derivatives – would find stress tests helpful in getting insight. By contrast, an institutional investor, or any other party going for alternative investments *deadly needs to do* stress testing. In terms of risk control, he will be absolutely blind without it.

> 'In this case, we need to be clear about this, but also provide other strategies for managing the potential risks from the manager's and investor's perspective,' insisted the reviewer.

By 'other', the reviewer probably means classical type tests that, as explained, are impotent with alternative investments and their potential risks. I find it sometimes difficult to explain that alternative investments are not for the faint hearted. *If* one finds it difficult to change his way of looking at risk by adopting a very rigorous attitude, *then* he better not become a prisoner of speculation and leverage.

> 'We need something here also about the limits of stress testing', continued the reviewer, 'how stress testing should be/can be used in combination with other risk assessment tools, so that it is not presented as a fait accompli for risk management'.

Nobody ever said that stress testing is a 'fait accompli', but it is a tool more powerful than the now classical testing methods. Of course, nobody is obliged to use stress testing. As explained in the previous sections, much depends on the complexity, leverage, and risks of the instruments with which one deals – and on his or her knowledge and skill to apply stress tests.

Indeed, on second thought, knowledge and skill alone are not enough because stress testing is based on both conceptual premises and mathematical models. Unfortunately, this book lacks the scope to describe the advanced statistical and mathematical tools in detail.[13] Instead, I take some examples of the type of practical stress tests that become necessary in a global economy that is characterised by:

- high leverage;
- on-and-off illiquidity; and
- an unprecedented amount of risk.

This risk is the result of several risk factors, which usually come into play. Typically, a *stress test scenario* would contain simultaneous moves in different *risk factors*. For instance two or more of the following:

- equity prices;
- interest rates;
- currency exchange rates; and
- commodity prices.

Ideally, the stress test would be designed as an *experiment* to reflect an event that the financial institution and its experimenters believe may occur in foreseeable future, prompted by a trigger, such as the collapse of a major institution, a political reason, or other outlier.

Down to basics, while the timing of such event may be hypothetical, the nature of the test may be based on a significant market twist experienced in the past, even if a rare one. This is a *historical stress test*, which examines analytically the aftermath of:

- a really exceptional happening; and/or
- a major change in market conditions.

Alternatively, the stress test may be based on a plausible market event, an outlier that has not yet taken place. This case is known as a *hypothetical stress test*, and it is essentially a *what if* scenario where the 'what' is usually something exceptional:

- the failure of a big hedge fund, like LTCM, is a historical scenario because such event took place in 1998;
- the bankruptcy of a major money centre bank with retail and wholesale operations around the globe is a hypothetical scenario.

The bankruptcies of the Bank of New England and of Continental Illinois, among others, are no precedents in global banking, the way we know it today, because while both were super-regional neither was a truly global player. By contrast, LTCM, Enron, and WorldCom – each in its own line of business – have been global players.

Even if the difference between historical and hypothetical stress tests is not always clear-cut, there is an urgency for factual and well-documented policies and practices on stress testing the potential impact of a catastrophe scenario on big banks, institutional investors and their portfolios. This is emphasised by the fact the Group of Seven (G-7) has been planning to conduct a *drill* in 2002. That is the first joint field test of coordinating measures aimed at:

- minimising panic in case of a major meltdown; and
- preventing a domino effect if megabanks and huge hedge funds collapse.

Below the level of a drill for global meltdown are other valuable tests to be undertaken by investment banks, commercial banks, and other institutions. These should include alternative investments and must focus on identifying weaknesses in the books: of the bank(s) making the drill, of its (their) correspondent banks, and of hedge funds to which it (they) made loans.

All four types of stress tests outlined in the previous sections are critical in regard to macromarkets and investments connected to them. They should involve all factors influencing the behaviour of financial markets: globalisation, deregulation, technology, and innovation. Most particularly, they should be focusing on the junction of growing business opportunity and every greater amount of risk, as Figure 8.4 suggests.

It is unavoidable that drills undertaken under this wider perspective will require educated guesswork expressed by means of hypotheses. For instance, in the 21 September 2001 teleconferencing at Merrill Lynch, Monte Carlo, on the state of the economy, which included macromarkets, Isaac Souede, the CEO of Permal, was to say that the dramatic events of September 11 made the recession deeper and more powerful. Therefore, he foresaw:

- minus 2 per cent growth of the US economy in the third quarter 2001;
- minus 3–4 per cent growth of the US economy in the fourth quarter 2001; and
- minus 3–4 per cent growth of the European economy in the first quarter 2002.

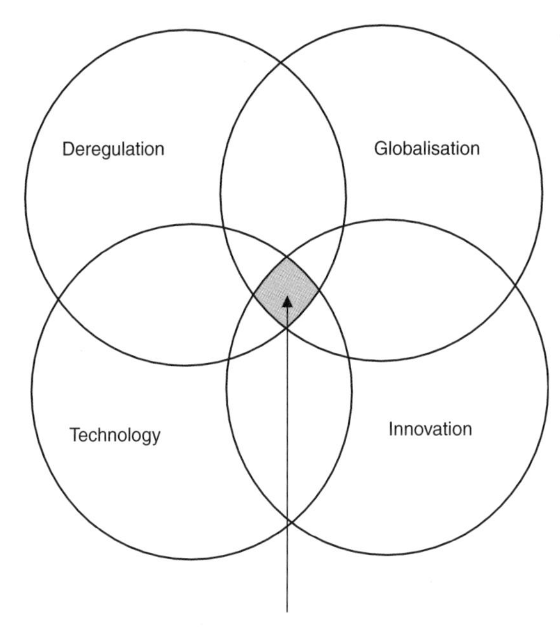

Figure 8.4 The main forces propelling rapid growth of business opportunity in finance and other industrial sectors.

These estimates were subsequently revised as monetary policy became more accommodating and the United States' government took measures, which amounted to an economic stimulus. Also it became evident that, while the US public was scared, it did not panic.

This is a different way of saying that values entering a stress test can change on short notice. To decide on tolerances and limits for risk management purposes, senior management need to go beyond the positive or negative growth projections and tackle the:

- issue of timing; and
- state of the macroeconomy.

Let me add that stress testing can be applied across the industrial spectrum. Manufacturing companies have the option of postponing new production runs till existing inventories are cleared out of the pipeline. The less they can predict future developments, the more reserved they will be in new manufacturing activities. Stress tests assist in developing worst-case scenarios which help to define how much more expensive their commitments will be *if* there is a high degree of uncertainty about their ability to pump their produce up the supply line.

The statement made in this last paragraph is applicable to hedge funds and all other financial institutions. Management should be keen to know the results of stress tests on credit risk and market risk inventoried in the entity's portfolio as soon as the evaluation is made. This must be a daily exercise, with intraday flashes as the situation warrants when markets are nervous, liquidity is low, or there are other reasons to believe that some miscalculation may have unexpected consequences for the entity and its investors.

6. Stress testing different types of risk

If the Enron and WorldCom mega-bankruptcies gave any clear signal, this is that reputational risk is a basic component of all other types of risk because it finds itself at their intersection. We do not have available, at least at the present time, stress tests for reputational risk. Yet, these would have been welcome because all businesses may be confronted with reputational and brand name risk (see Chapter 3).

Classically, credit risk present in the domain of reputational risk more than market risk, though the latter's share is on the increase. The same is true of legal risk, which is part of operational risk.

Malfeasance, including CEO malfeasance, is another reason for reputational risk. Since the Code of Hammurabi, in the eighteenth century BC, governments, regulators, and the courts (through jurisprudence) have added several factors to the roster, which leads to reputational risk:

- a lack of transparency, and with it the keeping of double books;
- an absence of clarity regarding conflict(s) of interest;
- lack of compliance and legal manipulations which might be uncovered too late; and
- inability to match the market moves compounded by highly leveraged positions that could wipe out the firm's capital.

Reputational risk and legal risk correlate. Apart from explaining the intricacies of legal risk, Chapter 3 has also shown that legal risks migrate and sometimes they combine with technology risks (also part of operational risk) to shake down management.

No stress tests are available to permit investigating this junction of several distinct risks, mainly because hard data is not available. Theoretically, because of lack of transparency, stress tests on the reputational risk of a fund of funds are nearly impossible. Over the course of my research, it has become apparent that monitoring every moment what hedge funds do with their portfolio, and therefore with alternative investment instruments sold to end-investors, is virtually impossible.

- There is a huge range of hedge fund strategies and nearly random market moves, which can upset even the best laid-out plan.
- But there might be coming a breach in the teflon coating of a secretive fund of funds' façade, and this should be exploited.

The breach in the teflon of hedge funds secrecy

The breach comes from the fact that to ease end-investors' fears, banks and SAIVs have the habit of printing a long list of entities working with them. As we have already seen, a list of 10 or 20 names is not unusual, and most of them suggest that they are the practitioners of 'scientific' investment policies. Practically, therefore, stress testing the reputational risk of a pool of funds of funds is easier than it sounds.

- The stress test must examine what would happen if 1, 2, or 3 hedge funds in that pool fail.
- Would the reputational risk for the whole alternative investment instrument explode? Will there be a hard landing?

Prospective investors need to be aware that behind the glamorous sounding names of the leveraged entities in the pool may be medium-size companies and one-man operations, with vastly divergent abilities to actively monitor and reallocate assets among investment styles, regions and asset classes. To be worthy of their salt, such relocations must be based on an ongoing assessment of global market conditions. At the same time, to survive these small entities need to:

- encounter in the longer run higher liquidity and lower volatility than is today the case; and
- be able to capture much of the upside performance while preserving capital on the downside.

A stress test would evaluate the hypothesis of whether or not they can do so. Alternative investments is a kind of financial acrobatics and the fact that transparency is minimum, or outright non-existent, is not only bad for the investors but also for the hedge funds and merchandisers of risk themselves, including SAIVs and commercial banks. The lower their visibility, the more likely they are to stumble in their deals. This is the reason why regulators look at transparency as the best way for *market discipline*.

> 'Hold information close to their chests – this is true of most hedge funds, although this is changing through the imperative of attracting institutional investors,' said a reviewer.

Till now this has been more wishful thinking than real life. Single-handed institutional investors cannot change the hedge funds. They need regulatory action to bring greater transparency or, alternatively, the panic created by some big hedge fund failures.

In the meantime, in the absence of hard data, stress tests should use experimental design and account for the fact that financial analysts are worried about high gearing. They also question some operational features of hedge funds, which provide for a culture of disincentives to posting small losses before they become a torrent.

Beware of mispricing

Stress tests should also focus on the risk of mispricing, by itself and in conjunction to gearing. These two issues correlate. One of the reasons for over-leverage by hedge funds is the fact that they are unlike traditional asset managers who in many cases receive (in good and bad years alike) a fixed percentage of the assets they administer.

The process of mispricing has some built-in incentives. All hedge fund managers, and in many cases their traders, are paid a direct percentage of the gains, which at times becomes a perverse set of personal incentives. In other cases, their compensation comes almost exclusively from the fund's profits. Since the absolute return dictates the fee:

- there is always a trend to mispricing instruments;
- at the same time, managers who post losses for a given year earn nothing.

Some hedge funds go further in their offer to lock-in clients. They assure them that they will resume payments to their own managers and traders only when a given investment goes beyond its historical high. This means that the asset manager must not only recoup the losses that come along but also exceed the previous profit level. This is called a *high-water market strategy*, and it is extremely dangerous because it pushes traders to take higher levels of risk.

The timing of financial reporting information also leaves much to be desired. There are no accounts of gains and losses, let alone quarterly reports, neither are there any estimates by analysts regarding profit figures. Gains, if any, are paid only at the end of a two- or three-year

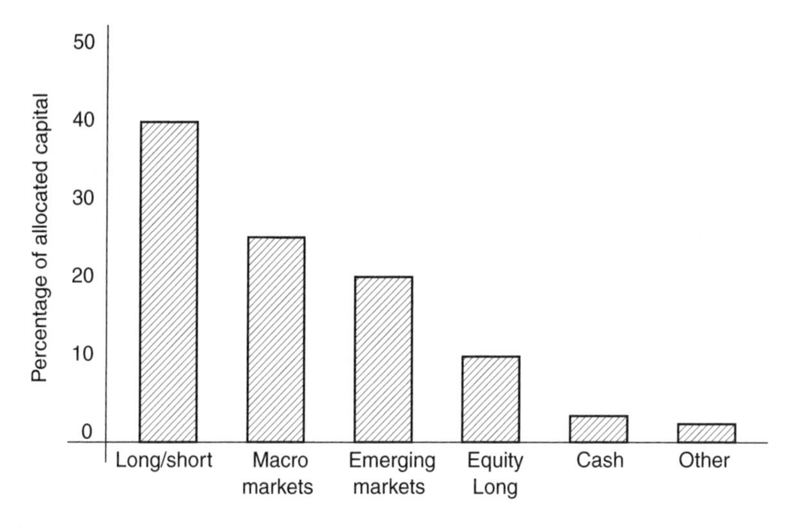

Figure 8.5 Asset allocation by one of the hedge funds with significant exposure to volatility.

period, which means that both the capital and the paper profits are at risk during that whole timeframe. Two stress tests are appropriate in this connection:

- will the company survive the three years? (a credit risk issue); and
- will the current strategy prevail three years down the line? Will it be able to adapt?

Problems of leveraging and of personal accountability

A most interesting stress test can be designed around the hypothesis that high leveraging and the associated exposure embedded in an alternative investment, would be enough to wipe out the investor's capital. Leverage and shorting can significantly alter overall returns as shown in Figure 8.5, which comes from a hedge fund. This should be kept in mind by investors who consider alternative investments as a method of diversification. In this asset allocation:

- the largest share, by far, is taken by long/short trades with all that this represents in exposure;
- next to it comes capital allocation to macromarkets;
- emerging growth claims third position, now that technology, media, and telecommunications have fallen from grace; and

- the next big chunk is emerging markets, which can be unpredictable: think of the East Asia meltdown in 1997 and Russia's bankruptcy the following year.

I have investigated this and other asset allocations to identify some of the best portfolio managers and strategies. This is a due-diligence process to select outstanding independent investment people in various categories, for instance, persons with different global or regional focus or objectives. Major hedge funds do exactly this. They interview more than one hundred potential investment managers each year, maintain a detailed database of potential candidates, and constantly monitor their existing managers.

- The CEOs of the better-run hedge funds say that they 'have to find the best managers and use them the best possible way'.
- But it is not possible to do that with 4,000–6,000 different hedge funds, big and small. As a result, everything has a tendency to become average.

Henry Ford once said, 'a committee cannot drive a company, like a committee cannot drive a car'. A leveraged, risk-taking hedge fund cannot optimise its risks and return through the averages of multi-style positions. Apart from the risk of misallocation of funds through averages, averages help precious little in terms of preservation of assets. Regarding assets and liabilities associated to alternative investments, there are also some other factors to consider, for instance, the instruments being sold by the merchandisers of risk are *not* rated by an independent agency.

7. Ways and means for exercising damage control

When it comes to alternative investments, which are by definition non-transparent, the investor's first move towards damage control in the event of high volatility should be to daily calculate capital at risk and withdraw from the investment if necessary, provided the clauses of the contract allow it and the instrument is liquid. The problem is that, with alternative investments, in the majority of cases their liquidity is low. This is a circular challenge:

- if an investment is non-transparent, you do not know at what point damage control becomes necessary;
- if there is, in addition, no liquidity, how can you withdraw from the investment?

Is there anything practical to be done? Let us address the question of liquidity, first. In mid-2001, one large financial institution offered me, as an individual investor, a pallet of alternative investment instruments. I asked the managing director who contacted me whether the institution was underwriting my capital, since the offer stipulated that capital preservation was guaranteed. His response was in the negative. Capital preservation was my stress test.

In some alternative investments offers I have received, there has been a curious clause about the form of delivery. What the investor receives is a sort of *global certificate*, which does not give the right to request an audit of individual instruments – yet these audits could be determinant of redemption price. Each end-investor would instead receive an amount of cash corresponding to the fair value of one underlying share. But there are problems with both transparency and accuracy in calculating the final redemption price:

- this 'fair value' is to be determined by the aggregator of risk, not by the market; and
- from that 'fair value' are to be subtracted the transaction costs, fees, premiums, commissions, and so on.

This is a 'win–win' situation for the issuer, but quite uncertain and unfavourable for the investor. Besides this, the use of the term *fair value* by the merchandisers of risk is utterly unfair to the end investor, for not to say outright that it stinks.

The FASB defines as fair value the market value set by a willing seller and a willing buyer under other than fire sale conditions. With alternative investments free market principles do not apply. The pseudo-fair value is set by the merchandiser of risk who acts as a dictator having got hold of other people's money.

One banker who wanted to sell me one of these investments saw that I was hesitant and produced an alternative. This was a structured instrument, a performance-linked note, which was not quoted anywhere. It was priced OTC, and it was managed by a number of hedge funds, each being assigned a quota from 2.5 to 7.5 per cent. (Each hedge fund is expected to manage that amount from the fund capital investors put into the fund of funds).

As every investor should know, structured finance transactions pool assets and transfer all or part of credit risk borne by the originator to the new investors – that is, the clients – who buy these instruments. In some cases, guarantors assume part of the credit risk embedded in structured instruments. With the offer I received, there were no guarantors, which is a rather general case with alternative investments. In this case, too, my query as to whether the salesman's bank would provide a guarantee to assure at least the capital, met with a negative.

- The credit institution selling the instrument acted as its designer (risk aggregator) and intermediary (merchandiser).
- This was not a product with principal protection. The institution that offered it assumed none of the risk. Indeed, it was eager to transfer to somebody else the likelihood of default.

These references are crucial to any investor who would like to be able to exercise damage control. When I studied the banker's offer, it was evident that the risks I was presented with were in no way compensated by the projected returns – a fact often unclear to the end-investor, whether an individual or an institution. Further, the promotional material I was given included the statement that:

> [This] investment has the same potential for gains or loss as a comparable investment in the underlying basket of non-traditional strategies.

This statement manages to be at the same time highly incoherent and false. What the bank suggested was a multi-style, non-traditional strategy whose gains and losses (particularly the latter) can be much higher than those of the underlier. In these and similar cases, tracking the risk is very complex, and it requires lots of skills as well as on-line database mining and real-time data streams.

In another case, where the capital was guaranteed, I built a model, which would have been able to track the investment's key components, then asked the bank selling the instrument to update it daily. The bank refused, saying that they did not get this information from the hedge funds in the first place, and therefore they were not in a position to provide it to end-investors.

Here is in a nutshell the stress test, which would have taken place if this information was forthcoming. The first step is to assume a leverage factor transpiring behind the alternative investment and based on experience as well as on the answers obtained to focused questions. Using this leverage factor, and some other criteria, the stress test should shift to the left of the distribution of past returns, by one or two standard deviations.

A shift by one standard deviation may be acceptable in a friendly market trending north, but the experimenter must be ready to shift by two (or more) standard deviations to the left, if the market turns ugly.[14]

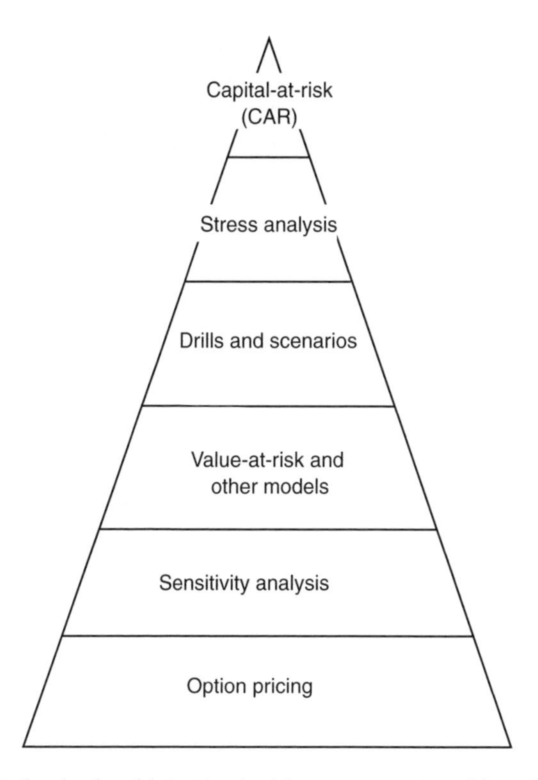

Figure 8.6 Six levels of sophistication in risk management models and procedures.

Note that within plus or minus one standard deviation from the mean is the highest frequency of the distribution; and the next highest frequency is between one and two standard deviations. The following step is to establish the triggers, which will give the warning sign for redemption.

Within the frame of reference which I have described, Figure 8.6 shows six levels of sophistication in risk management models and associated implementation procedures. All of them are vital to damage control. As a policy, quantitative methods should be complemented by qualitative approaches which account for risk factors not easy to model, such as the currency and credit crisis which gripped South America in mid-2001.

8. Is delta hedging and gamma hedging a solution?

In researching this book, I have encountered assertions that *rocket scientists* would undertake delta hedging on products, where it was apparent that some of the critical factors going into delta and gamma hedging were irrelevant to the nature of the product being sold. As a general statement, delta and gamma hedging are great in theory, but the deliverables do not always offer what they are supposed to give.

(For starters, delta hedging is a process, which requires not just analytics and real-time systems, but also a close-watch of price movements, transactions to compensate for increased risk, and liquid markets. Many vital factors come into play when banks combine the credit risk of loaning money to hedge funds with the market risk of their underlying investments, which are not necessarily covered by delta and gamma hedging.)

Some institutions seek a sort of protection in zero-coupon bonds. Others forego the investment in zero-coupon bonds by computing what they believe to be *virtual zero-coupons*. With the decline in interest rates, the virtual zero-coupon structures demand a higher proportion of the capital to protect the investment, leaving less to invest in the hedge fund deals. In turn, this reduces the would-be profits. Therefore, some institutions forego even the virtual protection by taking additional unhedged risks.

I have also encountered numerous other examples of similar practices in hedge funds, indicating at best ignorance on the part of salesmen about the products they are selling, and an evident reliance on investors being unable to press pertinent points. Essentially, there are no investment strategies that can protect the investor from all the dangers that exist in leveraged instruments sold in the market, regardless of any oral 'guarantee' to deliver the goods.

Due to these reasons, investors who go for this sort of deals are *risk buyers*, and it is essential that they should only assume those risks that they understand. They should use rigorous analytical approaches – including stress testing as described in this chapter – to reach a realistic estimate of market risk and of default, thereafter:

- sizing downwards the estimates of expected gains they have been given by the vendor; and
- sizing upwards credit risk, market risk, and operational risk.

Dr Alan Greenspan, the Federal Reserve chairman, told the Senate Banking Committee in one hearing, that the banking industry faces deterioration in asset quality, requiring bank supervisors to step up their scrutiny. While the banking industry has positioned itself in a way that it can greatly benefit from the advantages of globalisation, its leverage ensures that it suffers when the global financial health deteriorates.

For instance on 25 July 2002, Moody's Investors Service changed its outlook of J.P. Morgan Chase from positive to negative. Moody's gave the reasons for this decision:

- The assets quality in the bank's portfolio deteriorated.
- The credit institution was too much concentrated in telecommunications, media, and technology.
- There has been some damage in the bank's image and brand name.

This deteriorating assets quality of financial institutions often finds its way into alternative investments, and from there into the portfolio of end-investors. That is why the latter should always conduct stress tests and ingeniously develop worst-case scenarios to make sure that when worst comes to worst they can still preserve their assets.

Other risks of which the end-investor should be aware when considering alternative investments in a financial environment characterised by increasing globalisation as well as on-and-off illiquidity, have so far escaped stress tests. These are:

- Information concerning the strategic nature of such investments, in conjunction with their place of origin.

Persons and companies purchasing and selling assets in an alternative investment scheme should understand that the originator and its trading advisor will have absolute rights on selection procedures, design issues, timing, pricing, and other transactional characteristics which affect the value of the assets.

- The fact that subscribers are usually allocated very limited rights.

Contrary to the practice with exchange-traded securities, shares in alternative investments and other types of secretive assets generally have no voting rights. Therefore, their holders cannot exercise any management or control functions with respect to strategic moves, investment policies, and day-to-day operations – which are absolutely in the hands of hedge funds.

- There is only limited redemption of shares or other types of assets.

As I mentioned in regard to other issues concerning this sort of investing, shares will only be redeemable at the time specified in the contract. This not only means that the cash being paid becomes an illiquid asset, but also there is significant credit risk. When redemption time comes, the hedge fund may well have gone bust or lost most of its capital. However, different funds have different policies in regard to limited redemption of shares, and this should be investigated prior to commitment.

- The transferability of shares is limited or non-existent.

The ability of shareholders to sell all or a portion of their shares to qualified potential purchasers depends both on the clauses of the contract and upon current demand. There can be no guarantee that even if trading in shares is permitted by the contract, a market for such shares will successfully develop or that trading will not occur at a price well below NAV, if there is one.

> 'It is true that most hedge funds are unsuitable for widows and orphans, yet these contracts are designed by the lawyers of the hedge funds managers and buyers, most of whom are sophisticated investors (or like to think that they are), can take it or leave it,' said a reviewer.[15]

That is a fabulous stress test. *If*, and only if, the esoteric papers – written by lawyers working for a hedge fund, bank, or SAIV and its alternative investments, can be read and understood – in terms of risk and return – by Aunt Agatha, other widows and orphans, *then*, and only then, other investors should consider them. By 'other investors' I mean those who are sophisticated, or think they are, as the reviewer has suggested, including light-hearted pension funds and endowments.

Of all people, the person who thought about this type of stress test was Adolf Hitler. As I heard from Albert Speer, whom I interviewed after he made it out of the Spandau prison where he was interned for war crimes after the Nuremberg trial, Hitler had in his headquarters in East Prussia a sample of the most stupid soldiers that could be found in the Germany army.

The mission of these fellows was to read and understand each order which came out of HQ and send to the German field marshals and generals. Hitler believed that if a stupid soldier could not understand an order in the quiet environment of headquarters, a field marshal at the front would not understand it either.

That is an opportunity for Aunt Agatha to become advisor to hedge funds, SAIVs, and funds of funds. All she needs as extra luggage is training in *consumer protection acts* which exist practically in all western countries but are so often bypassed or outright forgotten.

9

Highly Leveraged Institutions, Regulators, and the New Lenders of Last Resort

1. Introduction

Globalisation and liquidity are pillars of modern capitalism, but there are unwritten laws as well. The first law of capitalism relates to globalisation. It says money will migrate to the business environment it considers to inspire more confidence and/or where the highest return is to be had.

- The pressure is relentless on money managers to care for the assets entrusted to them, and to better their past performance.
- One of the problems is that so much money pursuing relatively few alternative investment strategies reduces the potential returns to everyone.

There is no evidence that pursuing strategies such as arbitraging the statistical difference between one convertible bond and another eliminates market inefficiencies, or provides for sustained long-term returns. But there is plenty of reason to believe that a steady pressure on the most successful companies to continue their performance, such as fast growth despite the increase in their size following years of rapid development, leads to new inefficiencies.

This demanding environment is known as the *new economy*,[1] and it includes companies benefiting directly or indirectly from high technology: computers, communications, energy, and sophisticated software – and from extensive usage of the most advanced electronic systems, digitisation, the Internet as well as from novel financial instruments. By contrast, that section of the economy still embedded in classical business models: bread and butter financing, and old-fashioned production, purchasing, inventory management, or marketing, is labelled *old economy*.

'The new economy is a bit passé nowadays', said a reviewer.

If the new economy is passé, *then* alternative investments are dead in the water, because they are the wild kids of the new economy. However, down to basics, it is nearsighted to state that an economy based on high technology is 'passé'.

The railroads, which changed the economy of the mid- to late nineteenth century, went through many financial ups and downs. They also led to major financial crises, particularly in the United States. Yet, the railroad industry has made major contributions – and not only in transportation. The large amount of capital necessary to finance railroad construction in America has been at the root of the invention of capital markets, and this industry always bounced back to become the motor of what was *then* the new economy.

Many cognisant people today think of the new economy of the early twenty-first century as the latest metamorphosis of capitalism engineered by globalisation, deregulation, and technology. Capitalism's newly found vitality is a novel combination of open markets, rapid innovation, personal incentives, as well as fiscal and monetary policies that help to keep inflation low and limit the cost of money. In this evolving economy, companies that care for their survival:

- use financial strength to accelerate growth, while continuing to dominate the markets they serve; and
- build quality products, seeing to it their facilities are furnished with the best in equipment and tools for their staff.

Companies that do not take seriously the need to steadily adapt to business evolution and re-invent themselves do not survive. This is particularly true since the mid- to late 1980s. Survivability is also in doubt among companies which do not care or do not know how to be in charge of their *risks*. Down to the bottomline, this is precisely what is wrong with funds of funds, many hedge funds, SAIVs, and even credit institutions. This is, as well, what makes scary alternative investments and puts in doubt the future of capital invested in them.

2. Alternative investments and twenty-first century risks

Any reference to the first decade of the twenty-first century economy is also a reference to the able and steady management of risk. While the forces propelling the new environment are usually associated with economic growth and development that appears to go beyond time-established (therefore conventional) economic thinking, they also involve a great amount of exposure:

- since the beginning of time risk is often associated with fast growth; and
- new financial instruments have plenty of unknowns embedded in them.

To its proponents, the notions adding up to the new economy and its effects can be found at the intersection of social systems, physical assets, financial liabilities, and technology that affect the activities of specific industries and, most particularly, the service sector. To its critics, this approach to economic thinking would not make sense unless there is a new comprehensive, coherent, and efficient economic theory to sustain it. The truth lies somewhere in-between.

Such theory is not yet here. What there is, is amassed virtual wealth that dissolves as the equities indices dive. Down to the bottomline, wealth and the rate of growth are important yardsticks of performance. What the new capitalism is after is an optimisation of risk and return. But is risk appropriately managed? The answer is not self-evident because of the uncertainties of growing exposure: technical, financial, and social. All these references are important because the new economy is about:

- exponential technology;
- derivatives financial instruments; and
- increasing-return high-risk economics.

Central banks and other regulatory authorities have to develop a policy in the supervision of derivatives trades, the control of the leveraged wave of risk, and the alternative investments into which both preceding references are embedded. The growing amount of exposure is a direct reflection of the fact that, as George Soros suggests, one of the main uses of derivatives is to circumvent regulations.[2] Soros has the experience to know about what he is talking.

Regulation and the aftermath of excessive volatility

The globalisation of derivatives trades and of alternative investments at large, leads to an excessive amount of volatility in underlying commodities – as demonstrated by the crash of the bond market in March 1994 and of the continuing downtrend in the stock market from late March 2000 to today (December 2002). Many experts consider excessive volatility to be harmful, but there is no solution for dealing with it.

Since derivatives trades are global, regulation, too, should take place globally, which means throughout the world's financial markets. All derivatives traded OTC by banks, by treasurers, and by any type of funds, ought to be registered with the Bank for International Settlements and directly supervised by the Basle Committee. Today, with macromarkets, emerging markets, and other instruments, derivatives trades – and with them alternative investments – escape any single regulator's supervision.

Not only is risk management a different proposition with derivative financial instruments, because many of them are custom-made, novel, and include many unknowns but also – to the opinion of several experts – derivatives may be hiding bank failures which accumulate and might hit the economy all at once. Based on US statistics, Figure 9.1 shows a high correlation between the rapid growth of derivatives and a sharp drop in bank failures, because weak financial conditions have become much less transparent.

Another 'must' is personal accountability. According to new SEC regulations, post-Enron and post-WorldCom, CEOs and CFOs have to vouch their company's financial statement. Why should not hedge funds' and SAIVs' CEOs, as well as the chief executives of banks who

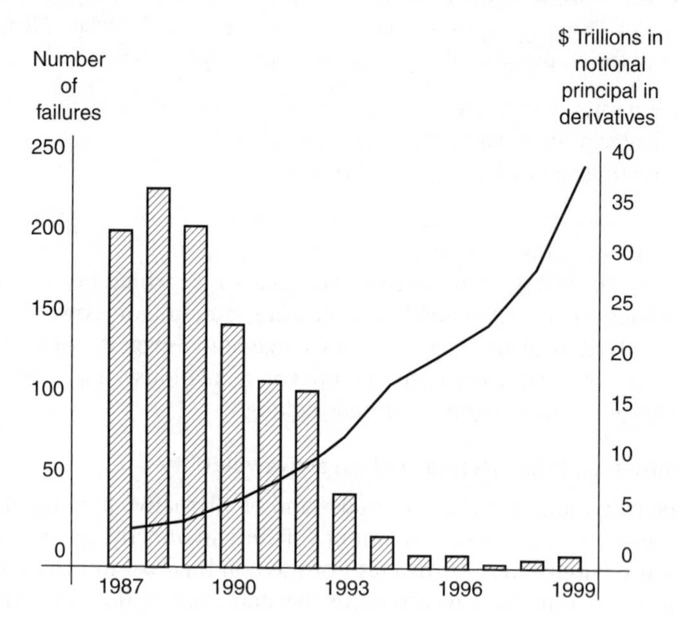

Figure 9.1 An interesting trend on bank failures and the growth of derivatives in the US market.

commercialise alternative investments, be responsible in the same way for promises made to investors, financial statements and statistics on past performance concerning their companies?

The issue of personal accountability

Personal accountability should be closely associated to the ability of putting all risks into perspective, and being able to present strategies to effectively manage them. The risks associated with leveraged financial instruments, derivatives, and alternative investments can be manageable not by 'risk reduction strategies' involving even more leverage, but through:

- a code of ethics;
- rigorous regulation; and
- real-time technology.

Some stock exchanges have taken a most welcome initiative regarding personal accountability. An example is the Toronto Stock Exchange which requires listed companies to disclose their approach to corporate governance in their annual reports, or information circulars, and make in this disclosure reference to published guidelines. The board and CEO, says the Toronto Stock Exchange, should *explicitly* assume responsibility for stewardship of the corporation and, as part of the overall stewardship, *assume responsibility* for:

- adoption of a strategic planning process;
- identification of principal risks;
- implementation of appropriate systems to manage those risks;
- succession planning, including appointing, training and monitoring management;
- a communications policy (read: transparency); and
- the integrity of internal control and management information systems.

A global adoption of this sound policy is urgently necessary because, as it can be extrapolated from past experiences:

- there will be steady controversy on the best way to judge the whims of the new economy; and
- there will be new types of risks, as well as a metamorphosis of old ones giving them much greater rigor.

Alternative investments are an example on the message carried by this second bullet. Chapter 8 brought home the notion that, in a highly leveraged economy, classical risk-testing methods are ineffectual. Therefore, it promoted stress testing.

As the careful reader will recall, in the background of a successful stress testing policy are sophisticated financial modelling solutions, factual and documented assumptions on market behaviour, cross-checks to verify that prices used are valid, ability to project extreme events, real-time computing, on-line datamining, and a plan of action.

A plan of action is an integral part of senior managers' personal accountability and it should be immediately put into effect if the stress test points to risks getting out of control. There are prerequisites to this type of interactive computational finance affecting top management's responsibility and the company's fortunes. These include:

- thorough analysis of each risk;
- definition of the range of stress tests;
- examination of effects of nonlinearities;
- consistency of experimentatal methodology; and
- comprehensive visualisation which is user-friendly.

While not all companies use technology in an able manner, those who position themselves to do so prosper, because they are instrumental in controlling their risks and in trimming their baseline. Wing-to-wing to risk control is cost control: the reduction in middle management layers in other terms organisational fat. Costs matter.

Correlation between different types of risk

For the new economy, a comprehensive view of major risks will involve correlation between two or more among them in ways which, by all likelihood, will be novel. Credit risk, market risk, and operational risk come to mind. The first two are the better known. As we have already seen, operational risk hit the market's eye with the 1999 first draft of the New Capital Adequacy Framework by the Basle Committee. It is a risk which pervades all other areas of exposure,[3] with top factors:

- the skill of managers and professionals, or lack of it;
- the ever more present aftermath of technology;
- execution risk which enters into any transaction;
- legal risk which increases with globalisation; and
- reputational risk which can hit a company at any time.

Even the best credit risk and market risk management systems necessarily exist within an operational risk environment. The New Capital Adequacy Framework advises that in countries subject to sizeable changes in economic conditions and banking practices, supervisors should consider imposing higher capital requirements to take account of operational risk, including legal risks.

Barings crashed due to failure of market risk management within a failure of operational risk control. It is easy to project a similar interaction with credit risk, for instance in the case of collateral. This leads to the conclusion that regulators are justified to want added capital requirements for operational risk. The problem is that nobody has, as yet, clear ideas about the method.

Facing the new economy's recasting of risks in an able manner requires action both at corporate and regulatory levels. At the corporate level, it is necessary to rethink and formalise risk management responsibilities. At the global regulatory level, solutions must be just as focused and they will eventually amount to nothing less than a new international financial architecture replacing Bretton Woods.[4] Recasting supervisory rules and regulations will necessarily demand rigorous answers to three issues:

- whether curbs on capital flows are necessary or are a profoundly bad idea;
- whether greater public resources should be made available to manage financial panics; and
- whether the IMF, BIS (or somebody else) should take on for itself the role of coordinating private-sector responses to a global financial crisis.

Opinions differ, and these differences have as much to do with the new economy as with the nuts and bolts of regulation. The debate over choosing among alternatives would not be resolved anytime soon. The IMF can be a fireman, dealing with crises as it has attempted to do till now, or a policeman aiming to prevent crises from happening. BIS can be the regulatory body; the club of global law makers. Or nothing may be done. In this case, left to its own devices and to tricky financial instruments like alternative investments, the future of the new economy may not be so bright.

3. As a bad precedent, LTCM is a prognosticator of 21st century failures

> One of the reviewers was quite concerned about using the precedent of LTCM, saying: 'Yes, it was a failure, but there have been similar failures in traditional investment houses as well'.

Business failures and lack of transparency correlate. Therefore, this chapter, in fact the whole book, pays a significant amount of attention to transparency and regulation, at present and in the future. Learning from what has gone wrong in the past is vital. As Dr Richard Bellman, one of my professors at UCLA taught his students 50 years ago: 'If we don't learn from the mistakes of the past we are condemned to repeat them'.

Of course, I could have chosen a different reference than LTCM. For instance, Barings. Barings was a venerable bank, not a hedge fund. However, the highly leveraged trades it did in Osaka and Tokyo, out of its Singapore office, were hedge fund stuff – the sort of risky instruments which today find themselves in alternative investments sold to institutional investors and to consumers at a level of *zero-transparency*.

Or, I could have taken as a bad precedent Enron, which also behaved as a hedge fund; Global Crossing, another highly leveraged entity which went bankrupt; WorldCom, tainted by the $3.8 billion scam and at the edge of the abyss; El Paso, whose shares fell by 25 per cent after the apparent suicide of its treasurer brought doubts about the company's finances; Tyco, which lost 30 per cent of its capitalisation in one single day; and a string of lesser company meltdowns. Correctly, *The Economist* has directed new attention to the ills of:

- personal greed;
- lousy accounts; and
- inadequate surveillance.[5]

In its heydays, LTCM was considered to be the Rolls Royce of Wall Street's hedge funds. But the two Nobel Prize winners and other well-known investments experts among its partners and consultants, showed a lack of prudence incompatible with their profession of investment advisors and asset managers. Post-mortem, some financial analysts even suggested that the hedge fund's high fliers could not really appreciate the synergy between market risk, liquidity and volatility.[6]

A mare's nest of self-made misfortunes

LTCM's self-made misfortunes offer an interesting case study because it continues to be the bogey of the hedge fund community, and investors are keen to discover whether the hedge funds, SAIVs, funds of funds, aggregators of risk, and merchandisers of risk have learned the lessons. Many of the macromarkets, emerging economies, and other investments found with LTCM, are alive and well today. The added flavour is the practice of going massively short in a market which changes its mood at an unprecedented pace.

'The world', says Nicola Meaden of Blackstone, 'is very different today than 40 days ago'.[7] There is an extreme volatility in credit markets making credit risk harder to hedge; and a depressed market magnifies the aftermath of strategies such as long-short, relative value, and plain shorting.

Greater risks showing up at faster pace see to it that hedge fund managers and others involved in alternative investments must pay significant attention to the liabilities side of their balance sheet.[8] The management of liabilities is a basic notion in the investment business; lack of it constitutes a source of exposure that increases exponentially with gearing.

- Liquidity risk sees to it that a leveraged institution may be unable to meet financial commitments to its counterparties, leading to credit risk.
- At the same time, price risk affects earnings. It arises from changes in interest rates, currency rates, equity, and commodity prices, as well as in their implied volatility.

Exposures due to liquidity risk and price risk develop in the normal course of business of a financial intermediary, and any other market player. Therefore, a rigorous risk management policy must ensure that there are in place appropriate internal controls and steady oversight by senior management.

In his excellent book *On Money and Markets*, Dr Henry Kaufman says LTCM 'had a derivatives exposure so huge – an estimated US$1.4 trillion – that its crisis threatened the viability of our financial system'.[9] Kaufman also adds that 'surprisingly, the firm's analytical wizards apparently did not take into account some financial market fundamentals'. They failed to understand that:

- sizeable positions in individual securities cannot be liquidated quickly, unless this is done at fire sale prices; and
- even fire sales do not attract buyers with cash when the assets being sold are of weak credit quality.

On these two bullets rests much of the drama at LTCM, Enron, Global Crossing, WorldCom, as well as that of many other highly leveraged companies and financial institutions. When LTCM's fortunes crashed in late September 1998, the hedge fund left gapping holes in major money centre banks, adding up to US$3 billion. Senior bankers know by experience that it is very difficult to fill a financial hole of these proportions, but the Federal Reserve Bank of New York succeeded in making the LTCM's shareholders pay. This was a vastly preferable solution than a fire brigade approach with taxpayer's money. It also created a good precedence, as a new lender of last resort was found: the shareholder in a leveraged deal.

Lack of supervision leads to conflict of interest

In the aftermath of LTCM's debacle, it was revealed that its management had signed up Bear Stearns as clearing agent at very low rates. With a contract stipulating rock-bottom prices, the partners sent much of their trading through Bear Stearns, making themselves the investment bank's largest hedge fund client. In fact, Bear Stearns was not just a clearing agent.

- The broker also handled futures, risk arbitrage, and mortgage trading with LTCM.
- Down to basics, this amounts to a concentration of exposure, if not a conflict of interest.

In its high gearing while sailing under a favourable wind, LTCM capitalised on the absence of supervision. This has not yet changed with hedge funds. The same is true about companies like Enron and WorldCom which use their treasury to speculate, *as if* they were hedge funds.

The salvage of LTCM from the abyss was an unquestionable success engineered at the 12th hour by the regulators. It was the successful outcome of a discrete, but very efficient, intervention by the Federal Reserve Bank of New York. It was also a feasibility test by regulators which should be generalised at a global scale.

The Federal Reserve acted not as a lender of last resort but as a broker, bringing together different distressed parties who were stakeholders. LTCM received a US$3.5 billion bailout from its lenders and trading partners, who were also its shareholders. This was at about the level of estimated billions of losses that had to be immediately covered. It was also the trigger that prompted the Fed to organise the rescue operation.

In all, senior executives from 16 banks and securities firms met with LTCM executives in the New York Federal Reserve Bank. By the time the salvage meeting took place, the hedge fund's net assets had sunk to about US$500 million from US$2.3 billion three weeks earlier; and that US$2.3 billion was what had remained to the overgeared hedge fund after having lost 40 per cent of its capital in the preceding 30 days.

Wall Street experts suggested that:

- for once, the alternatives were linear: receive an infusion of cash or go bust;
- without the support package, LTCM would probably not have been able to make payments to creditors.

The irony was that a great deal of these losses came from John Meriwether's speciality of fixed-income arbitrage, which he pioneered in the 1980s at Salomon Brothers where he and his proteges had become the firm's most profitable traders. Past experience is always helpful, but past bets do not have the same punch under current and future conditions – particularly when one is faced with the constraints resulting from huge loans and exotic derivatives, while at the same time being short of cash.

In 1998, at the 12th hour, the lenders had to advance the money to save LTCM. In 2002 with Enron, Global Crossing, Adelphia, WorldCom and the others, the markets rather than the regulators punished those who got involved and lost in huge leveraged deals as well as in trades whose ethics left much to be wanted. But the markets also punished the investors. As for the government, it saw that:

- many of those involved in conflicts of interest and in plain cheating are brought to justice; and
- new legislation is rushed through Congress to close some of the loopholes in CEO malfeasance.

One can only hope that personal accountability will become the rule. This should include fake promises like those of hedge funds assuring investors that they have devised a financial structure meant to protect them against misfortunes. Such assurances lack substance (see also the Appendix to Chapter 1); they are usually meant as counterweight to a double risk which can be found today with many alternative investments:

- investors have their money locked in for a minimum of two or three years; and
- most borrowing is short term, at maturities of three months to a year.

A lesson from LTCM is that in spite of the assurances that every care was taken about the handling of short-term liquidity problems, when the market turned against the hedge fund's bets its partners:

- could not put on the table the needed money;
- could not borrow; and
- could not get rid of unwanted positions.

As the value of its portfolio fell, LTCM could not reduce the risks that it had taken as fast as it had expected. The toxic waste had taken hold. As a result, its debt–equity ratio rose to levels that made lenders turn the other way, while banks that were owed collateral by LTCM started demanding it 'now'. This is what classically happens in a crisis, and that is why hedge funds managing among themselves over $500 billion, leveraged to between $20 billion and $25 billion, also funds of funds and alternative investments at large are so risky.

4. Market discipline and self-discipline

LTCM and all the other examples mentioned in Section 3 illustrate that both self-discipline and market discipline play a major role in controlling risks, and therefore in survival. On the bottomline, market discipline seeks to ensure that institutions adequately disclose financial and other information necessary for all financial players to:

- assess their risk profiles; and
- judge their performance.[10]

With respect to the investment process itself, prudent, self-disciplined management sees to it that, prior to reaching decisions, it calculates risk and reward – including future aftermath, expected, unexpected, and outlier events – and has available all elements which must definitely precede trading, loans, and investment activities. This means a methodology which encompasses:

- initial due diligence;
- steady reviews;
- critical evaluation; and
- judgement of outliers in risk.

All these need to occur in accordance with sound investment policies and principles. These usually set forth a good deal of analytical considerations, including exposure and liability issues. Prudent management should make steady reviews and evaluations using the best technology available, internal ratings-based (IRB) credit models,[11] market risk models, and operational risk models. Equally important, technologically, is the mining of rich on-line databases, in order to analyse patterns of precedence and establish:

- best case;
- worst case; and
- probable case scenarios.

Essential is the elaboration of *exit strategies* which can be supported through currently available resources, human and financial. Risk and return are very much affected by assumed and actual possibilities for orderly exit. Their computation is no routine business, but one that requires insight and foresight – and also reasonable and comprehensive primary and contingent take-out strategies.

Given the current and potential volatility of geared investments, even where hedge funds are not regulated their assessment of capital adequacy should go beyond compliance with regulatory capital requirements which are set for credit institutions. Institutions should have a sound methodology for internally allocating risk capital to the different types of investments, from going short to arbitrage operations and investing in the macromarkets, keeping this exposure associated with this allocation under lock and key.

As I never tire repeating, this requires both rigorous internal control policies and intraday risk management. Hedge funds, banks, brokers, corporate treasuries, pension funds, and other institutional investors going for alternative investments must have sophisticated systems in place to accumulate and exploit intraday information for risk control reasons, including:

- financial data streams,
- on-line database mining, and
- models permitting to judge exposure in real-time.

This is of course a tall call because the majority of banks, hedge funds, and other companies trading in derivatives are still in the middle ages in terms of technology and their financial reporting policies leave much to be wanted. Their managers and their traders do not have in place a system which permits to generate intraday balances, the way State Street Bank is doing. As a result, they are taking unreasonable risks.

- Intraday market valuation of derivatives positions is the best practice for banks, dealers, hedge funds, and, most recently, institutional investors.
- A corollary to this best practice is to always understand what the trader and the investor himself is trying to accomplish with derivatives trades – including the further out aftermath.

Without a full understanding of the purpose for which one enters into a trade it is nearly impossible to assess the effects of hedging in the sense of risk management. A different way of making this statement is that self-discipline is not a matter of words, nor is it solely based on board decisions. It needs a supporting system provided by organisation and technology.

Some (though certainly not all) credit institutions have the organisations and technology necessary to apply self-discipline, but the needed policies are not in place. Others are lacking even the technological fundamentals. A good way to finding out *if* a bank does so is to watch the volatility of its charges for bad and doubtful loans, as well as sour derivatives. Figure 9.2 is based on statistics from a money centre bank. To my experience:

- Credit institutions are more prone to have in place a system of checks and balances.
- By contrast, because they target double-digit returns, hedge funds have much lower self-defences.

A hedge fund is self-disciplined and prudently managed if it emulates in its internal governance the rules established by the Basle Committee on Banking Supervision, even if it is not obliged by law to do so. There should always be a balance between *economic capital* and *regulatory capital* – which is essentially economic capital matched to the realities of the market and of one's exposure.

Investors considering alternative investments need to ensure that the fund with which they are dealing can match capital adequacy requirements as established by the regulators for commercial banks.

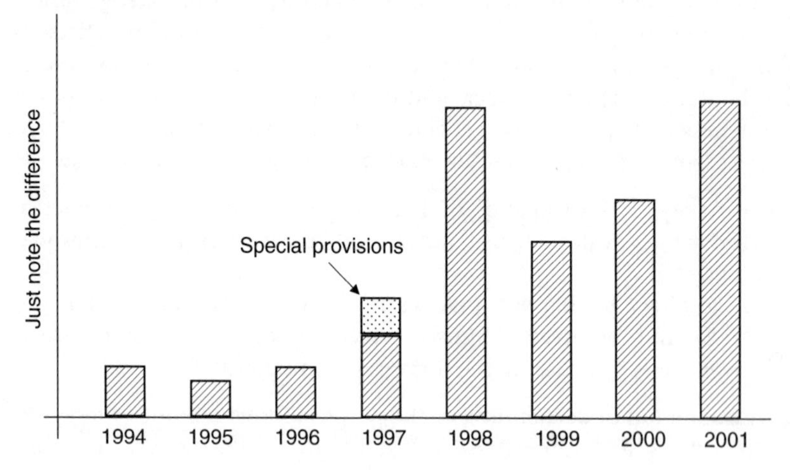

Figure 9.2 A money centre bank's charges for bad and doubtful debts. CAR skyrockets when the market goes into a tailspin.

This provides financial staying power and swamps leveraging. LTCM had none of that, and such practice is rare even today amongst hedge fund, fund of funds, and SAIVs.

The need for transparency is an integral part of the references which have just been made. We cannot speak with any degree of certainty of the opportunities associated with new, relative to old, financial instruments unless there is transparency in financial reporting. Risk and return is no abstract notion on which to report once in a while by word of mouth. It is a subject that should be taken very seriously. Reporting must be factual and documented, or left aside. Analytics, which lead to pragmatic risk and return evaluation, rest on three pillars:

- market discipline;
- transparency; and
- reliable financial reporting.

Markets must be characterised by a continuing increase in transparency, which helps to promote business confidence. Transparency makes management less complacent and it permits financial institutions to carry out increasingly comprehensive accounting and controlling functions, including dependable marking-to-model and marking-to-market practices.

Market discipline, transparency, and reliable financial reporting are precisely the domains where alternative investments – and the hedge funds, SAIVs, risk aggregators, and brokers/merchandisers behind them – *fail* to perform. Under these conditions, as Figure 9.3 suggests, the financial

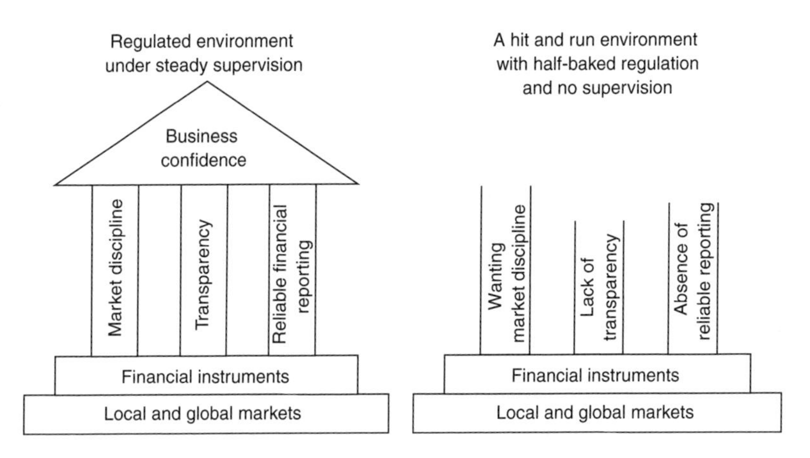

Figure 9.3 Market discipline, transparency, and reliable reporting in two different planets of finance.

edifice is in ruins. Well-managed companies cannot have confidence in it, because they know there are pitfalls and potholes.

Market disruptions are not unheard of as overleveraged bubbles burst: junk bonds in the late 1980s; CMOs and Mexico in 1994; the Asian Tigers in 1997; Russia and LTCM in 1998; Internet, technology, and telecommunications stocks in 2000; Enron in 2001; WorldCom and a host of other big ticket failures in 2002. The question which is compelling for both fund managers and investors in the future is whether the alternative investments' universe, or individual alternative investments strategies, will speed towards similar black holes.

5. The regulation of global financial institutions, hedge funds, and alternative investments

Markets cannot work without business confidence. There are plenty of responsibilities to be fulfilled in equities and other markets by entities which should continue to assume these responsibilities. Primary areas of responsibility in equity, equity-linked and equity derivative products include researching companies, industry sectors, and geographic markets for weaknesses in financial performance and for excesses in taking risk. The objects of such research and analysis should be:

- macro- and microeconomic conditions and trends;
- reliable reporting on sales and trading activities;
- prevailing transparency in financial transactions; and
- honest, accurate, and timely financial reporting.

Since in global markets these requirements are also global, there is a sincere need for transborder regulation and supervision, and for dependable worldwide capital adequacy guidelines matched by careful domestic reform. In terms of transborder standards, the Basle Committee on Banking Supervision is doing a commendable job, but with regard to domestic reform, in many cases this is still wanting.

All this is very relevant in a discussion on business opportunities and risks with alternative investments because without market discipline, transparency, and reliable financial reporting, any evaluation would be wanting if not outright misleading. Not only banks, but also all other institutions that work with alternative investments, should:

- adopt reliable and verifiable reporting practices; and
- show greater discipline with capital adequacy decisions in the economic environment(s) in which they operate.

This is despite fully accepting that globalisation and technology change the credit dimension, making markets more dynamic, and inciting (if not forcing) companies to take more risks. While risk is indivisible from doing business, in the past bankers have not been known for taking risks for risks' own sake. Other players, however, do so with other peoples' money.

If self-discipline by financial institutions was doable in a rigorous and reliable way, *then*, as I already underlined, there would have been no need for the SEC, the Fed, OCC, FDIC, FSA and the Bank of England. Financial history proves that self-discipline is ineffectual and, therefore, these supervisory authorities are cornerstones to the avoidance of systemic risk. But, as *The Economist* aptly asks:

> Who regulates Citigroup, the world's largest and most diverse financial institution?

With its operations in over 100 countries, selling just about every financial product that has ever been invented, probably every financial regulator in the world feels that Citi is only to some degree his problem. The lion's share of responsibility lies with the 'other' regulators. Therefore, in a sense, nobody truly regulates Citi: it is a global firm in a world of national and sectoral watchdogs.

- The same is true of American International Group (AIG), General Electric Capital, other non-banks and all of the hedge funds.

The Economist goes on to suggest that non-bank banks 'with big financial operations do not fit comfortably into the current regulatory framework. Enron, which has been plausibly described as an investment bank or hedge fund with an energy business on the side, was not regulated in America. In Britain, the firm itself was not regulated, though its financial subsidiaries were monitored by the FSA'.[12]

Indeed, these are urgent and important questionmarks over who regulates the growing number of firms now transforming themselves into huge financial conglomerates. Regulation cannot be improvised. It has to be established by law. Not only should it be universal, just like the financial markets are globalised, but also similarly interpreted and applied in all jurisdictions.

This is not easy. Yet, the fulfilment of such premises is vital in re-establishing confidence in the financial markets. Already in antiquity Demosthenes, the orator, had said that all business is based on confidence. LTCM, Barings, Enron, Global Crossing, NTL, WorldCom, and so many other man-made financial failures have given business confidence a severe beating. They have also led to distinguishing between:

- *normal risks* attached to traditional, widely led forms of investment, such as equities, bonds, units in mutual funds; and
- *extreme risks*, or development risks, which apply to new-style industries, like hedge funds and non-bank banks; and to new instruments, like alternative investments.

An example of the latter is the global hedge fund crisis in autumn 1998 and in mid-1999, when big funds have speculated against the yen with huge financial bets. The aftermath was the opposite of what was expected. In one case, only four days the dollar plunged by 18 per cent against the yen.

Among other extreme risks, bonds issued by telecommunications firms, which till 2002 were considered recession-proof, have been relegated to junk status or outright distressed through bankruptcies. This reference includes loans to the second largest US long distance telephone company WorldCom, whose equity became penny stock: down to US 6 cents, though it rebounced as speculation mounted that it may not go bankrupt. Finally, WorldCom filed for protection from creditors.

This is by no means a one-tantum case. Other mammoth state monopolies like France Telecom and Deutsche Telekom are saddled with loans of more than Euro 60 billion ($59.5 billion) *each*, which they cannot repay. These loans are projected to rise to Euro 70 billion or more for each firm, by the end of 2002.

The only way to be in charge of development risks, is that king-size loans, hedging-related operations, and all leveraged transactions provide information to enable investors, creditors, government supervisors, and other users of financial statements to appreciate an entity's exposure and its strategy for managing risks. Hedging through complex transactions requires transparency not only of transactions being done but also of instruments used to hedge anticipated transactions, and those inventoried in the portfolio.

A great deal of research on risk control, and evidently in global supervision, still remains to be done. Technology is another challenge. Many financial analysts believe that even if hedging of risk management was adequately defined, the majority of banks, hedge funds, institutional investors, and corporate treasuries would not have systems in place to identify and report assumed risks let alone to experiment on the optimisation and management of exposure.

6. Conclusion

The high-level negotiations to salvage LTCM from the abyss had the positive result of casting attention on the largely unregulated business of hedge funds. Central bankers have become much more concerned about institutions which use borrowed money to speculate on the direction of financial markets, and often miss the target. That is the dangerous side of globalisation:

- Hedge funds' web of international transactions has played a key role in linking financial crisis in one part of the globe to seemingly unrelated markets elsewhere.
- In their speculatory trades hedge funds and so many other players are hurt by the same market developments that led to losses at regulated investment firms – but with greater intensity.

Leveraging is risky and huge leveraging is deadly, as LTCM found out by mid-1998 in practically every channel it had bet, as the odds turned against the gamblers. The same is true of Enron in 2001 and WorldCom in 2002. In an age where rocket scientists are key ingredients in the panoply of market players, some of the failed companies had hired as consultants several of Wall Street's stars. The problem is that they used this talent for gearing rather than risk control. Rocket science is an important ingredient to the able management of a financial institution, But sound policies and steady supervision are the real keys to its sustained success.

End-investors who are attracted by alternative investments should appreciate that their capital may be subject to similar risks as LTCM, Enron, and WorldCom risk. It matters little if they make their bet to good luck and bad luck directly through hedge funds, or indirectly by means of funds of funds, SAIVs, and banks acting as aggregators of risk. In this fast-moving world of finance, where new risks replace old risks at a furious pace, some bets will be lost. The golden rule is that:

- Investors should not remain inactive but they should keep the control of their wealth. This is their responsibility.

Investors should not throw money at the problem. Given the strong inflow of assets to hedge funds and funds of funds, some experts are asking whether the inflows into speculative type investments are decoupling from realistic expectations. Others are worried by the fact that funds of funds increasingly capitalise on the activities of the underlying hedge funds, which typically leverage their capital by:

- entering into repo agreements;
- buying securities on margin;
- taking bank borrowing; and
- extensively using derivatives products.

The 1977 Asian crisis and subsequent negative events prompted little review of risk management procedures, nor did away with assumed exposure. If anything, today there is more credit risk, market risk, and operational risk, than in the past. The best advise for investors is to inform themselves about the risks they are taking before assuming them.

Governments in their turn have to be proactive, not reactive. *If* being proactive is the better policy, *then* it is indeed high time to regulate the hedge funds as well as the funds of funds and SAIVs; in short all the players in the field of alternative investments. As a general rule, financial institutions should become:

- less leveraged;
- transparent; and
- simpler in terms of structure.

A vital ingredient which will entice institutional investors into this market is the development of a regulatory framework based on efficiency, simplicity, transparency, and risk control guided by prudent rules. The various sectors of the economy should be supportive of effective regulation and supervisory activities in the areas of:

- ethical behaviour;
- reliable financial reporting;
- financial solvency; and
- investor protection.

The practice of alternative investments and the management of risk associated with them must be seen within this perspective. All four bullets contribute to the proper functioning of the markets and of the economy. Therefore:

- the management of risk is indivisible from their observance; and
- any regulatory system which bypasses one or more of these bullets will make more likely an alternative investments bubble.

It is self-evident that the more complex is the instrument the more difficult it is to develop and maintain a prudent supervisory environment. At the same time, there must be a level-playing field. The right sort of competition laws should regulate the nature of competition in the market, giving supervisors clear authority to prevent:

- collusive price setting;
- market sharing arrangements;
- aggressive off-loading of risk to end-investors; and
- excessive exposure which lessens the financial staying power of the entities assuming it.

In principle, the more dynamic and more competitive is a market, the more important is prudent regulation, but also the more complex and difficult are the issues to be addressed. For a regulated industry such as banking, the inclusion of specific principles like those described by the above four bullets is critical in setting the pattern of globalisation. Financial institutions and other companies are right to worry about both the other side of strategic risk, and the thresholds within which strategic drivers should be established. At the same time, adequate rules must be in place to protect the interests of all parties.

Alfred Nobel once said: 'I knew when I was ten years old that equity is only a figure of speech ...'[13] As this text has proved through practical examples and opinions from learned people who know how to evaluate new risks and assumed exposure, with alternative investment equity can become quicksand.

> One reviewer was concerned that readers would come away with this book with the view that there is nothing of any worth in alternative investments.

Investors often beg to differ, and the merchandisers of risks capitalise on this fact. The most important message this text brings to the reader is not to become prisoner of promotional literature and of salesmen talk, but to critically analyse what one is being told and to think for himself. If after being informed on the risks he or she comes away with a negative opinion about alternative investments, then let it be so.

In conclusion, it is the duty of both regulators and governments to assure that business confidence in a globalised economy is neither misplaced nor undermined, that asset quality is enough to satisfy capital requirements, and that the necessary policy provisions are in place. They also need to ensure that corrective action will be taken anytime an event occurs which threatens business confidence – whether this affects the corporate sector or the public.

'Comedy and tragedy', Socrates said, 'are the same thing and they should be written by the same authors'. In 2003, comedy and tragedy is being written by hedge funds, funds of funds, SAIVs, and commercial banks serving as aggregators of risk. Their script is alternative investments.

Acknowledgements

(Countries are listed in alphabetical order)

The following organizations, through their senior executives and system specialists participated in the recent research projects that led to the contents of this book and its documentation.

Austria

National Bank of Austria

Dr Martin Ohms
Finance Market Analysis Department
3, Otto Wagner Platz
Postfach 61
A-1011 Vienna

Association of Austrian Banks and Bankers

Dr Fritz Diwok
Secretary General
11, Boersengasse
1013 Vienna

Bank Austria

Dr Peter Fischer
Senior General Manager, Treasury Division

Peter Gabriel
Deputy General Manager, Trading

2, Am Hof
1010 Vienna

Creditanstalt

Dr Wolfgang Lichtl
Market Risk Management
Julius Tandler Platz 3
A-1090 Vienna

Wiener Betriebs- and Baugesellschaft mbH

Dr Josef Fritz
General Manager
1, Anschützstrasse
1153 Vienna

France

Banque de France

Pierre Jaillet
Director, Monetary Studies and Statistics

Yvan Oronnal
Manager, Monetary Analyses and Statistics

G. Tournemire, Analyst, Monetary Studies

39, rue Croix des Petits Champs
75001 Paris

Secretariat Général de la Commission Bancaire – Banque de France

Didier Peny
Director, Control of Big Banks and International Banks
73, rue de Richelieu
75002 Paris

F. Visnowsky

Manager of International Affairs
Supervisory Policy and Research Division

Benjamin Sahel
Market Risk Control
115, Rue Réaumur
75049 Paris Cedex 01

Ministry of Finance and the Economy, Conseil National de la Comptabilité

Alain Le Bars
Director International Relations and Cooperation
6, rue Louise WEISS
75703 Paris Cedex 13

Germany

Deutsche Bundesbank

Hans-Dietrich Peters
Director

Hans Werner Voth
Director

Wilhelm-Epstein Strasse 14
60431 Frankfurt am Main

Federal Banking Supervisory Office

Hans-Joachim Dohr
Director Dept. I

Jochen Kayser
Risk Model Examination

Ludger Hanenberg
Internal Controls

71–101 Gardeschützenweg
12203 Berlin

European Central Bank

Mauro Grande
Director
29 Kaiserstrasse
29th Floor
60216 Frankfurt am Main

Deutsches Aktieninstitut

Dr Rüdiger Von Rosen
President

Biebergasse 6 bis 10
60313 Frankfurt-am-Main

Commerzbank

Peter Bürger
Senior Vice President, Strategy and Controlling

Markus Rumpel
Senior Vice President, Credit Risk Management

Kaiserplatz
60261 Frankfurt am Main

Deutsche Bank

Professor Manfred Timmermann
Head of Controlling

Hans Voit
Head of Process Management, Controlling Department

12, Taunusanlage
60325 Frankfurt

Dresdner Bank

Dr Marita Balks
Investment Bank, Risk Control

Dr Hermann Haaf
Mathematical Models for Risk Control

Claas Carsten Kohl
Financial Engineer

1, Jürgen Ponto Platz
60301 Frankfurt

Volkswagen Foundation

Katja Ebeling
Office of the General Secretary
35 Kastanienallee
30519 Hanover

Herbert Quandt Foundation

Dr Kai Schellhorn
Member of the Board
Hanauer Strasse 46
D-80788 Munich

GMD First – Research Institute for Computer Architecture, Software Technology and Graphics

Prof. Dr Ing. Wolfgang K. Giloi
General Manager

5, Rudower Chaussee
D-1199 Berlin

Hungary

Hungarian Banking and Capital Market Supervision

Dr Janos Kun
Head, Department of Regulation and Analyses

Dr Erika Vörös
Senior Economist, Department of Regulation and Analyses

Dr Géza Nyiry
Head, Section of Information Audit

Csalogany u. 9–11
H-1027 Budapest

Hungarian Academy of Sciences

Prof Dr Tibor Vamos
Chairman, Computer and Automation Research Institute
Nador U. 7
1051 Budapest

Iceland

The National Bank of Iceland Ltd

Gunnar T. Andersen
Managing Director
International Banking & Treasury
Laugavegur 77
155 Reykjavik

Italy

Banca d'Italia

Eugene Gaiotti
Research Department, Monetary and Financial Division

Ing. Dario Focarelli
Research Department

91, via Nazionale
00184 Rome

Istituto Bancario San Paolo di Torino

Dr Paolo Chiulenti
Director of Budgeting

Roberto Costa
Director of Private Banking

Pino Ravelli
Director Bergamo Region

27, via G. Camozzi
24121 Bergamo

Luxembourg

Banque Générale de Luxembourg

Prof. Dr Yves Wagner
Director of Asset and Risk Management

Hans Jörg Paris
International Risk Manager

27, avenue Monterey
L-2951 Luxembourg

Clearstream

André Lussi
President and CEO
3-5 Place Winston Churchill
L-2964 Luxembourg

Poland

Securities and Exchange Commission

Beata Stelmach
Secretary of the Commission
1, Pl Powstancow Warszawy
00-950 Warsaw

Sweden

The Royal Swedish Academy of Sciences

Dr Solgerd Björn-Rasmussen
Head Information Department

Dr Olof Tanberg
Foreign Secretary

10405 Stockholm

Skandinaviska Enskilda Banken

Bernt Gyllenswärd
Head of Group Audit
Box 16067
10322 Stockholm

Irdem Ab

Gian Medri
Former Director of Research at Nordbanken
19, Flintlasvagen
S-19154 Sollentuna

Switzerland

Swiss National Bank

Dr Werner Hermann
Head of International Monetary Relations

Dr Christian Walter
Representative to the Basle Committee

Prof. Urs Birchler
Director, Advisor on Systemic Stability

Robert Fluri
Assistant Director, Statistics Section

15 Börsenstrasse
8022 Zurich

Federal Banking Commission

Dr Susanne Brandenberger
Risk Management

Renate Lischer
Representative to Risk Management Subgroup, Basle Committee

Marktgasse 37
3001 Bern

Bank for International Settlements

Mr Claude Sivy
Head of Internal Audit

Herbie Poenisch
Senior Economist, Monetary and Economic Department

Ingo Fender
Committee on the Global Financial System

2, Centralplatz
4002 Basle

Crédit Suisse

Ahmad Abu el-Ata
Managing Director, Head of IT Office

Dr Burkhard P. Varnholt
Managing Director, Global Research

12/14 Bahnhofstrasse
CH-8070 Zurich

Bank Leu AG

Dr Urs Morgenthaler
Member of Management
Director of Risk Control
32, Bahnhofstrasse
Zurich

Bank J. Vontobel and Vontobel Holding

Heinz Frauchiger
Chief, Internal Audit Department
Tödistrasse 23
CH-8022 Zurich

Union Bank of Switzerland

Dr Heinrich Steinmann
Member of the Executive Board (Retired)
Claridenstrasse
8021 Zurich

University of Fribourg

Prof. Dr Jürgen Kohlas

Prof. Dr Andreas Meier

Department of Informatics
2, rue Faucigny
CH-1700 Fribourg

Swiss Re

Dr Thomas Hess
Head of Economic Research & Consulting

Mythenquai 50/60
P.O. Box
CH-8022 Zürich

United Kingdom

Bank of England

Richard Britton
Director, Complex Groups Division, CGD Policy Department
Threadneedle Street
London EC2R 8AH

Financial Services Authority (FSA)

Lieselotte Burgdorf-Cook
International Relations
7th Floor
25 The North Colonnade
Canary Wharf
London E14 5HS

British Bankers Association

Paul Chisnall
Assistant Director
Pinners Hall
105-108 Old Broad Street
London EC2N 1EX

Accounting Standards Board

A.V.C. Cook
Technical Director

Sandra Thompson
Project Director

Holborn Hall
100 Gray's Inn Road
London WC1X 8AL

Barclays Bank Plc

Brandon Davies
Treasurer, Global Corporate Banking

Alan Brown
Director, Group Risk

54 Lombard Street
London EC3P 3AH

Abbey National Treasury Services Plc

John Hasson
Director of Information Technology & Treasury Operations

Abbey House
215–229 Baker Street

London NW1 6XL

ABN-AMRO Investment Bank N.V.

David Woods
Chief Operations Officer, Global Equity Directorate
199 Bishopsgate
London EC2M 3TY

Bankgesellschaft Berlin

Stephen F. Myers
Head of Market Risk
1 Crown Court
Cheapside, London

Standard & Poor's

David T. Beers
Managing Director, Sovereign Ratings
Garden House
18, Finsbury Circus
London EC2M 7BP

Moody's Investor Services

Samuel S. Theodore
Managing Director, European Banks

Alastair Graham
Senior Vice President, Director of Global Training

David Frohriep
Communications Manager, Europe

2, Minster Court
Mincing Lange
London EC3R 7XB

Fitch IBCA

Charles Prescott
Group Managing Director, Banks

David Nadrews
Managing Director, Financial Institutions

Travor Pitman
Managing Director, Corporations

Richard Fox
Director, International Public Finance

Eldon House
2, Eldon Street
London EC2M 7UA

Merrill Lynch International

Erik Banks
Managing Director of Risk Management
Ropemaker Place
London EC2Y 9LY

The Auditing Practices Board

Jonathan E.C. Grant
Technical Director

Steve Leonard
Internal Controls Project Manager

P.O.Box 433
Moorgate Place
London EC2P 2BJ

International Accounting Standards Committee

Ms Liesel Knorr
Technical Director
166 Fleet Street
London EC4A 2DY

MeesPierson ICS

Arjan P. Verkerk
Director, Market Risk
Camomile Court
23 Camomile Street
London EC3A 7PP

Charles Schwab

Dan Hattrup
International Investment Specialist
Crosby Court
38 Bishopsgate
London EC2N 4AJ

Charity Commission

Susan Polak

Mike McKillop

J. Chauhan

13–15 Bouverie Street
London ECAY 8DP

The Wellcome Trust

Clare Matterson
Member of the Executive Board and Head of Policy
210 Euston Road
London NW1 2BE

Association of Charitable Foundations

Nigel Siederer
Chief Executive
2, Plough Yard
Shoreditch High Street
London EC2A 3LP

IBM United Kingdom

Derek Duerden
Technical Strategy, EMEA Banking Finance & Securities Business
76 Upper Ground
London SE1 9PZ

City University Business School

Prof. Elias Dinenis
Head, Department of Investment
Risk Management & Insurance

Prof. Dr John Hagnioannides
Department of Finance

Frobisher Crescent
Barbican Centre
London EC2Y 8BH

TT International

Timothy A. Tacchi
Co-Chief Executive Officer

Henry Bedford
Co-Chief Executive Officer

Robin A.E. Hunt

Martin House
5 Martin Lane
London EC4R 0DP

Alternative Investment Management Association (AIMA)

Emma Mugridge
Director
10 Stanhope Gate
Mayfair
London W1K 1AL

Ernst & Young

Pierre-Yves Maurois
Senior Manager, Risk Management and Regulatory Services
Rolls House
7 Rolls Buildings
Fetter Lane
London E4A 1NH

Brit Syndicates Limited at Lloyd's

Peter Chrismas
Hull Underwriter

Anthony Forsyth
Marine Underwriter

Marine, Aviation, Transport & Space Division
Box 035
Lloyd's
1 Lime street
London EC3M 7DQ

United States

Federal Reserve System, Board of Governors

David L. Robinson
Deputy Director, Chief Federal Reserve Examiner

Alan H. Osterholm, CIA, CISA
Manager, Financial Examinations Section

Paul W. Bettge
Assistant Director, Division of Reserve Bank Operations

Gregory E. Eller
Supervisory Financial Analyst, Banking

Gregory L. Evans
Manager, Financial Accounting

Martha Stallard
Financial Accounting, Reserve Bank Operations

20th and Constitution, NW
Washington, DC 20551

Federal Reserve Bank of Boston

William McDonough
Executive Vice President

James T. Nolan
Assistant Vice President

P.O.Box 2076
600 Atlantic Avenue
Boston, MA

Federal Reserve Bank of San Francisco

Nigel R. Ogilvie, CFA
Supervising Financial Analyst
Emerging Issues
101 Market Street
San Francisco, CA

Seattle Branch, Federal Reserve Bank of San Francisco

Jimmy F. Kamada
Assistant Vice President

Gale P. Ansell
Assistant Vice President, Business Development

1015, 2nd Avenue
Seattle, WA 98122-3567

Office of the Comptroller of the Currency (OCC)

Bill Morris
National Bank Examiner/Policy Analyst,
Core Policy Development Division

Gene Green
Deputy Chief Accountant
Office of the Chief Accountant

250 E Street, SW
7th Floor
Washington, D.C.

Federal Deposit Insurance Corporation (FDIC)

Curtis Wong
Capital Markets, Examination Support

Tanya Smith
Examination Specialist, International Branch

Doris L. Marsh
Examination Specialist, Policy Branch

550 17th Street, N.W.
Washington, D.C.

Office of Thrift Supervision (OTS)

Timothy J. Stier
Chief Accountant
1700 G Street Northwest
Washington, DC, 20552

Securities and Exchange Commission, Washington DC

Robert Uhl
Professional Accounting Fellow

Pascal Desroches
Professional Accounting Fellow

John W. Albert
Associate Chief Accountant

Scott Bayless
Associate Chief Accountant

Office of the Chief Accountant
Securities and Exchange Commission
450 Fifth Street, NW
Washington, DC, 20549

Securities and Exchange Commission, New York

Robert A. Sollazzo
Associate Regional Director
7 World Trade Center
12th Floor
New York, NY 10048

Securities and Exchange Commission, Boston

Edward A. Ryan, Jr.
Assistant District Administrator (Regulations)
Boston District Office
73 Tremont Street, 6th Floor
Boston, MA 02108-3912

Microsoft

Dr Gordon Bell
Senior Researcher
Bay Area Research Center of Microsoft Research
455, Market Street
Suite 1690
San Francisco, CA 94105

American Bankers Association

Dr James Chessen
Chief Economist

Mr. Douglas Johnson
Senior Policy Analyst

1120 Connecticut Ave NW
Washington, DC 20036

International Monetary Fund

Alain Coune
Assistant Director, Office of Internal Audit and Inspection
700 19th Street NW
Washington DC, 20431

Financial Accounting Standards Board

Halsey G. Bullen
Project Manager

Jeannot Blanchet
Project Manager

Teri L. List
Practice Fellow

401 Merritt
Norwalk, CN 06856

Henry Kaufman & Company

Dr Henry Kaufman
660 Madison Avenue
New York, NY 10021

Soros Fund Management

George Soros
Chairman
888 Seventh Avenue, Suite 3300
New York, NY 10106

Carnegie Corporation of New York

Armanda Famiglietti
Associate Corporate Secretary, Director of Grants Management
437 Madison Avenue
New York, NY 10022

Alfred P. Sloan Foundation

Stewart F. Campbell
Financial Vice President and Secretary
630 Fifth Avenue, Suite 2550
New York, NY 10111

Rockefeller Brothers Fund

Benjamin R. Shute, Jr.
Secretary
437 Madison Avenue
New York, NY 10022-7001

The Foundation Center

79 Fifth Avenue
New York, NY 10003-4230

Citibank

Daniel Schutzer
Vice President, Director of Advanced Technology
909 Third Avenue
New York, NY 10022

Swiss Re

David S. Laster, PhD
Senior Economist
55 East 52nd Street
New York, NY 10055

Prudential-Bache Securities

Bella Loykhter
Senior Vice President, Information Technology

Kenneth Musco
First Vice President and Director,
Management Internal Control

Neil S. Lerner
Vice President, Management Internal Control

1 New York Plaza
New York, NY

Merrill Lynch

John J. Fosina
Director, Planning and Analysis

Paul J. Fitzsimmons
Senior Vice President, District Trust Manager

David E. Radcliffe
Senior Vice President, National Manager Philanthropic Consulting

Corporate and Institutional Client Group
World Financial Center, North Tower
New York, NY 10281–1316

Permal Asset Management

Isaac R. Souede
President and CEO
900 Third Avenue
New York, NY 10022
(telephone interview)

HSBC Republic

Susan G. Pearce
Senior Vice President

Philip A. Salazar
Executive Director

452 Fifth Avenue, Tower 6
New York, NY 10018

International Swaps and Derivatives Association (ISDA)

Susan Hinko
Director of Policy
600 Fifth Avenue, 27th Floor,
Rockefeller Center
New York, NY 10020-2302

Standard & Poor's

Clifford Griep
Managing Director
25 Broadway
New York, NY 10004-1064

Mary Peloquin-Dodd

Director, Public Finance Ratings
55 Water Street
New York, NY 10041-0003

Moody's Investor Services

Lea Carty
Director, Corporates
99 Church Street
New York, NY 10022

State Street Bank and Trust

James J. Barr
Executive Vice President, U.S. Financial Assets Services
225 Franklin Street
Boston, MA 02105-1992

MBIA Insurance Corporation

John B. Caouette
Vice Chairman
113 King Street
Armonk, NY 10504

Global Association of Risk Professionals (GARP)

Lev Borodovski
Executive Director, GARP, and Director of Risk Management, Credit Suisse First Boston (CSFB), New York

Yong Li
Director of Education, GARP, and
Vice President, Lehman Brothers, New York

Dr Frank Leiber
Research Director, and
Assistant Director of Computational Finance, Cornell University, Theory Center, New York

Roy Nawal
Director of Risk Forums, GARP

980 Broadway, Suite 242
Thornwood, NY

Group of Thirty

John Walsh
Director
1990 M Street, NW
Suite 450
Washington, DC, 20036

Broadcom Corporation

Dr Henry Samueli
Co-Chairman of the Board, Chief Technical Officer

16215 Alton Parkway
P.O.Box 57013
Irvine, CA 92619-7013

Edward Jones

Ann Ficken (Mrs)
Director, Internal Audit
201 Progress Parkway
Maryland Heights, MO
63043–3042

Teachers Insurance and Annuity Association/College Retirement Equities Fund (TIAA/CREF)

John W. Sullivan
Senior Institutional trust Consultant

Charles S. Dvorkin
Vice President and Chief Technology Officer

Harry D. Perrin
Assistant Vice President, Information Technology

Patty Steinbach
Investment Advisor

Tim Prosser
Lawyer

730 Third Avenue
New York, NY 10017-3206

Sterling Foundation Management

Dr Roger D. Silk
Principal

14622 Ventura Blvd
Suite 745
Sherman Oaks, CA 91403

Grenzebach Glier & Associates, Inc.

John J. Glier
President and Chief Executive Officer
55 West Wacker Drive
Suite 1500
Chicago, IL 60601

Massachusetts Institute of Technology

Ms Peggy Carney
Administrator, Graduate Office

Michael Coen, PhD Candidate,
ARPA Intelligent Environment Project

Department of Electrical Engineering and Computer Science
Building 38, Room 444
50 Vassar Street
Cambridge, MA, 02139

Henry Samueli School of Engineering and Applied Science, University of California, Los Angeles

Dean A.R. Frank Wazzan
School of Engineering and Applied Science

Prof. Stephen E. Jacobson
Dean of Student Affairs

Dr Les Lackman
Mechanical and Aerospace Engineering Department

Prof. Richard Muntz
Chair, Computer Science Department

Prof. Dr Leonard Kleinrock
Telecommunications and Networks

Prof. Chih-Ming ho, Ph.D.
Ben Rich- Lockheed Martin Professor
Mechancial and Aerospace Engineering Department

Dr Gang Chen
Mechancial and Aerospace Engineering Department

Prof. Harold G. Monbouquette, Ph.D.
Chemical Engineering Department

Prof. Jack W. Judy
Electrical Engineering Department

Abeer Alwan
Bioengineering

Prof. Greg Pottie
Electrical Engineering Department

Prof. Lieven Vandenberghe
Electrical Engineering Department

Anderson Graduate School of Management, University of California, Los Angeles

Prof. John Mamer
Former Dean

Prof. Bruce MILLER

Roundtable Discussion on Engineering and Management Curriculum (October 2, 2000)

Dr Henry Borenstein, Honeywell

Dr F. Issacci, Honeywell

Dr Ray Haynes, TRW

Dr Richard Croxall, TRW

Dr Steven Bouley, Boeing

Dr Derek Cheung, Rockwell

Westwood Village
Los Angeles, CA 90024

University of Maryland

Prof. Howard Frank
Dean, The Robert H. Smith School of Business

Prof. Lemma W. Senbert
Chair, Finance Department

Prof. Haluk Unal
Associate Professor of Finance

Van Munching Hall
College Park, Maryland 20742–1815

Notes

1 Alternative Investments Defined

1. The reader will find a definition of the terms end-investors, long/short, macromarkets, event-driven, emerging growth, emerging markets, and market-neutral strategies in Section 3.
2. This is also the reason why new regulations under study by the European Union aim to limit pension funds investments in private equity.
3. See D.N. Chorafas *Managing Derivatives Risk*, Irwin Professional Publishing, Burr Ridge, IL, 1996.
4. D.N. Chorafas *The Money Magnet. Regulating International Finance and Analyzing Money Flows*, Euromoney Books, London, 1997.
5. D.N. Chorafas and H. Steinmann *Off-Balance Sheet Financial Instruments*, Probus, Chicago, 1994.
6. D.N. Chorafas *Managing Operational Risk. Risk Reduction Strategies for Investment Banks and Commercial Banks*, Euromoney Books, London, 2001.
7. D.N. Chorafas, *Stress Testing*, Euromoney, London, 2002.
8. Global Equity Research, UBS Warburg, London, September 2001.
9. *The Economist*, 16 May 2002.
10. Audience poll in panel 'Alternative Investments: the Alternative Lifestyle?' *Euromoney Bond Investors Congress*, London, 19–20 February 2002.
11. D.N. Chorafas *Stress Testing*, Euromoney Self-Study Solutions, London, 2002.
12. *Business Week*, 25 February 2002.
13. D.N. Chorafas *The Management of Philanthropy in the 21*st *Century*, Institutional Investor, New York, 2002.
14. *Business Week*, 25 February 2002.
15. *Business Week*, 22 December 1997.
16. Merrill Lynch, *US Strategy Update*, 1 July 2002.

2 Are Alternative Investments Inherently Risky?

1. *Wall Street Journal*, 27 July 2001.
2. Felice A. Bonadio 'A.P. Giannini. Banker of America', University of California Press, Berkeley, 1994.
3. For a brief description of these different instruments see Chapter 1.
4. G. Soros, *'Soros on Soros'*, John Wiley, New York, 1995.
5. D.N. Chorafas *Liabilities, Liquidity and Cash Management. Balancing Financial Risk*, John Wiley, New York, 2002.
6. Sun Tzu '*The Art of War*', Wordsworth Reference, Ware, Hertfordshire, 1993.
7. *The Economist*, 8 June 2002.
8. D.N. Chorafas *Managing Operational Risk. Risk Reduction Strategies for Investment Banks and Commercial Banks*, Euromoney Institutional Investor, London, 2001.

9. D.N. Chorafas *Implementing and Auditing the Internal Control System*, Macmillan, London, 2001.
10. *The Economist*, 2 June 2002.
11. *Business Week*, 22 December 1997.

3 Globalisation, Legal Risk, Reputational Risk, and Technology Risk

1. G. Soros *Soros on Soros*, John Wiley, New York, 1995.
2. D.N. Chorafas *Managing Risk in the New Economy*, New York Institute of Finance, New York, 2001.
3. Named after their inventor, an Italian–American wheeler-dealer from Boston, Ponzi schemes are also known as *pyramiding*. They consist of taking money on the promise of very high, unrealistic returns, where the promoter pays the first depositors from the money he takes from the next wave. This is a confidence game which works up until the point where there is no more a mass of believers in the very high returns the Ponzi game is supposed to offer.
4. D.N. Chorafas *'How to Understand and Use Mathematics for Derivatives, Volume 1 – Understanding the Behaviour of Markets'*, Euromoney Institutional Investor, London, 1995.
5. D.N. Chorafas *Stress Testing*, Euromoney, London, 2002.
6. D.N. Chorafas *Agent Technology Handbook*, McGraw-Hill, New York, 1998.
7. D.N. Chorafas *Rocket Scientists in Banking*, Lafferty Publications, London and Dublin, 1995.
8. D.N. Chorafas *Network Computers versus High Performance Computers*, Cassel, London, 1997.
9. D.N. Chorafas *Understanding Volatility and Liquidity in Financial Markets*, Euromoney Institutional Investor, London, 1998.
10. D.N. Chorafas *How to Understand and Use Mathematics for Derivatives, Volume 2 – Advanced Modelling Methods*, Euromoney Institutional Investor, London, 1995.

4 The Financial Risks Taken with Alternative Investments

1. J. Grant *Money of the Mind*, Farrar Straus Giroux, New York, 1992.
2. D.N. Chorafas *Liabilities, Liquidity and Cash Management. Balancing Financial Risk*, JohnWiley, New York, 2002.
3. D.N. Chorafas *The Management of Philanthropy in the 21st Century*, Institutional Investor, New York, 2002.
4. *Business Week*, 29 July 2002.
5. See D.N. Chorafas, *Philanthropy in the 21st Century*, Institutional Investor, New York, 2002.
6. For example: Basle Committee on Banking Supervision 'Public Disclosures by Banks: Results of the 2000 Disclosure Survey', Bank for International Settlements, Basle, May 2002.
7. Invented as a mass market instrument in the 1980s, below investment-grade bonds fell out of favour in the early 1990s but returned to the fore after 1995.

8. *Wall Street Journal*, 27 July 2001.
9. I.e. somebody is daily pricing the instrument.
10. *Sigma*, No. 3/2001, Swiss Re, Zurich.

5 Hedge Funds, Multimanagers, and the Macromarkets

1. *Communications Week International*, 3 June 2002.
2. *Business Week*, 26 November 2001.
3. D.N. Chorafas *Reliable Financial Reporting and Internal Control: A Global Implementation Guide*, John Wiley, New York, 2000.
4. Crédit Swiss Private Banking, 'Global Investor', Zurich, July 2002.
5. D.N. Chorafas *Managing Risk in the New Economy*, New York Institute of Finance, New York, 2001.
6. G. Soros *Soros on Soros*, Wiley, New York, 1995.
7. Merrill Lynch 'Euroland Economics' Report, 6 June 2002.
8. Merrill Lynch 'Japan Macro Analysis', 6 June 2002.
9. *The Economist*, 8 June 2002.
10. The names in these case studies are fictitious but the strategies are ones taken by real hedge fund managers.
11. D.N. Chorafas *New Regulation of the Financial Industry*, Macmillan, London, 2000.
12. *Ibid.*
13. *Business Week*, 8–14 April 2002.
14. *Financial News*, 8–14 April 2002.

6 Risk and Return with Derivatives

1. STRIP is an acronym for Separate Trading of Registered Interest and Principal Securities.
2. D.N. Chorafas *Managing Credit Risk*, Volume 1 *'Analyzing, Rating and Pricing the Probability of Default'*, Euromoney, London, 2000.
3. D.N. Chorafas 'Modelling the Survival of Financial and Industrial Enterprises. Advantages, Challenges, and Problems with the Internal Rating-Based (IRB) Method', Palgrave/Macmillan, London, 2002.
4. D.N. Chorafas *Stress Testing*, Euromoney, London, 2002.
5. In 1994, Dr Fisher Black obtained the Chorafas Prize of the Swiss Academies of Sciences for having developed the option-pricing formula.
6. Institutional Investor, July 1992.
7. Federal Reserve, FDIC and OCC Joint Report 'Derivative Product Activities at Commercial Banks', Washington DC, 1993.
8. J. Gleeson *The Moneymaker*, Bantam Books, London, 1999.
9. *Business Week*, 25 February 2002.
10. D.N. Chorafas *Managing Credit Risk*, Volume 2 *The Lessons of VAR Failures and Imprudent Exposure*, Euromoney Institutional Investor, London, 2000.
11. *Ibid.*
12. D.N. Chorafas *The 1996 Market Risk Amendment. Understanding the Marking-to-Model and Value-at-Risk*, McGraw-Hill, Burr Ridge, IL, 1998.

13. D.N. Chorafas *Advanced Financial Analysis*, Euromoney Institutional Investor, London, 1994.
14. D.N. Chorafas *Credit Derivatives and the Management of Risk*, New York Institute of Finance, New York, 2000.
15. D.N. Chorafas and H. Steinmann *Off-Balance Sheet Financial Instruments*, Probus, Chicago, 1994.

7 Scrutinising Alternative Investment Strategies Intended to Give Higher Returns

1. E. Bergengren *Alfred Nobel*, Thomas Nelson and Sons, London, 1962.
2. D.N. Chorafas *Advanced Financial Analysis*, Euromoney Institutional Investor, London, 1994.
3. G. Hector *Breaking the Bank. The Decline of Bank America*, Little Brown and Co., Boston, 1988.
4. Swiss Bankers Association. 'Special Risks in Securities Trading', Basle, 2001 Edition.
5. D.N. Chorafas *Managing Risk in the New Economy*, New York Institute of Finance, New York, 2001.
6. D.N. Chorafas *Integrating ERP, Supply Chain Management and Smart Materials*, Auerbach/CRC Press, New York, 2001.
7. *Business Week*, 10 April 2000.
8. *International Herald Tribune*, 20 July 2002.
9. *Business Week*, 29 July 2002.
10. Audience vote at panel discussion 'Alternative Investments – The Alternative Lifestyle?' *Euromoney Bond Investor's Congress*, London, 19–20 February 2002.
11. D.N. Chorafas *Reliable Financial Reporting and Internal Control: A Global Implementation Guide*, John Wiley, New York, 2000.
12. *Business Week*, May 14 2001.

8 Assessing Strategic Risks through Stress Testing

1. G. Soros *Soros on Soros*, Wiley, New York, 1994.
2. For a more indepth look at the methods of stress testing for alternative investments, including credit risk, market risk, and operational risk see D.N. Chorafas *Stress Testing: Euromoney Self-Study Solutions*, London, 2002.
3. D.N. Chorafas *Liabilities, Liquidity and Cash Management. Balancing Financial Risk*, John Wiley, New York, 2002.
4. D.N. Chorafas *The 1996 Market Risk Amendment. Understanding the Marking-to-Model and Value-at-Risk*, McGraw Hill, Burr Ridge, IL, 1998.
5. D.N. Chorafas *Modelling the Survival of Financial and Industrial Enterprises. Advantages, Challenges, and Problems with the Internal Rating-Based (IRB) Method*, Palgrave/Macmillan, London, 2002.
6. *The Economist*, 27 July 2002.
7. D.N. Chorafas *Stress Testing: Risk Management Strategies for Extreme Events*, Euromoney, London, 2003.

8. D.N. Chorafas *Modelling the Survival of Financial and Industrial Enterprises. Advantages, Challenges, and Problems with the Internal Rating-Based (IRB) Method*, Palgrave/Macmillan, London, 2002.
9. Marcus Tullius Cicero, Roman senator and orator, 106–43 BC.
10. D.N. Chorafas *Understanding Volatility and Liquidity in Financial Markets*, Euromoney Books, London, 1998.
11. The MIT Report, June/July 1996.
12. D.N. Chorafas *Chaos Theory in the Financial Markets*, Probus, Chicago, 1994.
13. D.N. Chorafas *Modelling the Survival of Financial and Industrial Enterprises. Advantages, Challenges, and Problems with the Internal Rating-Based (IRB) Method*, Palgrave/Macmillan, London, 2002; and D.N. Chorafas *Stress Testing*, Euromoney, London, 2002.
14. This method is described further in D.N. Chorafas *Stress Testing*, Euromoney Self Study Solutions, London, 2002.
15. This argument forgets that the future of orphans and widows is put at risk when pension funds speculate in alternative investments.

9 Highly Leveraged Institutions, Regulators, and the New Lenders of Last Resort

1. D.N. Chorafas *'Managing Risk in the New Economy'*, New York Institute of Finance, New York, 2001.
2. George Soros 'Soros on Soros: Staying Ahead of the Curve', Wiley, New York, 1995.
3. D.N. Chorafas *Managing Operational Risk. Risk Reduction Strategies for Banks Post-Basle*, London and Dublin, Lafferty, 2000.
4. D.N. Chorafas *New Regulation of the Financial Industry*, London, Macmillan, 2000.
5. *The Economist*, 8 June 2002.
6. D.N. Chorafas *Understanding Volatility and Liquidity in Financial Markets*, London, Euromoney Institutional Investor, London, 1998.
7. *The Economist*, 27 July 2002.
8. D.N. Chorafas *Liabilities, Liquidity and Cash Management. Balancing Financial Risks*, New York, John Wiley, 2002.
9. Henry Kaufman *On Money and Markets*, New York, McGraw-Hill, 2000.
10. D.N. Chorafas *Reliable Financial Reporting and Internal Control: A Global Implementation Guide*, New York, John Wiley, 2000.
11. D.N. Chorafas *Modelling the Survival of Financial and Industrial Enterprises. Advantages, Challenges, and Problems with the Internal Rating-Based (IRB) Method*, London, Palgrave/Macmillan, 2002.
12. *The Economist*, 16 May 2002.
13. Erik Bergengren: 'Alfred Nobel', Thomas Nelson and Sons, London, 1962.

Index